DEATH in the SNOW

McGill-Queen's Iberian and Latin American Cultures Series
Series editor: Nicolás Fernández-Medina

The McGill-Queen's Iberian and Latin American Cultures Series is committed to publishing original scholarship that explores and re-evaluates Iberian and Latin American cultures, connections, and identities. Offering diverse perspectives on a range of regional and global histories from the early modern period to twenty-first-century contexts, the series cuts across disciplinary boundaries to consider how questions of authority, nation, revolution, gender, sexuality, science, epistemology, avant-gardism, aesthetics, travel, colonization, race relations, religious belief, and media technologies, among others, have shaped the rich and complex trajectories of modernity in the Iberian Peninsula and Latin America.

The McGill-Queen's Iberian and Latin American Cultures Series promotes rigorous scholarship and welcomes proposals for innovative and theoretically compelling monographs and edited collections.

1 Populism and Ethnicity
Peronism and the Jews of Argentina
Raanan Rein
Translated by Isis Sadek

2 What Would Cervantes Do?
Navigating Post-Truth with Spanish Baroque Literature
David Castillo and William Egginton

3 The Pen, the Sword, and the Law
Dueling and Democracy in Uruguay
David S. Parker

4 From the Theater to the Plaza
Spectacle, Protest, and Urban Space in Twenty-First-Century Madrid
Matthew I. Feinberg

5 Death in the Snow
Pedro de Alvarado and the Illusive Conquest of Peru
W. George Lovell

DEATH in the SNOW

PEDRO de ALVARADO and the ILLUSIVE CONQUEST of PERU

W. GEORGE LOVELL

McGill-Queen's University Press
Montreal & Kingston ◆ London ◆ Chicago

ISBN 978-0-2280-1440-9 (cloth)
ISBN 978-0-2280-1546-8 (ePDF)
ISBN 978-0-2280-1547-5 (ePUB)

Legal deposit fourth quarter 2022
Bibliothèque nationale du Québec

Printed in Canada on acid-free paper that is 100% ancient forest free (100% post-consumer recycled), processed chlorine free

This book has been published with the help of a grant from the Canadian Federation for the Humanities and Social Sciences, through the Awards to Scholarly Publications Program, using funds provided by the Social Sciences and Humanities Research Council of Canada.

Funded by the Government of Canada | Financé par le gouvernement du Canada | Canada | Canada Council for the Arts | Conseil des arts du Canada

We acknowledge the support of the Canada Council for the Arts.
Nous remercions le Conseil des arts du Canada de son soutien.

Image on page vi amended from an engraving of Chimborazo and Carihuairazo (1881) by Edward Whymper (1840–1911), a renowned explorer and mountaineer as well as an illustrator of books and periodicals.

LIBRARY AND ARCHIVES CANADA CATALOGUING IN PUBLICATION

Title: Death in the snow : Pedro de Alvarado and the illusive conquest of Peru / W. George Lovell.
Names: Lovell, W. George (William George), 1951- author.
Series: McGill-Queen's Iberian and Latin American cultures series ; 5.
Description: Series statement: McGill-Queen's Iberian and Latin American cultures series ; 5 | Includes bibliographical references and index.
Identifiers: Canadiana (print) 20220287112 | Canadiana (ebook) 20220287163 | ISBN 9780228014409 (cloth) | ISBN 9780228015468 (ePDF) | ISBN 9780228015475 (ePUB)
Subjects: LCSH: Alvarado, Pedro de, 1485?-1541. | LCSH: Conquerors—Central America—Biography. | LCSH: Peru—History—Conquest, 1522-1548. | LCGFT: Biographies.
Classification: LCC F3442 .L68 2022 | DDC 985/.02—dc23

In fond remembrance of Patrick S. Werner,
even in death larger than life,
a soulmate with whom I got to Realejo and there conjured up
Pedro de Alvarado and the illusion of Peru

Armed with imperial edict and with gold [in mind],
Herding his slaves by forest, shore, and stream,
Under the lash they wrought, and, 'ere the moon
Had withered to a shred in the pale dawn,
The banners of his fleet rose on the wind –
Twelve ships, a galley, and the lesser craft,
Freighted with men and beasts, and food and arms,
New lands, new seas, new peoples, conquering …

Charles Warren Stoddard,
"Pedro de Alvarado" (1881)

CONTENTS

PART THREE
Arrival

PART FOUR
Up, Over, and Down

PART FIVE
Saving Face

PREFACE

I was in Seville, working in that marvellous city's Archivo General de Indias, when *Los nacimientos* (1982), the first volume of Eduardo Galeano's *Memory of Fire* trilogy, auspiciously appeared. Archival investigation, it must be said, has its moments of euphoria and delight – nothing compares, for instance, with coming across an item long considered lost, or not known about to begin with. Poring over centuries-old documents, however, can be an exhausting grind, as many a colleague might attest. After one extended stint, with pertinent data accumulated but no semblance of closure in sight, reading about Galeano in the literary supplement of the newspaper *El País* and then buying *Los nacimientos* at a local bookstore came as something of a relief. Compared to the contents of the thick bundle of documents I was sifting through, his succinct, distilled, superbly crafted cameos, which narrate what occurred when and where in the Americas from earliest times to the year 1700, were (and are still) a kind of epiphany, a pleasure to read, a cornucopia to peruse time and again. I revelled in his revelations, rejoicing at learning so much from so few but such honed, incisive words.

A gifted man of letters Galeano surely was, but a historical geographer he was too, mapping out *Los nacimientos* period by period, place by place, with grounded authority and poetic grace – to say nothing of an impressive command of the sources upon which he cast his 308 vignettes of time/locale/episode. My thrill at combing his Spanish original was actually enhanced three years later, after Cedric Belfrage's dextrous rendering of it appeared in English. As Galeano himself acknowledged, when *Los nacimientos* became *Genesis* (1985), Belfrage opened up another world to the Uruguayan writer, cultivating a readership among which his voice was acclaimed and appreciated even more.

One vignette in *Los nacimientos*, "Riobamba," particularly intrigued me. It concerns the ill-fated attempt by Pedro de Alvarado, not content with the spoils he had accrued in the conquest of Mexico (1519–21) and

Guatemala (1524–26), to muscle in on the conquest of Peru (1534–35) and thereby seize a prize piece of wealth in a domain already ceded, under royal licence, to Francisco Pizarro and Diego de Almagro. Alvarado's South American exploits begat a debacle that few, even specialists in colonial history, know much about, and are the subject of this book. There is no better way to impart a sense of what was at stake, and how it all tragically came to naught, than to reprise Galeano's evocation, courtesy of Belfrage's translation:

> Half a year before, the ships anchored in Puerto Viejo. Inspired by promises of a virgin kingdom, Pedro de Alvarado had sailed from Guatemala. With him went five hundred Spaniards and two thousand Indian and [Black] slaves. Messengers had reported: "The power that awaits you makes what you have seem like dirt. To the north of Tumbes [Túmbez] you will multiply your fame and wealth. To the south, Pizarro and Almagro have now become the masters, but the fabulous kingdom of Quito belongs to no one."
>
> In the coastal villages they found gold, silver, and emeralds. Loaded with quick fortunes, they set off for the mountains. They faced jungles, swamps, fevers that kill in a day or leave one mad, and terrifying rains of volcanic ash. In the Andean foothills, snowstorms and winds that cut like knives broke the bodies of the slaves, who had never known cold, and many Spaniards left their bones in the mountains. Soldiers dismounting to tighten their horses' girths remained permanently frozen. The booty was thrown to the bottom of ravines: Alvarado offered gold, and the soldiers clamored for food and shelter. His eyes burned by the blinding snow, Alvarado kept charging up the trail to cut off with one sword-blow the heads of slaves who fell and of soldiers who wished they hadn't come.
>
> More dead than alive, with muscles iced and blood frozen, the toughest ones managed to reach the plateau. Finally, today they have hit the royal highway of the Incas, the one that leads to Quito, to paradise. No sooner do they arrive than they find in the mud fresh hoof-prints. Captain Belalcázar has beaten them to it.[1]

Galeano's vignette is wrought from two of his published sources, Francisco López de Gómara's *Historia general de las Indias* ([1554] 1863) and Frederick A. Kirkpatrick's *Los conquistadores españoles* ([1934] 1970). What *Death in the Snow* seeks to do is to put flesh on the bones Galeano unearthed, contextualizing key events and circumstances and elaborating on them with recourse to documentation, much of it archival in nature, to which Galeano did not have access. This material includes correspondence penned or dictated by Alvarado himself – John E. Kelly (1932) tried his hand at translating two such items – and an array of other contemporary protagonists. These include Almagro and Pizarro as well as informed observers who came after, the likes of Pedro de Cieza de León ([1553] 1998) or Antonio de Remesal ([1619] 1964–66) and the "Coronista Maior de su Magestad de las Indias – His Majesty's Chief Chronicler of the Indies," Antonio de Herrera ([1615] 1728). These sources, and myriad others, I comment on in the references – but also, as the story unfolds, in the text and its attendant notes, their contents informing and enriching the narrative from start to finish.[2] Besides filling a gap in the literature, *Death in the Snow* has its own sorry tale to tell, one suffused by incidents as dramatic as any marked by imperial Spain's relentless pursuit of empire.[3]

ACKNOWLEDGMENTS

A book leans, customarily, on many a shoulder, and this one – the idea for which arose four decades ago – is no exception. As I note in the preface, it was learning of Eduardo Galeano's first instalment in his *Memory of Fire* trilogy, *Los nacimientos* (1982), that got me started, the vignette "Riobamba" piquing my curiosity and causing me to wonder why the attempt by Pedro de Alvarado to meddle in the conquest of Peru, its calamitous consequences for Indigenous peoples in particular, was so little known. How could six years of graduate studies, and two years of post-doctoral inquiries, not have brought to light even an inkling of the episode? Did the trajectory of my research on Latin America to date end in a vanishing point?

The glimmer that Galeano represented became a beacon after Alexandra Parma Cook and Noble David Cook informed me of their undertaking to translate into English the hitherto missing part 3 of Pedro de Cieza de León's *Crónica del Perú* (1553). Sasha asked if I knew about the fate of Indigenous Guatemalans forced to toil, and perish, under Alvarado's tyranny in Ecuador in 1534. Yes I did, I replied, invoking Galeano. But Cieza has written about it at length, Sasha divulged, whetting my appetite by sharing with me a couple of extracts from her labours with David, which resulted in the publication of *The Discovery and Conquest of Peru* ([1553] 1998). After reading the translation, an enthralling experience, I realized that a millennial project awaited me. *Death in the Snow*, however, was put on hold until two prior commitments had been fulfilled, both of them also involving Alvarado but grounded in a Mesoamerican, not an Andean, setting (Lovell, Lutz, and Kramer [2016, 2017] 2019 and Lovell, Lutz, and Kramer 2020).

When I finally buckled down to the task, much of the actual composition coincided with the lockdown and restrictions imposed by COVID-19. But the present book is not a COVID creation: its pre-pandemic provenance has been established. Though the twenty months between

March 2020 and December 2021 can hardly be considered propitious – I was most fortunate to get out of Spain and return to Canada when COVID-19 initially struck – I trust to have something to show, and share, for the shrinking of my usually much-farther-flung spatial orbit during those most untoward of times.

I discussed my work on the project and presented my preliminary findings at numerous conferences, foremost among them those convened by the American Society for Ethnohistory, the Conference of Latin American Geography, and the Latin American Studies Association. Especially fruitful in terms of feedback and suggestions was the seminar I attended in March 2018 at the Universidad Nova de Lisboa on "Historia, culturas y realidades andinas." The stimulation of my Seville colleagues from the Universidad Pablo de Olavide – Nayibe Gutiérrez Montoya, Juan Marchena Fernández, José María Miura, and Tristan Platt – was crucial at the gathering in Lisbon, as was interaction with an array of Ecuadorian scholars who attended the forum "Perspectivas Multidisciplinarias sobre el Ecuador" organized in Ottawa in October 2019 by Luis Abanto Rojas. Luis introduced me in Ottawa to Ramiro Molina Cerdeño, who proved a pivotal contact when I headed to Ecuador two months later. Ramiro's knowledge of his native Manabí enhanced my exploration of it, during the course of which I retraced Alvarado's plunderous path from the Bahía de Caráquez to Riobamba.

Kris E. Lane was an equally bountiful source of information, and I profited from his savvy counsel in both the archive and the field. Archival sleuthing in Ecuador was confined to Quito, where time spent in the Archivo Metropolitano de Historia was particularly productive, director Diego Chiriboga Murgueitio affording me one-on-one attention that bolstered my morale. I also logged profitable spells at the Archivo Histórico and the Archivo Histórico Nacional as well as at the Instituto Geográfico Militar. Consultation there of J. Gualberto Pérez's *Carta geográfica de la República del Ecuador* (1922) assisted me in figuring out Alvarado's perilous route of rampage, besides allowing better appreciation of the lay of a complex, captivating land. Home base in Quito was the Residencia Manuela Sáenz at the Universidad Andina Simón Bolívar, whose library became a veritable refuge. The warm welcome given me by the founder of the university, Enrique Ayala Mora, to say nothing about his insights into Ecuadorian history, was a highlight of my stay.

In Seville, the Escuela de Estudios Hispano-Americanos was the optimum choice of where to be based, its library a treasure, its location a walk of twenty minutes to the Archivo General de Indias (AGI). I thank Antonio Sánchez de Mora, head of the AGI's Reference Department, for his speedy attention to requests for copies of pertinent materials. My gratitude is also extended to Esther González Pérez, who transcribed the roll call of men who accompanied Alvarado to Peru. With painstaking poise, Wendy Kramer perused Esther's transcription alongside me, clarifying and contextualizing line by line as we progressed.

At the Bancroft Library in Berkeley, California, Theresa Salazar unearthed for me microfilms of the *Revista Peruana* and kindly ran off hard copies of Alvarado-related correspondence. Staff of the Manuscripts and Archives Division at New York Public Library were similarly helpful, as was Bonnie Brooks at Queen's University in acquiring numerous books via interlibrary loans. When a doctoral student at Queen's, Alexandra Pedersen transcribed key texts and made them more manageable to work with.

The encouragement of John Hemming, Christopher H. Lutz, Linda A. Newson, Tony Pasinski, Margarita Suárez, Nancy E. van Deusen, and Ronald Wright spurred me on, as did the always incisive critiques of Maureen McCallum Garvie. Patrick Philpott helped me locate the bust of Sebastián de Belalcázar in the conquistador's birthplace north of Córdoba, where local historian Feliciano Casillas Sánchez welcomed us, walked us around, and anchored Belalcazar's most renowned offspring firmly in place. Yet again the map-making skills of Jennifer Grek-Martin transformed sketchy drafts into a finished product. At McGill-Queen's University Press the support of Philip Cercone has been stalwart, the strategic prompting of Richard Ratzlaff timely and apt. So too the editorial prowess of Kathleen Fraser embellished the book's design and layout, while Curtis Fahey enhanced its narrative thrust and flow. Funding for my endeavours from the Social Sciences and Humanities Research Council of Canada is gratefully acknowledged.

The once indomitable Patrick S. Werner may no longer be with us, but his trace runs throughout.

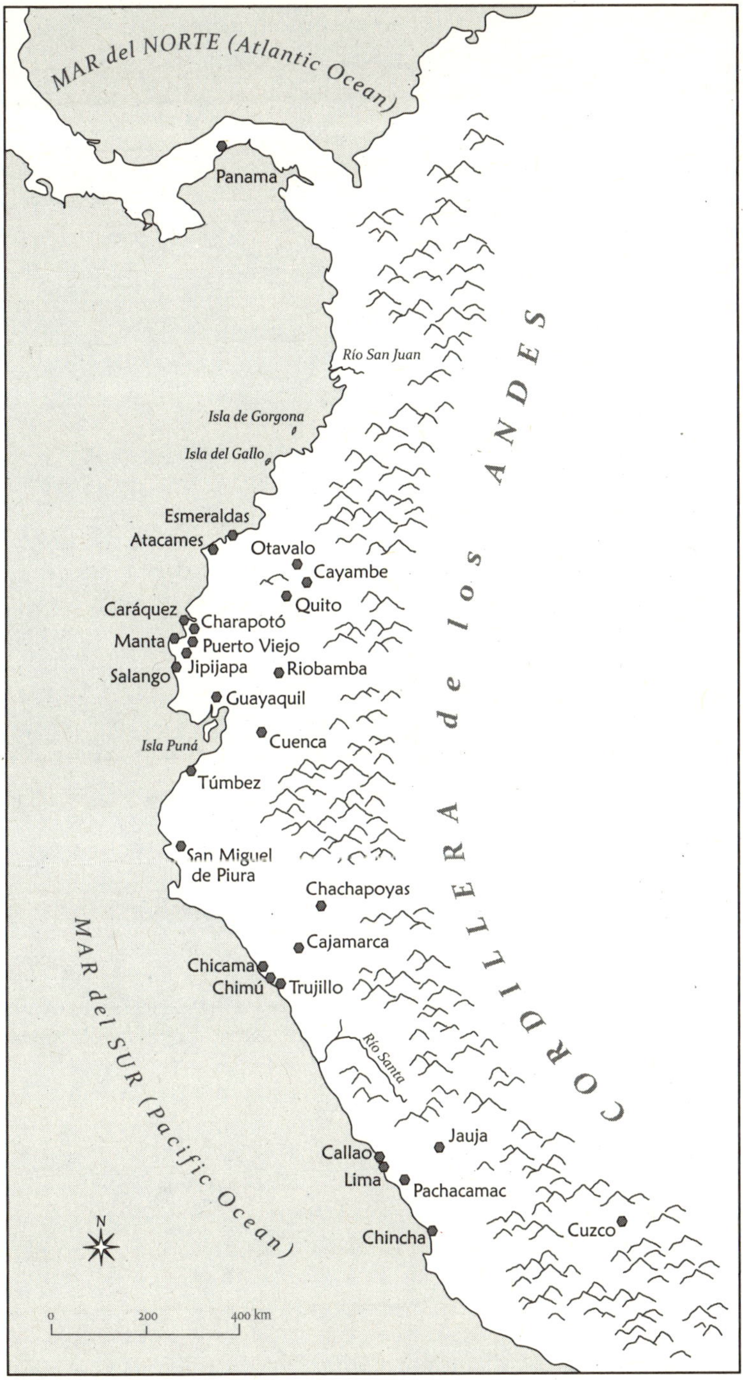

Map 1

The Pacific Littoral, Panama to Peru

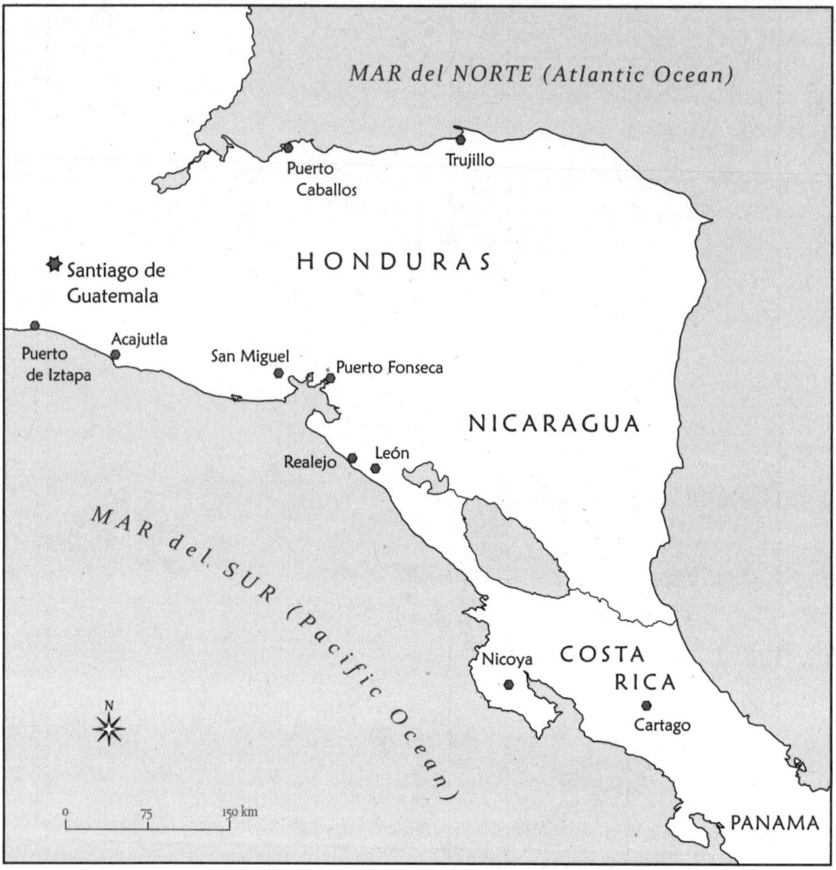

Map 2

Central America

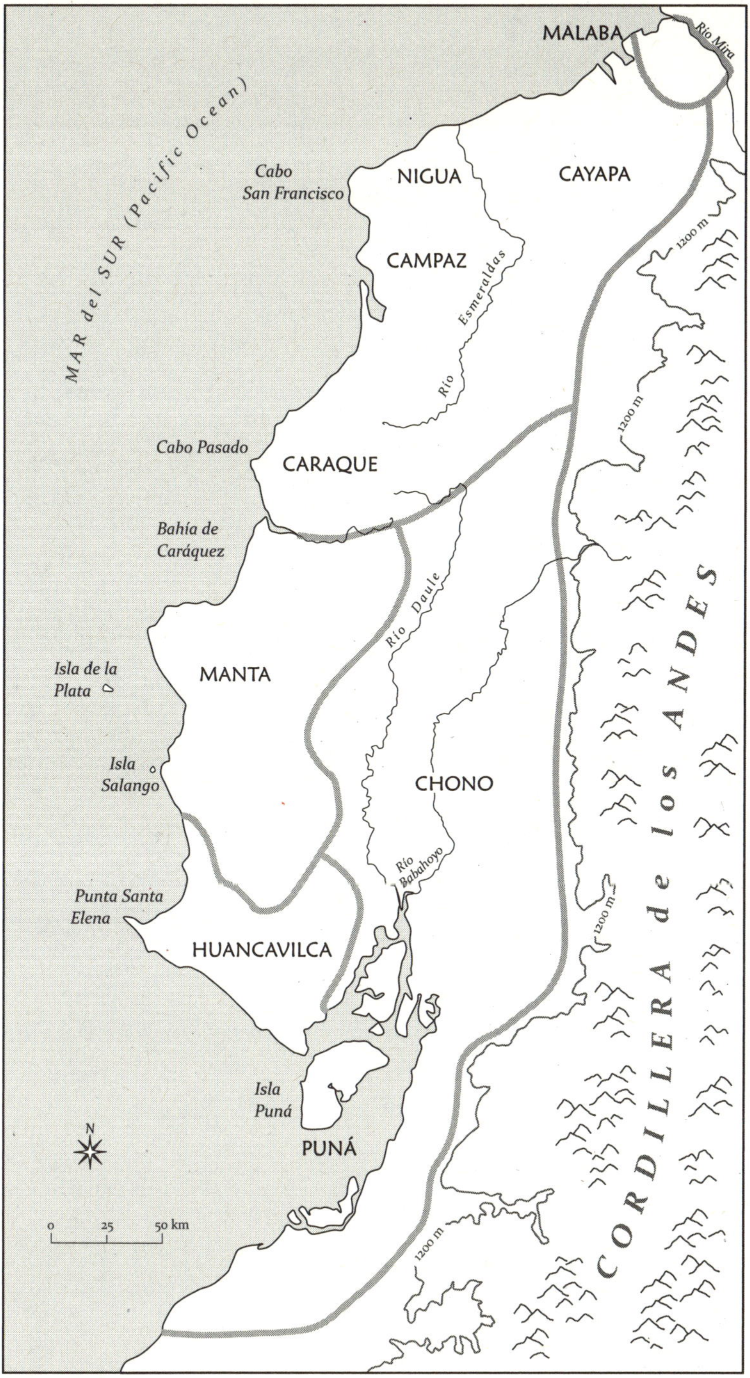

Map 3

Ecuador: Cultural-Linguistic Affiliations at Spanish Contact (after Newson 1995)

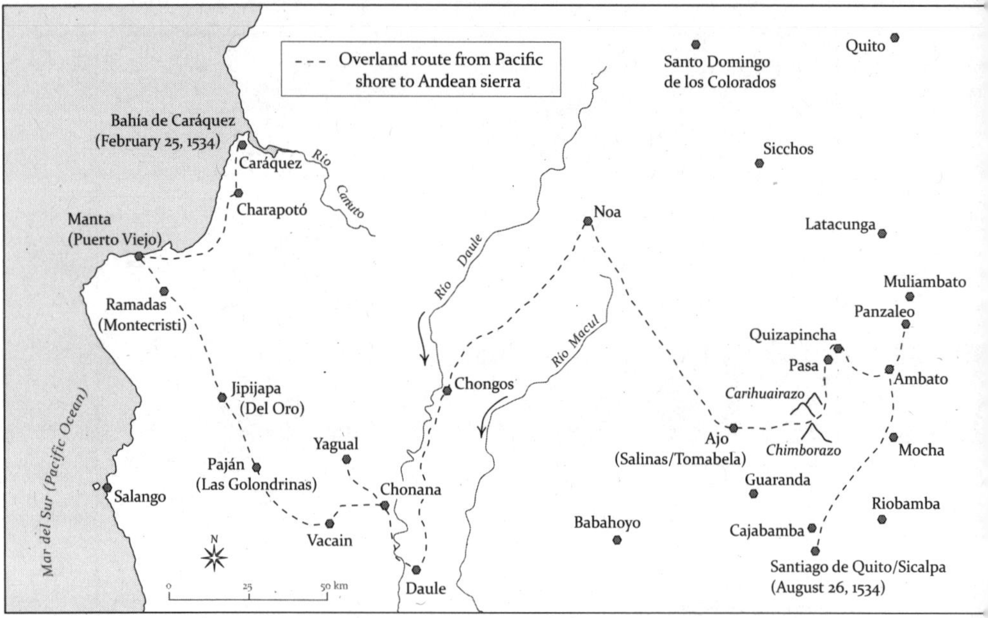

Map 4

Peregrinations of Pedro de Alvarado in Ecuador
(25 February–26 August 1534)

Figure 1

Two-masted Indigenous raft resembling that encountered by the pilot Bartolomé Ruiz during the second expedition of Francisco Pizarro, 1526–27. Source: Spilbergen ([1619] 1943) in Edwards (1965, 156).

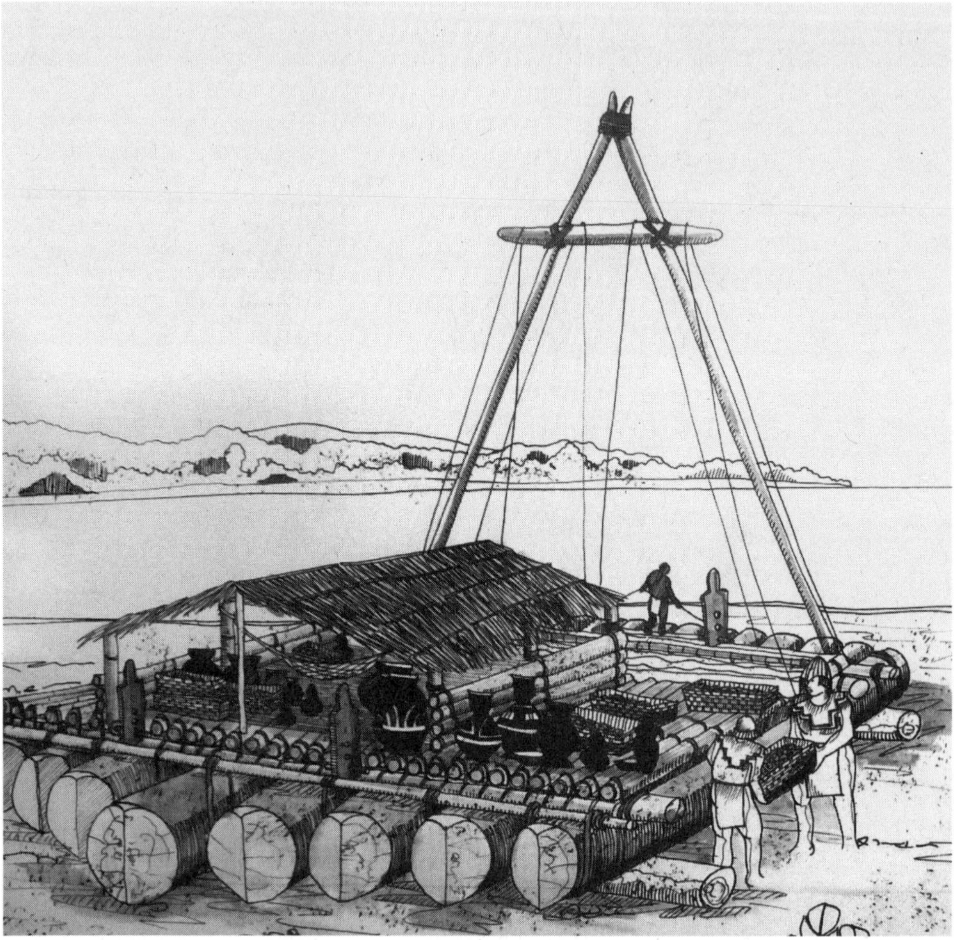

Figure 2

One-masted Indigenous raft being loaded with goods prior to embarking on long-distance commerce along the Pacific littoral. Courtesy of the Museo Nacional del Ecuador.

Figure 3

The Puerto de Yztapa on the Pacific coast of Guatemala, as rendered in 1598 by Pedro Ochoa de Leguiçamo (Torres Lanzas [1903] 1985, 7–8). North is top, south bottom. Eight square blocks at the top end of the figure indicate the city of Santiago de Guatemala, eight smaller squares at bottom the *villa* (town) of Iztapa. The triangular shape east of town is its fortress (*velarte/baluarte*) across the entrance to the port from the *arenal* (sand bar). Courtesy of the Archivo General de Indias (Mapas y Planos, Guatemala 2).

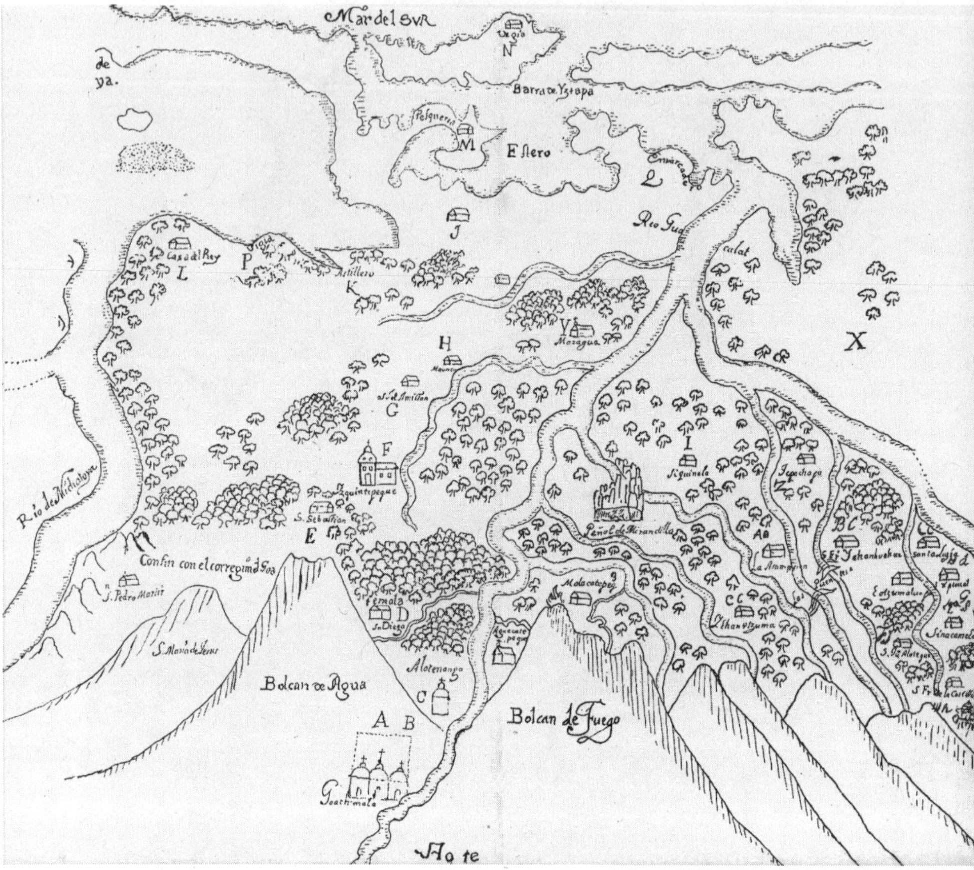

Figure 4

The Pacific coast of Guatemala (Costa del Mar del Sur) as depicted by Francisco Antonio de Fuentes y Guzmán in his *Recordación florida* (1690–99). South is top, north bottom. Indicated by the letters A and B is Santiago de Guatemala ("Goathimala"), Agua volcano to its south, Fuego volcano to its west. Yztapa (Iztapa) is indicated by the letter J, Escuintla (Yzquintepeque) by the letter F, and Masagua (Mozagua) by the letter Y.

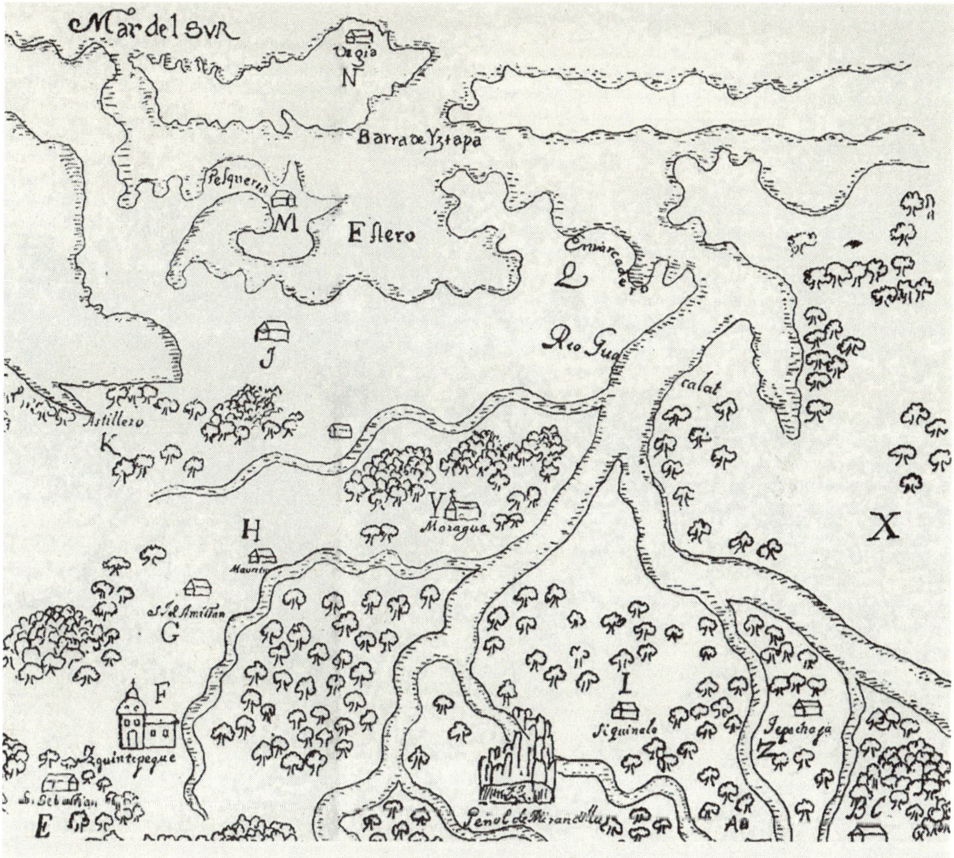

Figure 5

Detail of Figure 4. South is top, north bottom. The *envarcadero* (jetty or pier) at Iztapa is indicated by the letter L, the port's *astillero* (shipyard) to its east by the letter K. Indicated by the letter N is the *vigía* (lookout or watchtower), on an island guarding the entrance to the estuary, plagued by ever-shifting sand.

Figure 6

Shipyard slip at Realejo, Nicaragua, long since past its colonial heyday as second only to Guayaquil in terms of shipbuilding activities on the Pacific coast. Photograph by the author.

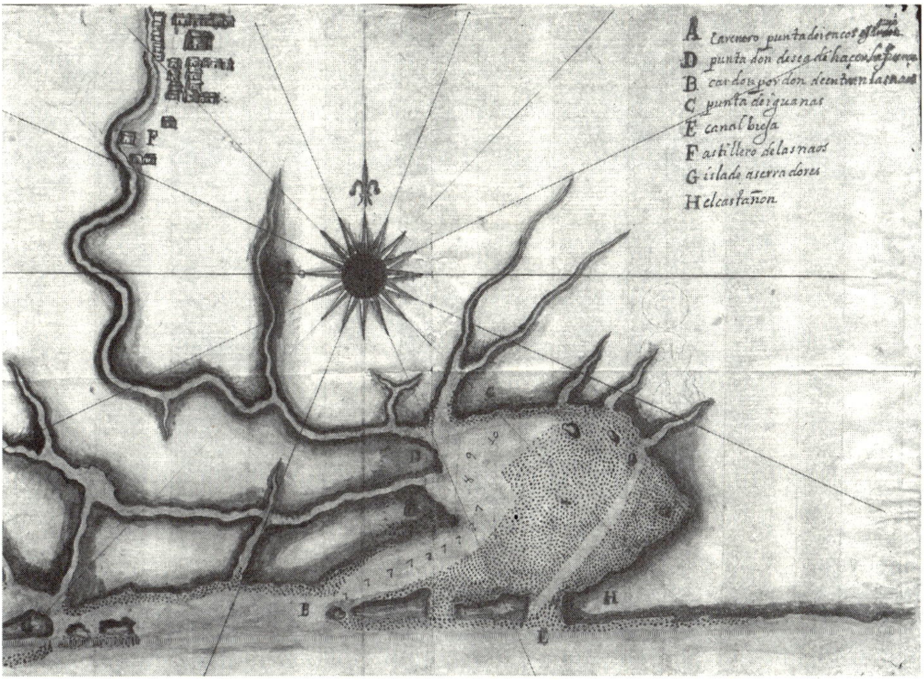

Figure 7

The Puerto del Realejo as rendered by Martín de Andújar in 1673 (Torres Lanzas [1903] 1985, 9–0). North is top, south bottom. Beneath a depiction of Realejo itself, the *astillero de las naos* (shipyard) is indicated by the letter F. Courtesy of the Archivo General de Indias (Mapas y Planos, Guatemala 6).

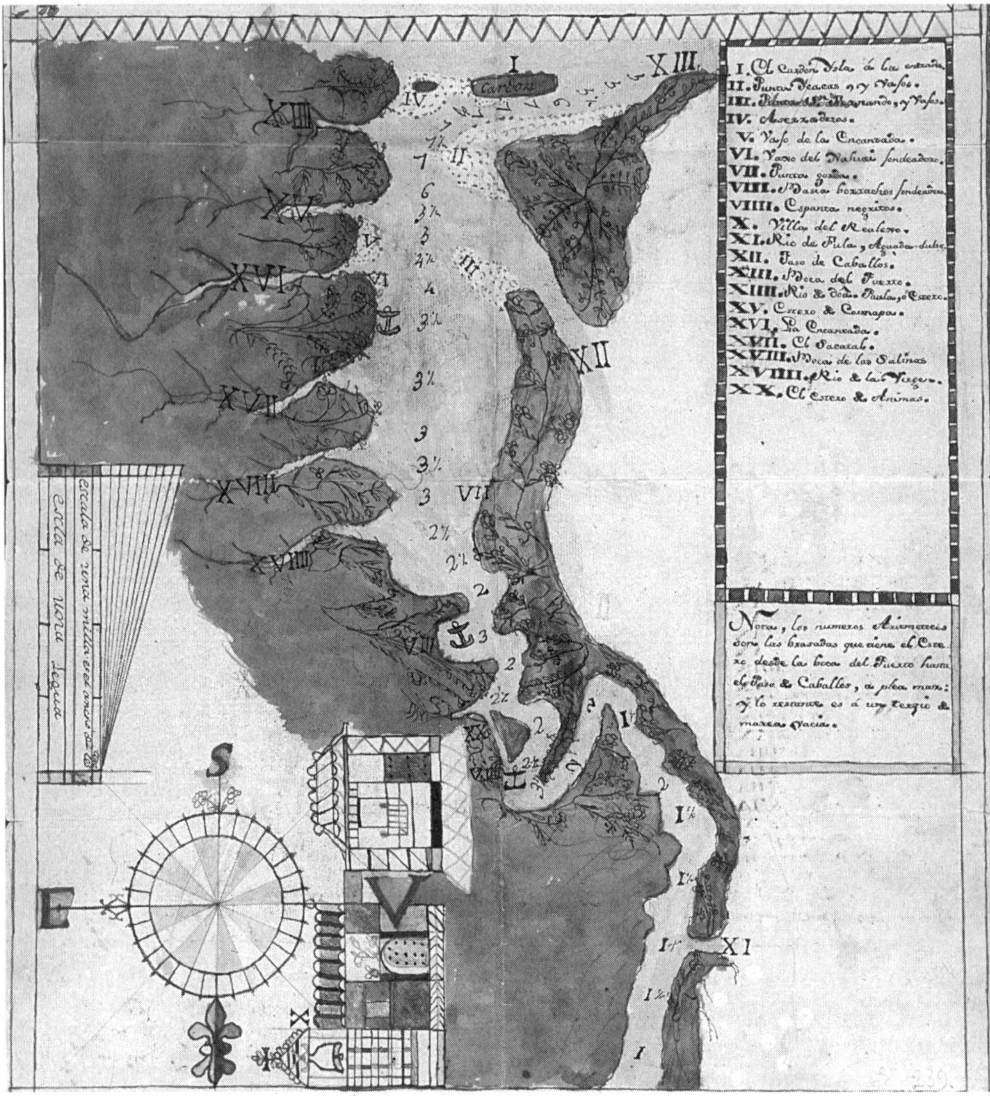

Figure 8

The port and estuary of Realejo, as rendered by Juan Gordoñez in 1779 (Torres Lanzas [1903] 1985, 142). South is top, north bottom. The Villa del Realejo is indicated by the letter x, next to the church belltower. Courtesy of the Archivo General de Indias (Mapas y Planos, Guatemala 239).

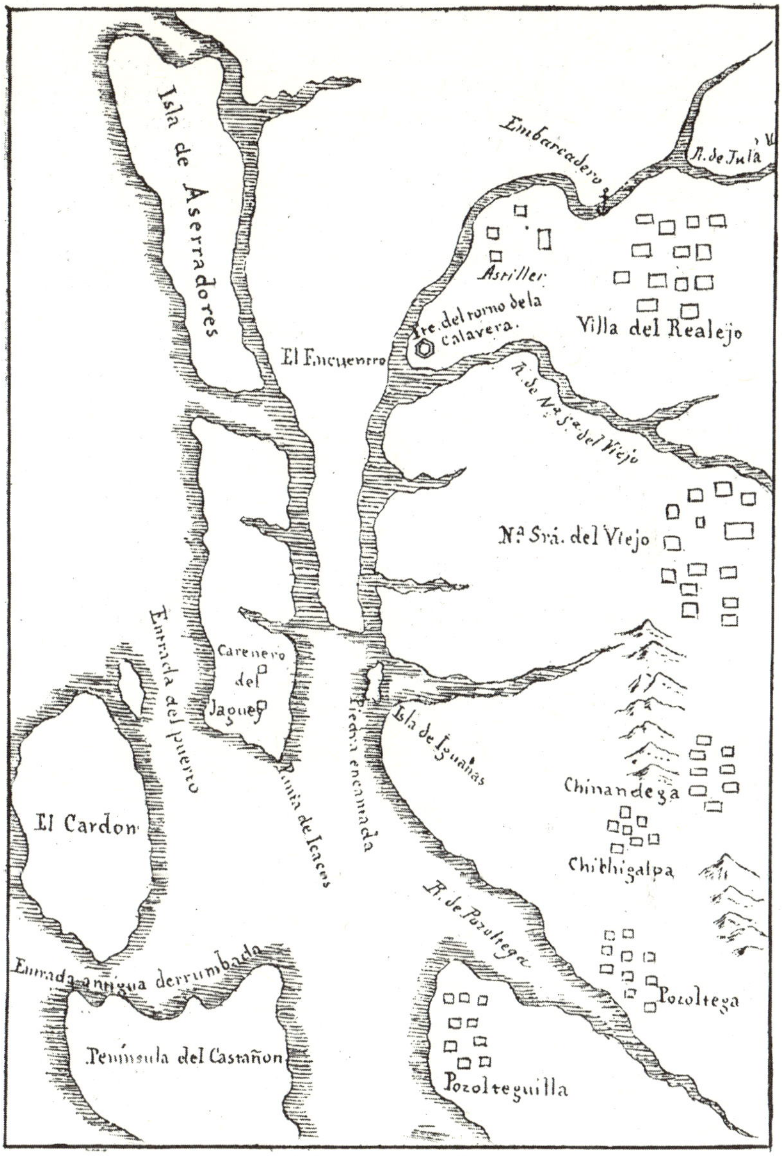

Figure 9

The port and estuary of Realejo, as depicted by Francisco Antonio de Fuentes y Guzmán in his *Recordación florida* (1690–99). The Villa del Realejo (thirteen small squares) is at the top right, its *astillero* (shipyard) the four small squares to the left. The *embarcadero* (jetty or pier) is on the river between the two. The Isla de los Jagüeyes, at the mouth of the estuary, is identified as the Carenero de Jagüey, at the tip of which is the headland known as the Punta de Icacos.

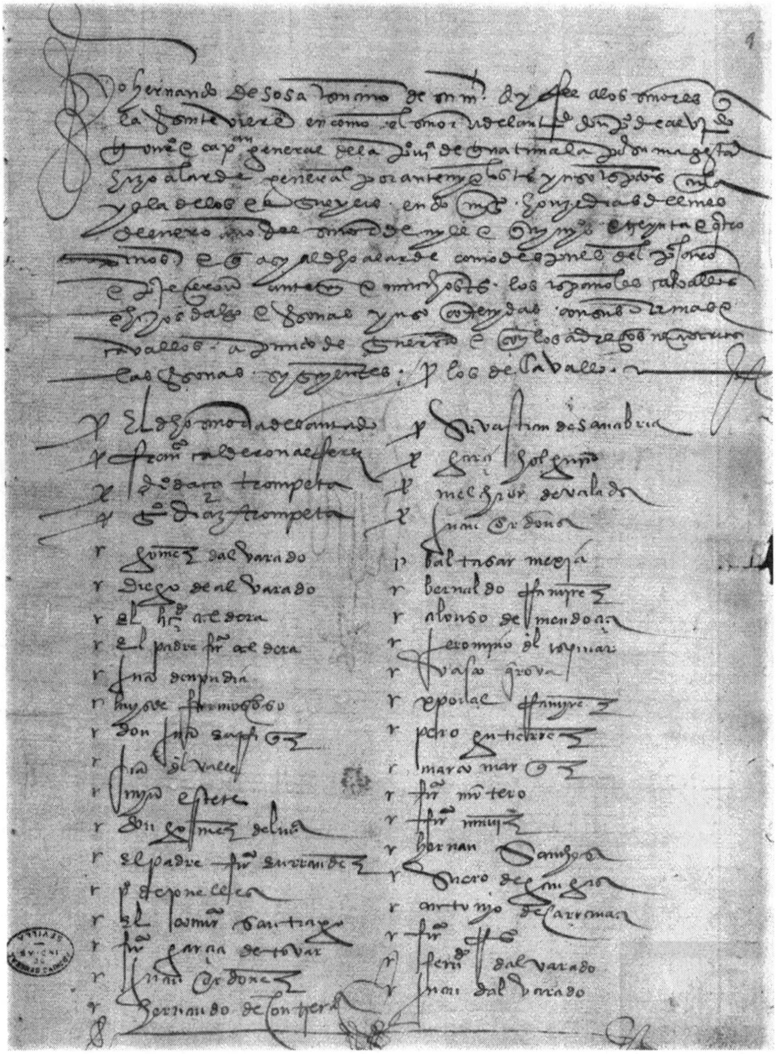

Figure 10

Folio 32 recto of the *alarde* (roll call) of men who accompanied Pedro de Alvarado on his expedition to Peru, recorded 11 January 1534 on the Isla de los Jagüeyes by the notary Hernando de Sosa. Courtesy of the Archivo General de Indias (Guatemala 41).

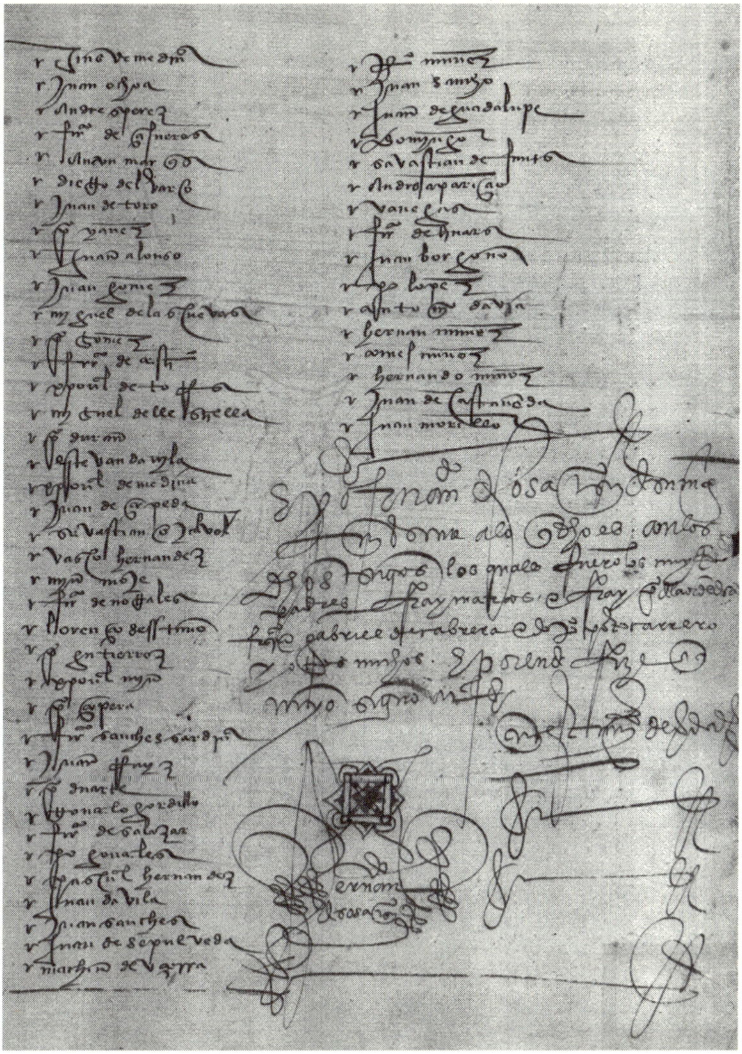

Figure 11

Folio 35 recto of the *alarde* (roll call) of men who accompanied Pedro de Alvarado on his expedition to Peru, recorded 11 January 1534 on the Isla de los Jagüeyes by the notary Hernando de Sosa. Courtesy of the Archivo General de Indias (Guatemala 41).

Figure 12

The Caráquez shore to the west of the town bay.
Photograph by the author.

Figure 13
Dated 1726, an engraving of San Miguel de Piura, founded by Francisco Pizarro in 1532, depicting a battle that Hernando de Soto is said to have had with Indigenous opponents. San Miguel is considered the first Spanish settlement to be founded in Peru. Artist unknown.

Figure 14
Chimborazo. Photograph by the author.

Figure 15

Carihuairazo. Photograph by the author.

Figure 16

Statue of Hernán Cortés, the work of Eduardo Barrón González (1858–1911), in Medellín, Spain. The words on the stone (middle left) state that "here stood the room [in the dwelling] where Hernán Cortés was born in 1485." Photograph courtesy of Sandra Taborda.

Figure 17

Statue of Francisco Pizarro, the work of Charles Cary Rumsey (1879–1922), in Trujillo, Spain. Photograph by the author.

Figure 18

Statue of Diego de Almagro, the work of Joaquín García Donaire (1926–2003), in Almagro, Spain. Photograph by the author.

Figure 19
Bust of Sebastián de Belalcázar, the work of Francisco Núñez García (1936–2018), in Belalcázar, Spain. Photograph by the author.

Figure 20

Statue of Pedro de Alvarado, the work of Estanislao García Olivares (b. 1959), in Badajoz, Spain. Photograph by the author.

PART ONE

–

Rainbow of Illusions

1. ALWAYS WANTING MORE

Having served Hernando Cortés as his *mano derecha* (right-hand man) in the conquest of Mexico, Pedro de Alvarado had seen the bounty of that land with his own eyes, and well appreciated the wealth it constituted. As ambitious as he was avaricious, upon being dispatched by Cortés to head the conquest of Guatemala, Alvarado was quick to realize that the place to where he had been sent did not compare favourably. Aptly describing Central America, situated "between the great mining centers and Indian populations of the Andes and Mexico," as "a rainbow of Spanish illusions and frenzied activity between the two pots of gold," William B. Taylor sums up not only Alvarado's geographical predicament but also his resolve to change that by moving on to more lucrative locations.[1] Writing closer to the times, the chronicler Antonio de Remesal (1575–1627) is equally perceptive. "Don Pedro was a man of proud and lofty will, intent on achieving great things," the Dominican friar asserts. "Guatemala was too small, just not enough for him, hence his search for something bigger and better."[2]

The conquest of Guatemala, however, proved no easy task and took an immense toll on natives and newcomers alike, not least because of Alvarado's reckless behaviour and wanton greed, which turned erstwhile Maya allies, the Kaqchikels, against him. Their enemies, the K'iche's of Utatlán, had been soundly defeated by the end of April 1524, two months after Alvarado's invasion, in which Indigenous warriors from Tlaxcala and other Mexican polities fought alongside the Spaniards, whom they far outnumbered. A pact with the Kaqchikels following K'iche' capitulation lasted barely six months; the *Memorial de Sololá*, which articulates the vicissitudes of conquest from a Maya perspective, records the Kaqchikels having abandoned their capital, Iximché, for the refuge of nearby mountains on 26 August. From their secluded redoubt they staged a rebellion that lasted six years, only to flare up again in 1533.[3] When Alvarado set sail for Peru a year later, in search of the riches that eluded him in Guatemala, the conquest of its tenacious Maya peoples was far from over. His brother Jorge in this regard accomplished more than he did, notably during Alvarado's lengthy absences elsewhere.[4]

Alvarado, it seems, always wanted more – recognition as much as riches. He was forever on the lookout to better himself, even if that meant jeopardizing the interests of other parties, disobeying orders or not taking them into due consideration, and running the risk of reprimand. The trait surfaced several times in his relationship with Cortés, triggering tension and discord between them, but was apparent even before they joined forces to undertake the Mexican campaign. A recounting of some pivotal incidents affords us a better appreciation of the man who saw fit to defy both king and high-court ruling by staking out a share of the booty in the conquest of Peru.

THE ALVARADO-CORTÉS RELATIONSHIP

Born the same year (1485) not far from one another in Extremadura – Alvarado's birthplace, Badajoz, lies some seventy kilometres west of Medellín, the birthplace of Cortés, downstream along the Río Guadiana – the two men first met in 1510, not on Spanish soil but in the Indies, on the Caribbean island the Spaniards named La Española, today Haiti and the Dominican Republic. Both would have been some twenty-five years of age. Cortés had already logged five years' experience in the New World prior to Alvarado's arrival, living in "the small town of Azúa, close to the city of Santo Domingo." There, Adrián Recinos informs us, Cortés "held the post of public notary, profiting from the work of Indians on lands granted him by Governor [Nicolás de] Ovando and don Diego Colón,"[5] the latter the son and successor of Cristóbal Colón (Christopher Columbus).

Alvarado must surely have been impressed at the social standing and economic assets of his fellow *extremeño*, and so moved quickly to ingratiate himself, besides touting the virtues of the brothers who accompanied him.[6] Under the command of Diego de Velázquez, in 1511

Alvarado and Cortés took up arms and waged war in the conquest of Cuba. In the wake of this engagement Alvarado "prospered for a number of years as a landholder," the historical record noting that he held property in the Villa de la Trinidad, "a person who enjoyed the confidence of the otherwise suspicious governor Velázquez."[7] Being on good terms with Velázquez resulted in Alvarado being named as one of the captains of a fleet the governor had built to set sail and explore Mexico, an expedition led by Juan de Grijalva that left Cuban shores in May 1518, nine months before the departure of Cortés. It was on this expedition that Alvarado, at the helm of "a very fine ship called the *San Sebastián*," revealed his impetuous bent, leaving without Grijalva's permission the harbour the *San Sebastián* shared with three other ships to explore "a wide river that the Indians referred to as the Papaloapan."[8] Alvarado's sortie upriver did not please Grijalva, who believed it put the enterprise at risk. After the *San Sebastián* had been reunited with the rest of the fleet, Grijalva ordered Alvarado to return to Cuba as a form of censure.[9]

The *San Sebastián* arrived back in Santiago de Cuba "carrying gold, textiles, and other objects acquired during the expedition." Alvarado cleverly turned Grijalva's censure to his advantage, currying favour with Velázquez, who "listened with great joy to the tale of newly discovered lands, upon hearing of which he decided to send another expedition, one even stronger and more numerous, to explore the riches of that far-flung territory."[10] The man chosen to lead the expedition, however, was not Grijalva – who was received by Velázquez on his return with no ceremonial tidings, these having been usurped by Alvarado – but Cortés. His armada of eleven ships left Santiago de Cuba on 18 November 1518, stopping at the Villa de la Trinidad for a period of three months to take on more men, arms, horses, and supplies. "From that port," fellow combatant and future chronicler Bernal Díaz del Castillo tells us, "sailed Alvarado and three of his brothers – Jorge, Gonzalo, and Gómez, along with a half-brother called Juan, the elder, as well as Alonso de Ávila, Cristóbal de Olid, and other notable men."[11] Alvarado boarded ship once again at the helm of the *San Sebastián*. Among his crew of some sixty soldiers was Díaz del Castillo, perhaps our most informative eyewitness. The *San Sebastián*'s contingent of men made up about one-tenth of Cortés's expeditionary force, which numbered approximately five hundred in all. Despite himself aspiring, as Recinos puts it, “to head the armada, and feeling slighted for not having been designated to do so,” Alvarado “settled nonetheless for the important role of serving Cortés as his second in command.”[12] A fortnight or so after departure, recorded as 18 February 1519, their relationship suffered its first of three notable rifts.[13]

COZUMEL

Compared to the gravity of what was to follow on the Mexican mainland, the incident that occurred after Alvarado made landfall on the island of Cozumel was of far less import, but it indicates the tense atmosphere of Spanish-Indigenous encounters whenever Alvarado was involved, especially when Cortés was not present to restrain him. Having set sail from Cuba with express orders that the armada was to make the passage to Mexico in unison, Alvarado’s pilot steered the *San Sebastián* ahead of the other vessels, arriving on the shores of Cozumel three days before Cortés himself did. Alvarado had been on Cozumel during the Grijalva expedition the year before, so he would have been reasonably familiar with the lay of the land. An attempt to round up native inhabitants saw them instead take flight, although two Indian men and one Indian woman were captured. Adornments from a temple and small chests that contained jewels also were seized, actions that displeased an irate Cortés. Upon his arrival in Cozumel, “the first thing Cortés did was to have the pilot Camacho put in irons for failing to obey orders and wait for him at sea.” According to Díaz del Castillo, he also scolded Alvarado sternly, “as angry with our captain as he had been with the pilot, telling him that he would never pacify the country by robbing the natives of their possessions.”[14] The Indians held captive were released and the stolen items returned, along with gifts of beads, bells, and Castilian clothing. Alvarado’s maverick behaviour, however, was a sign of things to come.

CHOLULA

By 12 March, no great wealth on Cozumel to detain them, the armada reached the estuary of the river in Tabasco named after Grijalva. There, ashore, Alvarado is reputed to have distinguished himself on the field of battle. Skirting the Gulf Coast littoral, on Good Friday (22 April 1519) the armada dropped anchor off the island of San Juan de Ulúa (Uluacan), across from which the Villa Rica de la Vera Cruz was founded two months later.[15] Thereafter, Veracruz served as a strategic base, Spaniards venturing from there west into interior Mexico and the seat of the Aztec empire, Tenochtitlán, about which Cortés was well informed by the Indigenous allies who sided with him.

Of these, despite initial opposition, the Tlaxcalans proved the most crucial, Cortés entering the city of Tlaxcala as a friend, not a foe, on 23 September 1519. Tlaxcalan loyalty to the Spanish cause was sealed by their leader, Xicoténcatl, offering his daughter (Tecuilvaztzin, baptized Luisa) to Cortés, who in turn passed her on respectfully to Alvarado.[16] That union was to prove not only fruitful – Doña Luisa bore Alvarado two sons, Pedro and Diego, and a daughter, Leonor, born in Guatemala[17] – but mutually advantageous.[18] It was also, given the turbulent times, relatively long-lasting: Doña Luisa died in Guatemala in 1536, a year after her return with Alvarado from his expedition to Peru. Horacio Cabezas Carcache notes that the union between Alvarado and Tecuilvaztzin/Luisa was "a lawful, religious marriage in the full sense of the word."[19] Commitment to it, he contends, swayed Alvarado to view the challenge that lay ahead, the defeat of the Aztecs most of all, through a Tlaxcalan prism, aligning himself with their interests and acting accordingly.

The Aztecs were the sworn enemies of the Tlaxcalans – and so, therefore, were those who were their allies. One such group was the Chololteca of Chololلan (Cholula), whose city-state lay thirty kilometres southwest of Tlaxcala. Between 14 and 18 October 1519, a vile massacre took place at Cholula, a slaughter that, in the view of Cabezas Carcache, had Alvarado as its intellectual author. "Grateful for such a special gift," he writes, alluding to Alvarado having been given the hand of Tecuilvaztzin/Luisa, "Pedro de Alvarado counseled Cortés to punish the Chololteca, allies of the Aztecs, in exemplary fashion, the execution of which resulted in a cruel massacre."[20]

Matthew Restall, however, allows for interpreting the Cholula massacre as an act of self-defence, one in which (believing the Chololteca were intending to attack the Spaniards within the confines of the city) Cortés struck first, or had the Tlaxcalans do so for him. "The alleged

Chololtec ambush," Restall concludes, "was probably a Tlaxcalteca ruse devised to manipulate the captains," foremost among whom was Alvarado.[21] Whether or not he, or Cortés, were taken in by Tlaxcalan claims does not negate an atrocity that, by all accounts, took thousands of Chololteca lives.

TENOCHTITLÁN

Alvarado and Cortés, as best Hubert Howe Bancroft could discern, were polar opposites: he considered the latter a statesman – prudent and careful, measured and circumspect, disciplined and analytical, a man of vision. Alvarado he saw as innately the contrary – duplicitous and egocentric, cunning and deceitful, impulsive and vengeful, a man of arms given to violent outbursts rather than an astute, level-headed thinker.[22] No better instance of his explosive temperament is the massacre he was responsible for at the Temple of Huitzilopochtli in Tenochtitlán on or around 19 May 1520.

To mark the festival of Toxcatl, thousands assembled with their lords to honour the Aztec deity Tezcatlipoca. A throng gathered in front of where Spanish forces and their Tlaxcalan allies were stationed. Cortés had departed Tenochtitán for Veracruz to fend off the challenge to his authority by Pánfilo de Narváez, sent from Cuba by Velázquez to bring Cortés to account for having set off inland on the conquest of Mexico without the governor's express consent. Left behind to serve as acting commander, Alvarado was wary and on edge. Construing that paying homage to Tezcatlipoca was nothing but cover for an imminent attack, he moved quickly, targeting a group of leaders, attired in all their finery, clothes embroidered with gold, feathers, and precious stones, just as they were about to take part in a closing ceremony. "The outcome of this assault," Recinos observes, "was the death at the hands of the Spaniards of the flower of Mexican nobility, which turned the entire city against the invaders."[23]

When Cortés returned with reinforcements to a tumultuous Tenochtitlán and was informed of the outrage, he declared it "a very wrong thing to do" – according to Díaz del Castillo, an act that proved a "considerable setback" to Spanish objectives.[24] López de Gómara, who served as secretary to Cortés, describes his master's response more subtly. "Cortés, who must have felt badly about the affair," he writes, "dissembled his feelings so as not to irritate the perpetrators, for it happened at a time when he had need of them, either against the Indians, or to put down trouble among his own men."[25] Given the severity of the episode, a backlash was inevitable. Stones from Aztec catapults pelted down relentlessly, trapping the Spaniards in their garrison, to which an incensed horde had laid siege, intent on starving them out.

A retreat to the safe haven of Tlaxcala was deemed the best chance of survival. On the evening of 30 June – enshrined in Spanish annals as La Noche Triste – Cortés and his men began a five-day battle to save themselves. This they achieved, but at enormous cost. Besides the death of two thousand "yndios amigos," according to Cortés some 150 Spanish lives were lost, six times that many in the reckoning of Díaz del Castillo. "There were few left in the end," he records, "about 440 of us, with twenty horses, a dozen crossbowmen, and seven musketeers. We had no powder, and everyone was wounded, crippled or maimed."[26] Having caused the calamity, Alvarado made amends by spearheading rearguard action during the retreat, adding to his legend in the making by an acrobatic feat at Tacuba. As the pounded party fought its way to safety, he is said to have gripped his lance as a pole and vaulted across a body of water, "one that today is called El Salto de Alvarado – Alvarado's Leap."[27]

Cortés regrouped in Tlaxcala, where the Spaniards considered their options and planned a counterattack. With vital Indigenous assistance, in a little over a year, by 13 August 1521, Cortés had executed what amounted to the reconquest of Mexico.[28] After doing so, he chose not only to overlook Alvarado's impetuosity in triggering the Aztec uprising but to entrust him, two years later, with the conquest of Guatemala. Why Cortés decided this is a matter of conjecture: perhaps he thought that Alvarado was by then too risky a partner and that having him operate farther afield was a better option for the plans he had in mind for Mexico – and the wealth he was certain to amass. In any event, it was to Guatemala that Alvarado departed in December 1523, a destination hundreds of leagues and many weeks' march away.

DISAFFECTION, DISABILITY, AND DISAPPOINTMENT

Seven months later, addressing Cortés from the Kaqchikel stronghold at Iximché after many a fray and countless setbacks, Alvarado makes clear his disgruntlement at the lack of recognition afforded him – and the meagre prospects the conquest of Guatemala entailed. "I pray Your Grace to give [His Majesty] an account of who I am and of how I have served [him] in these parts," he wrote on 28 July 1524. "And how, in his service, I am lamed in one leg, and how little return I and these *hidalgos* [noblemen from Spain] in my company have received up to the present, and the little profit that we have made so far." Sorely displeased that "His Majesty has no notice of me, which does not surprise me," Alvarado states bluntly that "for this nobody is to blame but Your Grace."[29] Aware of the riches up for grabs in Mexico, and bearing a grudge that he had nothing remotely like them to show for his efforts in Guatemala, only a war wound that left him with "one leg shorter than the other by four finger-widths,"[30] Alvarado once again let his volatile nature get the better of him. Soon after penning these lines, or more likely narrating them for a scribe to record, he turned on his Kaqchikel associates without remorse, insisting that they furnish copious amounts of tribute to compensate for the "little return" and "little profit" that until then had fallen his way – or suffer retribution for not delivering. In a matter of months, his comportment turned allies into enemies, triggering an insurrection that the Kaqchikels sustained for years.[31]

His being at odds with Cortés, despite hailing him as the person "who had given him all that he had, and that with him he wished to die,"[32] was not lost on Alvarado's mentor. Cortés pulled no punches when he wrote to Emperor Charles V on 3 September 1526:

> Otatlán [Utatlán] and Guatemala [Iximché], where Pedro de Alvarado [has] always resided, having rebelled in consequence of various offences done to them by the Spaniards, have never since become peaceable, but on the contrary have done, and are still doing, much harm to the Spaniards settled in their neighborhood, and to their Indian friends. Your Majesty must know that the country there is very broken, and the population very dense, and the people so warlike and

> brave and at the same time so trained in all kinds of warfare, offensive as well as defensive, that they have invented pits and other engines to kill the horses. And although the said Pedro de Alvarado has never ceased making war upon them with upwards of 200 horses and 500 foot, all Spaniards, besides 5,000, and at other times even 10,000 Indians, he has hitherto been unable to reduce them under Your Majesty's rule. On the contrary, they become stronger every day through the people who join them.[33]

So much for Alvarado bringing troublesome adversaries to heel, as Cortés had succeeded in doing in Mexico, notably on account of alliances struck and adhered to with "yndios amigos." Cognizant of how much Alvarado was to blame for the perilous state of affairs in Guatemala – he states plainly that the natives have rebelled "in consequence of various offences done to them" – Cortés signs off in matter-of-fact fashion. "I believe," he asserts, "that were I to go among them, I could, by mild treatment or otherwise, bring them to knowledge of what, God permitting, they owe to Your Majesty."[34] How the conquest of Guatemala would have unfolded had Cortés assumed control of it, rather than continue to delegate duties to Alvarado, is but a chimera, but one Cortés clearly envisioned as having different outcomes than those engendered by Alvarado.

2. THE LURE OF PERU

Spaniards first made contact with Inca civilization, seeing for themselves the precious items it was capable of producing, when the pilot Bartolomé Ruiz de Estrada came across a seafaring raft off the coast of Ecuador around the time that Cortés was voicing his concerns about Alvarado, as the year 1526 was drawing to a close.[1] Ruiz was venturing south at the helm of a lateen-rigged *carabela* (caravel), having left his commanding officer, Francisco Pizarro, and a party of followers farther up the Pacific coast at the mouth of the Río San Juan, in present-day Colombia.[2] This was the second expedition led by Pizarro, whose partner Diego de Almagro "figured with increasing prominence as a near equal and a potential rival."[3] In the wake of encountering, and then seizing, the laden raft, Ruiz returned to notify Pizarro, who welcomed the news.[4] He broke camp, boarded ship, and reconnoitered where Ruiz had come from, reaching as far as Atacames (Map 1), which had only lately fallen under Inca rule.[5]

According to John Hemming, twenty men had been on the raft when Ruiz seized it. Eleven of them jumped into the sea to avoid capture; it is not known whether or not they drowned, or somehow survived. Of the remaining nine, six were taken ashore and released. Three were held on to, with the idea of teaching them Spanish so that they could serve as interpreters.[6] A document that Raúl Porras Barrenechea attributes to Pizarro's secretary, Francisco de Xerez, and sent to Emperor Charles V, describes the lavish objects Ruiz found on the raft, placed there so as to facilitate commerce with partners in trade along the Pacific coast, as far as Central America and Mexico beyond.[7] Lines from the document run:

> They were carrying many pieces of silver and gold as personal ornaments … including crowns and diadems, belts and bracelets, armour for the legs and breastplates; tweezers and rattles and strings and clusters of beads and rubies: mirrors decorated with silver, and cups and other drinking vessels. They were carrying many wool and cotton mantles and Moorish tunics … and other pieces of clothing coloured with cochineal, crimson, blue, yellow and all other colours, and worked with different types of ornate embroidery, in figures of birds, animals, fish, and trees. They had some tiny [steelyards] to weigh gold … There were small stones in bead bags: emeralds and chalcedonies and other jewels and pieces of crystal and resin. They were taking all this to trade for [*Spondylus*] fish shells from which they make counters [ornaments], coral-covered scarlet and white.[8]

While the natives aboard the raft were dealt with summarily, those of Atacames were more numerous and proved hostile. "More than two hundred assembled in order to wage war," the chronicler Pedro de Cieza de León informs us, "because the Spaniards were in their land without reason or justice and against their will." The situation became fraught and precipitated an altercation between Pizarro and Almagro about whether to continue the expedition or return to Panama, from where they had set out. "They had a heated exchange about this," Cieza reveals, "so that friendship and brotherhood turned to animosity, and they reached for their swords." Ruiz and others "intervened and pulled them apart, mediating between them." It was agreed that "Pizarro would remain with the men wherever was best and that Almagro should return to Panama for succor." This he did aboard one ship while another took Pizarro to the Isla del Gallo, an island off the southernmost coast of Colombia where Ruiz had stopped over the year before (Map 1). "At the end of the first month that they had been there," Cieza relays further, "Pizarro decided that the other ship would also go to Panama."[9] On board were malcontents for whom no room had been found to leave earlier with Almagro, the vessel placed "under [the] command of the loyal and determined pilot, Ruiz."[10] A desperate period of hunger and sickness ensued for those left behind.[11]

In September 1527 two ships sent by the governor of Panama, Pedro de los Ríos, arrived to alleviate the suffering. Guided by Ruiz, they had been placed under the charge of "a cavalier named Tafur," instructed by Ríos to order Pizarro to return with his men to Panama. On the Isla del Gallo, Pizarro drew his sword and with it, from east to west, traced his fabled line in the sand. As recounted by Prescott, he then declared, pointing north: "Friends and comrades! On that side are toil, hunger, nakedness, and drenching storm; on this side," pointing south, "ease and pleasure. There lies Peru with its riches; here, Panamá and its poverty. Choose, each man, what best becomes a brave Castilian. For my part, I go to the south." So saying, he stepped across the line.[12]

The pilot Ruiz is said to have been the first of thirteen men to follow suit and cast his lot with Pizarro. Most of the men chose not to, "many of them disillusioned or disaffected," relieved at the prospect of again being on terra firma in Panama.[13] The two ships dispatched by Governor Ríos sailed back, Tafur incensed at what he regarded as not only wilful folly but also rank disobedience on the part of Pizarro.[14] Ruiz left with Tafur for Panama, arranging there to return with a ship that would continue the expedition beyond where it had been terminated earlier.[15]

On makeshift craft, Pizarro moved with his faithful to the Isla Gorgona, an island to the north of the Isla del Gallo (Map 1). On it "there are no people," Cieza divulges, "nor would there be any reason for them to populate such a wretched land" – but Pizarro "wanted to stay in a place he believed was safer than the Isla del Gallo or the mainland."[16] The Spaniards languished on the Isla Gorgona some six or seven months, until March 1528, when Ruiz again arrived from Panama.[17] After joyous celebration, Pizarro and his diehard supporters boarded the ship, which continued to bear south, with the loyal Ruiz steadfastly at the helm. The intrepid pilot steered around the Punta de Santa Elena and into the Gulf of Guayaquil, at the far end of which lay the Inca city of Túmbez (Map 1). Its merchants were the ones said to have stocked the pillaged raft so plentifully, their activities and products indicative of an advanced civilization. Incursions ashore as far south as the Río Santa convinced Pizarro even more of the booty that awaited the successful conqueror of the land the Spaniards called "Perú," a corruption of "Birú" or "Virú."[18] But how might that be effected if the influential governor of Panama refused to give it his backing?

ROYAL LICENCE AND ENDORSEMENT

Pizarro acted in partnership not only with Diego de Almagro but also with Hernando de Luque, an accord between the three having been struck on 10 March 1526.[19] Opposition on the part of Governor Ríos to their mounting any further forays led to Almagro and Luque agreeing that Pizarro should return to Spain and there seek the sanction unforthcoming in Panama.[20] This he was able to secure from Emperor Charles V in meetings that culminated in the *Capitulación de Toledo*, a contract or royal licence acknowledged in a document signed by Queen Isabel on 26 July 1529.[21] The endorsement authorized Pizarro to proceed with the conquest of Peru, whose wonders he extolled even though his two expeditions to date had taken him primarily to coastal locations, the wealth of a vast interior surmised, its dividend believed to be certain. "You may continue with the discovery, conquest, and colonization of Peru," it is stated, "two hundred leagues along the coast from the settlement the Indians call Tenumpuela, known now as Santiago, until reaching the settlement of Chincha" (Map 1).[22] Pizarro was directed to recruit 250 men to accompany him on the mission, a number in the end he was unable to muster, despite his success in rallying a good many conscripts in his native Trujillo.[23] Among them were his younger brothers Gonzalo, Juan, Fernando, and Francisco Martín de Alcántara.[24] In recognition of his services as "our chief pilot of the Southern Sea," Pizarro was able to negotiate that an annual salary of 75,000 *maravedís* be assigned Bartolomé Ruiz, "to be drawn from income emanating from the said land."[25]

Pizarro's being in Spain coincided with Cortés being there too, the latter basking in the glory of his Mexican exploits and newly anointed as Marqués del Valle de Oaxaca, a noble title to one of Mexico's most resource-rich provinces. Convinced that Peru would be the next prize catch for Emperor Charles V, Cortés championed the cause of Pizarro with gusto. "It is even said that Pizarro would have found it difficult to raise the necessary funds," Prescott observes, "but for the seasonable aid of Cortés, a native of Estremadura, like himself, his companion in arms in early days, and, according to report, his kinsman."[26]

Also in Spain around this time, hoping to convince the king to approve another expedition of conquest, was Pedro de Alvarado.

PART TWO

–

Preparations

3. ARRANGEMENTS IN SPAIN

Alvarado set sail for Spain on the first of two return journeys in February 1527, staying there until July the following year.[1] Pizarro's passage to Spain saw him reach Toledo by mid-1528.[2] Whether or not the two men crossed paths, perhaps in Seville, we do not know. Alvarado and Cortés were also in Spain at the same time, during the months of April and May 1528, but they avoided meeting, by then not being on the best of terms.[3] Cortés and Pizarro overlapped and communed, both well received at court.

Alvarado was not so lucky, at least at the outset. His hitherto close association with Cortés meant that his mentor's enemies targeted him too. Known and connected, Cortés could fend things off, but Alvarado found himself hard pressed. What he desired most was an audience with Emperor Charles V, which would allow him not only to tell of what he had achieved to date but also to propose plans for future undertakings, ones from which the Crown would benefit considerably. Upon arrival in Seville, however, Alvarado was beset by obstacles related to word of his excesses in Mexico and Guatemala reaching the Council of the Indies. Just as incriminating as his blatant abuse of Indigenous populations was his alleged malfeasance in not giving his comrades-in-arms their due share of the spoils and, even more remiss, failing to furnish the Crown its official cut, the *quinto real* or royal fifth. Prior to Alvarado's departure, a thick dossier detailing these charges had been dispatched from Mexico to the Council of the Indies. Its officers perused the missive and held the culprit to account, impounding the gold, precious stones, and other valuables he had brought with him.[4]

THE MAKING OF A NEW MAN

Serious accusations that would flummox even the most resilient saw Alvarado draw on his resolve and talk his way out, relaying to anyone who would listen tales of his daring triumphs and valiant accomplishments. This effusive baring of soul won him friends and admirers, his insistence that he knew how best to serve His Majesty eventually coming to the attention of one who had the king's ear, the influential Luis de la Cueva. Before currying royal favour, however, the dashing Alvarado first worked his charm on the De la Cueva family itself, contracting a vow of matrimony with the elder of don Luis's daughters, Francisca. Wooing Francisca served only to distance Alvarado from Cortés further, for Cortés had harboured hope that Alvarado would marry his cousin, Cecilia Vázquez, to whom Alvarado had previously been committed.[5] Not alluded to in Alvarado's wedding plans was his Tlaxcalan consort in Guatemala, doña Luisa Xicoténcatl, far removed from where the nuptials would take place. Marriage with Francisca, Recinos informs us, was celebrated "toward the end of 1527 or in January 1528, because on the nineteenth of that month, in Burgos, Alvarado acknowledged by letter a dowry in his favour of 7,000 gold pesos."[6]

Prior to the ceremony, as son-in-law-to-be of Luis de la Cueva, Alvarado endeared himself to none other than the secretary of the Council of the Indies, the powerful Francisco de los Cobos, *comendador mayor* (senior commander) of Castile, "privy to the Emperor and friend, relative, and protector of the De la Cueva family."[7] Allegations of butchery, greed, gross misconduct, and embezzlement were laid aside as Alvarado received, in effect, a royal pardon. His assets were freed up and the insignia of Santiago, rank of commander, was bestowed on him.[8] The crowning glory came when, by royal decree, signed in Burgos on 18 December 1527, he was named governor and captain general of Guatemala, a position that carried "a salary and benefits of 562,500 *maravedís* each year in office" and that entitled him to be referred to as, and call himself, "Adelantado" – supreme ruler, a designation formally conferred on him two days later.[9]

The concessions granted Alvarado pertained to Guatemala, but he took the opportunity of being at court to convince the king and his counsellors that, released from the grip of Cortés, he was capable of greater feats of conquest. We have no record before Remesal's assertion years later, but, during his stay in Spain, Alvarado raised the matter of enhancing Emperor Charles V's dominion by constructing a fleet that would explore the Pacific and navigate west across it to the Islas de la Especiería, the Spice Islands or Moluccas.[10] Although news of Peru already circulated, especially notions of its wealth and grandeur, its subjugation was still a long way off and did not then figure in any scheme of Alvarado's imagining. That would come later. His priority concern was to return to Guatemala, secure its pacification, and begin the task of building the ships that would allow Pacific exploration to be pursued.

4. CONSTRUCTING THE FLEET

On 26 May 1528 Alvarado registered his intent to return to Guatemala with the Casa de la Contratación, the House of Trade, in Seville, making his way thereafter down the Guadalquivir to Sanlúcar de Barrameda, at the mouth of the river. Not until early July was he actually seaborne, in the company (besides his new wife, Francisca) of an entourage of followers, government officials, and members of the clergy. A noteworthy representative of the Church was Licenciado Francisco Marroquín, a priest who formerly conducted spiritual duties at the court of Emperor Charles V and who later became the first bishop of Guatemala – and a lifelong defender of Alvarado. Twenty-four Dominican friars also boarded ship. Among officers of the Crown were three individuals destined to play prominent roles in assisting Alvarado to govern Guatemala responsibly, a formidable task: Francisco de Zurrilla, *contador* or accountant; Francisco de Castellanos, *tesorero* or treasurer; and Gonzalo Ronquillo, *veedor* or inspector.[1]

A stormy passage of some three months, likely with stops en route in the Canary Islands and at ports in the Island Caribbean, ended in tragedy with the death of doña Francisca. The cause of her demise is inconclusive: Recinos attributes it, vaguely, "to a rough crossing or the effects of the tropical climate" but intimates also that the young woman may have died giving birth in Veracruz.[2] After her burial, a forlorn Alvarado made the journey to Mexico City with his offloaded goods – "considerable baggage and valuable items," in the parlance of Bishop Juan de Zúmarraga – only to find himself subjected to the same fate as upon arriving in Seville the year before.[3] Charged once more with multiple acts of wrongdoing, great and small, he had his belongings confiscated and discriminately plundered while, clapped in chains, he himself was imprisoned and prosecuted.[4] Again only by royal decree, notice of which reached Mexico City on 5 April 1530, a year after the trial began, was Alvarado released from captivity and the embargo lifted on his possessions, or rather what remained of them.[5] Diminished but by no means defeated, he arrived back in Guatemala later that month after an absence of some three and a half years – "deprived of his worldly goods," Recinos reinforces, "but with his head full of adventurous ideas for the near future."[6] A change of fortune beckoned, one Alvarado must surely have believed would be for the better.

IZTAPA AND THE SOUTH SEA

"When the Adelantado was in Valladolid in 1527," Remesal relays, "in return for all the grand rewards he received from Emperor Charles V, he promised to construct a fleet he would either dispatch or himself command to explore the Pacific." On lands yet to be discovered, Alvarado insisted, abundant riches lay waiting – besides the fact that such an expedition "would also find a way to reach the Spice Islands, something much desired by the Emperor and all the kingdoms of Castile."[7]

Upon his return to Santiago de Guatemala, Alvarado moved quickly into action, deploying his nephew Luis de Moscoso to reconnoitre coastal areas with a view to advising him of the best site at which to locate a shipyard where his fleet would be built. Moscoso's commission was no easy task: sheltered, deep-water locations on the Pacific littoral of Guatemala were non-existent. After a survey of options, none of them ideal, Moscoso recommended Iztapa (Map 2), some fifteen leagues (a little over seventy kilometres) to the south of the highland capital, founded three years before (on 22 November 1527) by Alvarado's brother Jorge, on the lower slopes of Volcán Agua overlooking the valley of Almolonga.[8] Meanwhile, Cortés, back in Mexico after his sojourn in Spain, was informed of Alvarado's initiatives and, much taken himself with the notion of exploring the Pacific, demanded that his former right-hand man either desist or that they mount a joint venture. But Alvarado was having none of it. This venture was for him alone: he did not wish any partner to be involved, least of all the commander he believed he had served most loyally but from whom due recompense was yet to come.

His contract was with the Crown, with the sovereign who had received and favoured him, not with a rival he now wished to disassociate himself from, never again to be beholden.[9]

Iztapa (Figure 3) lay on the coast at the mouth of the Michatoya and Achuiat rivers, reached by descending from the cool, energizing elevation of Santiago (1,550 metres above sea level) to the humid, enervating heat of Izcuintepeque (Escuintla, 338 metres above sea level) and then skirting through Masagua and Amayuca (Figure 4). Upstream on the Río María Lindo, a short distance from shore, an *astillero* or shipyard (see Figure 5) was established, at the present site of Puerto Viejo, a *caserío* or hamlet in the *municipio* (township) of Iztapa in what is today the Department of Escuintla.[10]

How many ships were built at the Iztapa yards with Peru now in mind is not easy to ascertain. Bancroft puts the number at merely three, but in a letter penned to Emperor Charles V when taking stock of the situation, Alvarado mentions eight.[11] His search for a team of carpenters, caulkers, and skilled craftsmen had resulted, in short order, in the construction of the flagship *San Cristóbal*, a *galeón* (galleon) of three hundred tons "as beautiful as anything made in Vizcaya," and two other sizable ships, the *Santa Clara* (a *nao* or carrack of 160 tons, "a very nice piece of work") and the *Buena Ventura* (a *nao* of 150 tons). Reference is also made to five vessels on which names had not yet been bestowed – another *nao* of 150 tons, a *carabela* of sixty tons and two of medium tonnage, and a *patax* (tender) of fifty tons, to ensure that material necessary for any repairs ("pitch and tar, iron, rigging, and sails") would readily be at hand.[12] Enlisting only the best for the job, whose labours were responsible for creating "the most beautiful fleet ever seen in these parts," had cost the much-indebted Alvarado "more than 50,000 castellanos."[13]

The heavy lifting, of course, fell on native locals, especially those who lived in closest proximity to where the ships were built. "Because of the armada," judge Alonso de Maldonado noted in legal documents penned later, "Iztapa and other towns on the south coast are worn out and much diminished."[14] Kaqchikel populations also suffered greatly, made to pay for having sided with Alvarado upon his invasion of Guatemala only to rise up in rebellion after being treated so abusively.[15] Indigenous travails were witnessed first-hand by none other than Bartolomé de las Casas, "Defender of the Indians," who bemoans: "He took the lives of countless people building boats. From the Caribbean to the Pacific, a distance of 130 leagues, anchors weighing three and four *quintales* were carried on the backs and shoulders of the Indians. By the same means, too, on sad, naked shoulders, heavy artillery; I beheld many as such on the roads, laden and distressed."[16] Writing much later, though with the benefit of hindsight, Las Casas's fellow Dominican, the chronicler Francisco Ximénez, also deplored Alvarado's actions: "He began by looking for suitable locations for a shipyard, felling timber, sewing riggings, hauling iron, making tar, transporting pieces of artillery – all at the expense of the poor Indians, removing them from their homelands and taking them far away to very remote shores. Building boats cost the lives of many Indians."[17]

The scale of the venture, and fears among Crown officials of the ruination it would cause, eventually triggered moves to have it stopped.

5. OPPOSING FORCES

The contract drawn up between Alvarado and the Crown is a mundane piece of paperwork, the bureaucracy of empire at its plodding best. One thing is stipulated clearly, however, and spelled out most unequivocally: that whatever peregrinations befell Alvarado's fleet as it explored the Pacific, the Spice Islands far to the west ostensibly the destination, at all costs it must avoid encroaching on, and intruding into, territory that had been laid claim to by another party, with whom Emperor Charles V already had struck an accord.[1]

"Having pacified this province of Guatemala," the document begins, "you now wish to serve and aggrandize our Royal Crown, as you always have done, by constructing a fleet near the city of Santiago, in order to discover the secrets of the South Sea. This you have embarked upon having heard of very rich islands and of other lands on the shores of that sea, to which end you have requested licence to conquer, a request granted under the following conditions."[2] The first stipulation then painstakingly states: "Permission, power, and authority is hereby extended you, in the name of the Royal Crown of Castile, to discover, conquer, and colonize whatever islands there are in the South Sea [Pacific] to the west of New Spain, these not being located where currently there are governors in place. Likewise, permission and authority are granted you to discover whatever part of the southern mainland also lies to the west – not yet discovered, and respecting the north-south boundaries of lands that have been assigned the governance of other persons."[3] Ponderous it may be, but with regard to heeding existing arrangements, the *capitulación* leaves no doubt as to what should *not* transpire – entering areas ceded to a fellow Spaniard with *his* own agenda of conquest. Neither Peru nor Pizarro are mentioned by name, but Alvarado surely knew to whom and where the contract referred when it called for him to honour prevailing circumstances.

CHANGING COURSE

The contract authorizing Pizarro to undertake the conquest of Peru, we will recall, was signed by the Empress Isabel in Toledo on 26 July 1529, pre-dating Alvarado's *capitulación* by three years.[4] In the interim, however, word of Pizarro's exploits and Peru's riches spread far and wide, resonating with the ever-vigilant Alvarado as the construction of his fleet was underway at Iztapa. Why not make Peru its objective, he convinced himself, and not the Spice Islands? The more he thought about it, the more that made sense – at least to him: the Spice Islands would still serve as pretext, to avoid any perceived breach of contract. Peru, however, insinuated itself and took over.

It soon became apparent that this was indeed Alvarado's intention – to muscle in on the conquest of Peru, from which nothing would deter him. His friend, Bishop Marroquín, perhaps put it best when he wrote a decade and a half later: "This was the time when the call of Peru rang loud, so loud that captain and soldiers alike abandoned where they were to go there. The mind of Alvarado was fixed on higher stakes best forget the small corner that is Guatemala."[5]

Two constituencies opposed what they considered Alvarado's obsession with Peru: the Audiencia (High Court) of New Spain in Mexico City and prominent officials of Santiago de Guatemala, including Spaniards who represented the Crown in administering Guatemala and who were challenged at every turn by the actions, behaviour, and decisions of the governor of the province himself. The Audiencia, presided over by Bishop Sebastián Ramírez de Fuenleal, urged Alvarado repeatedly "to attend to the business of governing, not with constructing a fleet for purposes of exploration" that he did not have licence to carry out. Opposition was lodged on two grounds: first, that Alvarado's boat building detracted from, and thus endangered, the pacification, settling, and development of Guatemala; and second, that the undertaking subjected the native population to excessive demands that were deemed egregious even for a servile race. One of the Audiencia's censures is dated 10 July 1532;

behind its unwelcome interference – it ordered that ship construction be brought to an immediate end – Alvarado discerned the hand of Cortés, by now his nemesis.[6]

Three men – the accountant Francisco de Zurrilla, the treasurer Francisco de Castellanos, and the inspector Gonzalo Ronquillo, all royal appointees who had accompanied Alvarado on his return voyage from Spain – wrote directly to Emperor Charles V on 28 September 1531, levelling strong criticism at the Adelantado.[7] While the Audiencia addressed the king from afar – three hundred leagues (some 1,665 kilometres) lay between Santiago and Mexico City – the three Crown officials, being residents of Guatemala, could relay their concerns from closer proximity. What they have to say warrants rendition in detail.[8]

HIS MAJESTY INFORMED

Zurrilla, Castellanos, and Ronquillo begin by stating, "[W]e are not at liberty to write about what we see and feel," an articulation of their fear that simply by putting pen to paper they run the risk of any letter composed being seized and falling into the wrong hands, so autocratic is Alvarado's rule. But the king must be informed of what is seriously amiss, thereby allowing the situation to be remedied and God and His Majesty properly served. They elaborate:

> We have written Your Highness before about Governor Alvarado constructing a fleet to explore the Pacific and there discover certain provinces of which he says he has been informed. After the city attorney dispatched that last missive, along with Your Majesty's share of gold valued at 5,000 pesos, one of the Adelantado's ships returned to Guatemala from that part of the mainland [Castilla del Oro/Panama] governed by Pedro de los Ríos, bringing news of the great riches that Pizarro has discovered in Peru. The desires of Governor Alvarado were whetted and he promptly determined that he would sail to these parts with his armada. To that end ships have been made or bought in considerable haste, and the necessary accoutrements of war amassed, all with a view to

> sailing for Peru without awaiting orders or receiving licence from Your Eminence to do so. We do not know if he is thinking of heading to where Pizarro is or to another part of the same territory. What we do know is that, were he to go where Pizarro currently is, or reach the borders of his governance, that could result in much harm and the deaths of Spaniards on both sides.[9]

The three declare themselves "absolutely certain" that, were Alvarado to leave Guatemala, he would take with him "many Spaniards, arms, and horses – and a great number of Indians." Considerable damage would be wrought because "much of this territory is still at war." Removing fighting men who have put down roots in it, become landowners, and have natives working for them could easily lead to insurrection, "so belligerent and indomitable are the Indians here, unable to be brought to heel and prone to rebellion, as we witness every day for ourselves." If Alvarado personally assumes command of the armada, as he plans to, and departs with the contingent of men, horses, and weaponry he says he will, then "we guarantee that this province would be in great danger of being lost and in need of being conquered all over again." The prospect of such a reverse is only made worse by Alvarado naming his brother Jorge to serve as governor in his absence, for he would dispatch reinforcements out of province when ordered to do that, threatening the security of Guatemala even more.

Alvarado, they say, has let it be known that there is simply not enough wealth in Guatemala for a man of his ambition, that it means nothing to him to forsake it in search of greater things. That being manifestly the case, then why doesn't His Majesty assign someone to govern as His Majesty would wish, and the land and its peoples deserve? Guatemala is not so worthless as to be neglected and abandoned, especially given the effort it took to conquer it, a conquest paid for by untold Spanish lives. They urge the king to decree that any Spaniard assigned Indians to work for him not be allowed to leave Guatemala and take his charges with him – Alvarado included.

Why is the Adelantado so dissatisfied with his lot, the three men wonder – does he not enjoy, and live very well from, the fruits of half the province already? He most emphatically does, yet he has his eyes on, and no doubt will lay his hands on, certain native communities close to Iztapa that at the moment furnish tribute and labour to other conquistadors and residents of Santiago. Unlawful appropriation will see them deprived of their privileges, as has happened elsewhere; Alvarado routinely seizes assets for himself and on occasion passes them on to one of his cronies. His goal is to be lord of *all* the land, not just a massive chunk of it, even if he is consumed by delusions of grandeur vis-à-vis Peru.

As to how Alvarado finances the construction of his armada and the ancillary costs involved, the letter makes mention of the source of significant parts of his income. In 1530 alone, the toil of 1,500 Indigenous slaves earned him 12,000 pesos from his mining operations, and each year he receives 4,000 pesos from the tribute owed him by two native communities in Mexico, Yçacar (Izúcar) and Suchimilco (Xochimilco). His salary as royal governor nets him 2,000 *ducados*.[10]

Zurrilla, Castellanos, and Ronquillo repeat, again and again in their three-folio missive, that removal of hapless natives is bound to end in calamity. "Your Majesty should know that Governor Alvarado openly declares that, when he departs for the conquest of Peru, he intends to take with him all the lords and leaders of this land, along with one or two thousand Indians. He maintains that their being taken away will foster peace, because those remaining would not dare rebel. We tell Your Majesty that, were this to occur, it will be completely the opposite. Having seen their friends and relatives carried off, knowing that they might be next, Indians would be quick to rebel." The natives live in fear, believing that the boats they are building could ferry them to death thousands of leagues from home. The three officials implore the king "not to be taken in and deceived by what the Governor tells him," pleading that he enforce a recent decree, adhered to in Mexico but ignored in Guatemala, "that Indians not be displaced from one land to another, because it is clear that such measures cause them to fall ill and perish." Is it not the case already that native numbers in Guatemala diminish by the day, without their being hauled off to die by the thousands elsewhere?[11]

Given Alvarado's destructive bent, the exhortation ends with three summary recommendations:

> First, that whoever stays to govern after Alvarado departs be someone placed in charge by Your Majesty, not by Alvarado. Second, that no conquistador awarded Indians to work for him be allowed to leave; if he chooses to do so, restrictions should apply, namely that his horses and arms stay behind. Third, and most importantly, that no Indigenous leader or free Indian be removed; should any natives be taken away, they must have been branded as slaves, and recognized as such, prior to departure. This is what is called for to serve God and Your Majesty. It is simply not right to allow conquered land to be lost, for Alvarado to head off into the unknown under the guise of serving Your Royal Highness. If Alvarado wishes to make an armada then have him bring in people from afar, as Pizarro agreed to do – neither a Spaniard nor an Indian did he take from Panama. He lured men from Spain to assist him in the conquest of Peru, where Alvarado wants to conquer also.[12]

The appeal made by the three men that Alvarado "bring in people from afar, as Pizarro agreed to do," underscores their concern that the Peruvian venture would empty the land not only of natives but of Spaniards as well.[13] As recent arrivals themselves, with matters of governance to attend to, they had no desire to see fellow countrymen move on elsewhere but rather wished to have them stay put and help the fledgling colony prosper.

That what Zurrilla, Castellanos, and Ronquillo had to say reached the king's ears, or at least was read and duly noted by clerks in his Council of the Indies, is evidenced by the document in question having pertinent words written on it. In the left-hand margin of folio 1 it is stated: "Make duplicate copies of the provision concerning this matter – send one to Guatemala, the other to Pizarro."[14]

When Alvarado's copy reached him, if ever it did, he was actually not in Guatemala but in Nicaragua, at the port of Realejo, preparing to set sail for Peru.

6. REALEJO

Some eight meandering kilometres upstream from the modern port of Corinto, tucked and hidden away in swamps of thick mangrove, lies Realejo, a desultory, ramshackle place even by the standards of poor, eviscerated Nicaragua. Though forlorn and forgotten today, its oppressive year-round heat as relentless as its September rains, Realejo was once a key station in imperial Spain's Pacific seafaring.[1] It was here (Figure 6) that Alvarado put the finishing touches to the fleet he had begun to construct in Iztapa, convinced to head to Realejo on account of its sheltered location – close to the ocean (Figure 7) but not on it – and its access to top-quality shipbuilding materials, species of prized pine foremost among them.[2] His decision was vindicated, albeit at a cost, by the loss of two vessels during a howling gale while anchored three-quarters of the way between Iztapa and Realejo (Map 2) in the Gulf of Fonseca, where he had sailed to in early 1533.[3] Alvarado's fleet was depleted only temporarily, however, restored to its intended size after a spell in Realejo, known then also as Puerto de la Posesión, that proved to be more prolonged than had been anticipated.[4]

Before arriving in Nicaragua – the Adelantado also attended to business in León, the capital of the province not far from Realejo – Alvarado had written to Emperor Charles V from Santiago de Guatemala with characteristic sleight of hand regarding where his fleet was bound. Knowing full well the king's dictates ordering him to steer clear of Peru, he suggests to "Your Sacred Royal Catholic Majesty" that "in view of the slim chance Governor Pizarro has of conquering all of Peru, I believe that with my armada I can lend him the necessary assistance to carry it out fully" – by which he means the conquest of territory and peoples within the boundaries of Pizarro's *capitulación*. "I would be willing to change my plans and go to Peru," Alvarado states candidly, adding that to serve His Majesty better, and "with greater goals in mind," he has already begun to build, at considerable expense, "bigger ships." The Spice Islands he says he has not given up on – two Portuguese pilots with thirty years' experience there, familiar with the language spoken by some of its peoples, have passed on valuable information – but Peru looms large.[5]

THE WAITING GAME

Patience was never a virtue of Alvarado's, so he was much displeased at having to wait in Realejo (Figure 8) month after month for the king's decision to reach him. When it did – courtesy of Gabriel de Cabrera, the attorney general who had taken Alvarado's correspondence to Spain to deliver it to Emperor Charles V in person – he responded promptly, unable to resist commenting that he wished the monarch had done so too. "Having finished building the armada and being ready to depart some time ago," he complains, "I have been awaiting word from Your Majesty indicating His pleasure with the order to set sail. As the instructions from Your Majesty were so late in coming, I have been forced to maintain both ships and men at a cost as great as mounting the expedition itself. In constructing the fleet, I exhausted all my capital, and fell 40,000 gold pesos in debt. All told I have expended more than 130,000 gold pesos, as laid out in the accounts I enclose. However, I believe that sum to be well spent, considering what is at stake and the hope of it bearing fruit."[6]

Alvarado continues:

> Reading the instructions from Your Majesty, I note that Your Highness obligates me to furnish a fleet of twelve ships and four hundred Spaniards for the purpose of exploration and conquest. While this requirement might be judged impossible by others, in view of the fact that men and ships are so scarce in these new and far-flung lands, I consider it a mark of royal favour that I be asked to do what no one else would be able to. As my desire is to comply with everything that Your Majesty commands, God willing I set sail today [18 January 1534] with twelve craft ranging from forty to three hundred tons, of

> which eight are not less than one hundred tons, all of them equipped with munitions and supplies as well as they could be in Seville. I am heading out with 450 Spaniards, of whom 260 are horsemen, one hundred musketeers and crossbowmen, and the remainder armed with swords and lances. In addition I have a crew of 140 sailors to man the ships, besides two hundred Black slaves belonging to the Spaniards. Never before, Your Majesty, has there been seen in these parts anything like this, an expedition equal to any demand that may be asked of it, men accustomed to these lands and to the fatigues of war, veterans with experience whom I value highly. Among those recently arrived from Spain, I have recruited very good pilots, skilled in the art of navigation, who will receive top salaries, deservedly so.[7]

While Alvarado notes that two hundred Black slaves would accompany their Spanish masters, no mention is made of an Indigenous contingent. Royal representatives Zurrilla, Castellanos, and Ronquillo, we should recall, were distressed at Alvarado's declared intent of having "one or two thousand Indians" aboard ship when he sailed, the majority of them from Guatemala but many purloined in Nicaragua and some too from Mexico.[8] Given later reports of two thousand and upward of three thousand native fatalities by the end of the expedition, a figure of "one or two thousand Indians" carried off at the start may be an underestimation.[9]

As for his course at sea, the instructions issued to Alvarado conformed to those of the original *capitulación* – he was to head west across the Pacific to the Spice Islands – but allowance was made for him to explore in a southerly direction between the thirteenth degree of latitude and the twentieth, which he acknowledged, and "where it may prove best to conquer and settle."[10] No allusion is made in this letter to Pizarro and his acts of conquest – at the time of its being written, the Inca Atahualpa had been captured and executed, and Cuzco had fallen – but Alvarado prides himself on being "so fortunate that I may perform for Your Royal Crown the greatest services ever undertaken in these lands." Furthermore, he states, "in addition to what already has been embarked upon, I will send two ships custom-built for the purpose to navigate and measure the Strait of Magellan so that this route can facilitate maritime passage, the most important matter for Your Kingdoms."[11]

Challenging if not daunting feats of navigation called for a pilot of exceptional ability to assume charge of safe sailing and steady steering, an honour that Alvarado saw fit to bestow on Juan Fernández, whom he befriended while biding his time in Realejo. Fernández's partnership with the conquistador Sebastián de Belalcázar had taken him to Peru early on, in 1531, but he never felt sufficiently rewarded for his efforts, bearing Belalcázar – "like Pizarro, a man of eminence" – a grudge for having done better, as Alvarado did Cortés.[12] There is evidence that Fernández also had dealings with Almagro, the two involved in the Nicaraguan slave trade that "transported many free Indians to Peru and other places."[13] In Realejo, the pilot mixed easily among his fellow countrymen, who were enthralled by tales he could relay from personal experience – Fernández is said to have been present when Pizarro orchestrated the ambush of Atahualpa at Cajamarca, a ransom thereafter placed on the Inca's release reckoned to have been worth more than 1.5 million pesos.[14] Listening to these tales only fanned the flames of Alvarado's desire to wrest a share of the spoils. "If Pizarro, with his diminutive force, had secured such booty," Bancroft mused, "what might not Alvarado now hope for with his powerful fleet and veteran army?"[15] The dictates of the Crown, however, were adamant: the parameters of Pizarro's *capitulación* must be respected. What ruse could be conjured to flout royal decree yet not be accused of violating it?

Fernández was able to furnish a pretext at the same time as captivate his audience. He alleged, and had no trouble convincing Alvarado, that the northern reaches of the Inca empire, which had been governed by Atahualpa from Quito, lay beyond the limits of Pizarro's *capitulación* and had yet to be conquered. No doubt great treasure remained there for the taking. Fernández's assertions were confirmed by the arrival in Realejo of another pilot, García Holguín de Cáceres, earlier dispatched by Alvarado on a mission of reconnaissance "for the purpose of ascertaining the actual state of affairs and the nature of the country."[16]

What García Holguín had to say likely only reinforced a decision already made. Peru, not the Spice Islands, beckoned.

7. MANOEUVRES BEFORE DEPARTURE

God, it turned out, was not willing to have Alvarado depart Realejo on 18 January 1534, nor on the morning of 21 January, when he wrote to the *cabildo* (city council) of Santiago de Guatemala to confirm the choice of his brother Jorge as the person who would serve as *lugarteniente*, lieutenant governor, during his absence.[1] Jorge was the man singled out by Crown representatives as being the least desirable replacement, but not so in the eyes of Alvarado.[2] He sang Jorge's praises to the highest, asking members of city council to extend him "the respect and good will he rightly deserves to take care of the land," above all that they commit to ensuring the province "be governed in harmony, love, and devout zeal in the service of His Majesty."[3] Alvarado signed off with obsequious wishes for the good health and prosperity of "your most noble selves," reminding the city fathers that "my every success is in *your* best interest" and promising "to write a full report to Your Honourable Gentlemen from the land where God will guide me."[4]

On 23 January 1534 Alvarado finally set sail. A poem penned by Charles Warren Stoddard three and a half centuries later evokes the grandeur of the fleet: "Twelve ships, a galley and the lesser craft / Freighted with men and beasts, and food and arms / New lands, new seas, new peoples, conquering …"[5] The months prior to departure, however, were fraught with drama as final preparations drew to a close. Most of the ships, Alvarado could claim, were constructed under his direction, but at least two, perhaps as many as five, were acquired by other means, dubious if not unlawful. One vessel belonging to Juan Rodríguez, so Recinos informs us, was seized without payment.[6] Non-payment after acquisition proved also the case with a galleon owned by Antonio Diosdado.[7] It was certainly so with a ship jointly owned by Álvaro de

Paz, Santos de Figueroa, and a Spaniard whose surname was Cisneros.[8] Two more, one belonging to Hernán Ponce de León and a captain Soto, another to the *provisor* (bishop's deputy) Pedro Bravo and Cristóbal de Burgos, Alvarado maintained he had been forced to buy and equip to compensate for "the two" that he had acquired at public auction from the estate of the late Pedrarias Dávila, then "taken from me by [Governor] Castañeda and friends of his."[9] Their owners asserted otherwise, that the ships had been stolen.[10] Documentation pertaining to the *Concepción*, owned by Soto and Ponce de León, and the *Victoria*, owned by Bravo and Burgos, indicates just how far Alvarado was prepared to go to ensure that his needs were met – and that arrangements made by a powerful rival were conveniently nixed by his actions.[11]

A STAB AT PIZARRO

The *Concepción* and the *Victoria* had been procured by Pizarro to transport men, horses, and essential supplies to assist him in his campaign of conquest, the two ships and three more supposed to sail from Nicaragua to Peru under the command of Pizarro's friend and associate, the pilot Gabriel de Rojas. His testimony and that of seven others was recorded by the notary Sebastián de Saavedra in San Miguel in Peru on 23 October 1533, after which a copy was made and couriered by Saavedra himself to Panama. There, on 29 November, his counterpart Hernando del Castillo acknowledged receipt. Del Castillo and the governor of Panama, Licenciado Antonio de la Gama, perused the documentation before sending it on to the king and his Council of the Indies in Spain.

The *probanza* (legal documentary evidence) begins with a summary statement by Saavedra to the effect that "Captain Gabriel de Rojas arrived here in San Miguel with ten companions, saying that he had come to Peru from Nicaragua on the orders of Governor Francisco de Castañeda, sent to inform the honourable governor Don Francisco Pizarro of some of the things that have taken place in Nicaragua, on account of which no men and assistance, as was anticipated, are now forthcoming."[12] After the testimony of Rojas come the depositions, in turn, of his *compañeros* Juan Rodrigues, Juan de la Calle, Diego de Aguilera, Baltasar Vázquez, Diego Rodrigues, Francisco Rodrigues de los Arrieles, and Cristóbal Rodrigues. Of these eight men, two (Juan de la Calle and Cristóbal Rodrigues) are unable to sign their depositions, "not knowing how to write – no sabe escrivir," but all swear what they state to be true, "jurado de decir verdad."[13]

The witnesses concur that, in July 1533, Alvarado stole into Realejo one night with heavily armed men aboard ship. Under cover of darkness, he snatched from their berths two vessels on which informants must have told him work had been completed. Three others lay in slips on dry land, as yet unfinished. From them Alvarado looted vital accoutrements – anchors, cables, sails, and rigging – and made off, returning to where he then was stationed, Puerto Fonseca, some one hundred kilometres north and west along the coast. Though the incident caused no casualties, it provoked great uproar, resulting in Governor Castañeda convincing the deprived parties to go to Puerto Fonseca, confront Alvarado, and demand that the ships either be returned or paid for. Bravo, Burgos, and Ponce de León courageously did so – a face-to-face encounter with Alvarado under these circumstances surely ran considerable risk – but to no avail. They managed to exact a promise from him to give back the pilfered items from the three ships still in dock at Realejo, thereby making them seaworthy.

The promise, however, was never kept. Not addressed in the disclosures is whether or not Alvarado sought to justify his depredation by alluding to the ships of Pedrarias Dávila that had been impounded after he bought them, the Adelantado asserting he had bills of sale to prove that he had. The three men who went to Puerto Fonseca returned to Realejo empty-handed and relayed their lack of success to Castañeda, who was incensed at such scandal and rampage ("mucho escandalo e alboroto") giving his governship of Nicaragua a bad name.

Also having occasion to discuss matters with Castañeda was Luis de Moscoso, Alvarado's nephew. Moscoso had been sent by his uncle to negotiate a deal with the governor, whose seat of authority was in León, the old capital of Nicaragua lying inland fifty kilometres to the east of Realejo. The deal, if such it can be called, involved Castañeda throwing a cordon around Realejo and environs "so that no ships, or men on them, could leave Nicaragua to be with [and help out] Francisco Pizarro, governor of Peru, until the Adelantado packs up and heads off to those parts with his armada." Alvarado was prepared to enforce his demand by having a "300-ton galleon, armed and equipped, stand guard at the mouth of the port to make sure that no vessel left Nicaraguan waters for any part."[14] Moscoso is said to have sweetened the deal with Castañeda by offering him four thousand pesos – not so much a bribe as a proposal of payment, one that would see money change hands in exchange for "certain horses and Black slaves that the governor owned, and on the condition that no ship leave port."[15]

Castañeda was not swayed. Instead, he moved in short order to fit out a brigantine of his own, the *San Pedro*, and dispatched Rojas to advise Pizarro of Alvarado's marauding and his intent to invade Peru. The *San Pedro*, minimally stocked and manned to make the journey as swiftly as possible, secretly left Realejo, so Rojas testified, in mid-September 1533, "escorted for safety's sake from port to the mouth of the estuary by two armed ships, for it was suspected that there, to obstruct passage to the high seas, a vessel of Alvarado's lay waiting."

The brigantine slipped past any watch without incident and made its way south. After a transit of "thirty-five or thirty-six days," the *San Pedro* reached San Miguel, bringing word of "people in Nicaragua about to come to Peru on one of the eleven or twelve ships in the Adelantado's armada." Alvarado's justification for butting in, Rojas stated, was because "Pizarro, according to the Adelantado, is operating beyond the boundaries of his territory, on territory that has been awarded to him."[16] An encroachment of "two hundred leagues," Cristóbal Rodrigues is recorded as stating, had taken place, Alvarado bent on going to Peru to serve notice of trespass to Pizarro in person and "to take the gold from him" that he believed to be his. Meanwhile, Rodrigues worried that, if preventative measures aimed at having Alvarado desist from further pillage in Nicaragua were delayed, "a ship called *Santiago*, and others still there [in Realejo], will be stolen," as were the *Concepción* and the *Victoria*, as well as the "anchors, sails, cables, and dinghies" of the three vessels in dry dock.[17]

Two weeks after the *San Pedro* snuck away, Castañeda, seething at the challenge to his rule that Alvarado's comportment (or lack thereof) represented, and mindful that nothing in what had transpired, or was about to, was to the Crown's benefit, issued a stern command:

> I order that no one, be they a resident, denizen, or inhabitant of Nicaragua, sell the Adelantado Don Pedro de Alvarado any provision of corn, or meat, or any foodstuff whatsoever. Nor, as well, to sell to anyone who comes looking for them, with Alvarado's needs in mind, whether they arrive in person or send by messenger a written request. Any conduct to the contrary will be charged and incur the death penalty, as well as the loss of the offender's estate, which will accrue to His Majesty.
>
> With respect to the Adelantado forcibly entering Realejo, removing and making off with two of its best ships, he now has returned with an armed vessel and men, and is anchored at the mouth of the port, set to take the remaining ships, then abscond and cause trouble with Governor Francisco Pizarro, who is undertaking in His Majesty's name the conquest of Peru. Preventing necessary assistance from reaching Pizarro is Alvarado's aim. I order that this be publicly proclaimed, so that no one can allege not to know.[18]

Castañeda entrusted Rojas with a missive he had penned to be hand-delivered to Pizarro, thereby letting the governor of Peru know what manoeuvres were afoot and warning him what to expect. Rojas was able to comply with Castañeda's red alert five weeks after leaving Realejo, three months before Alvarado departed. One of the crew aboard the *San Pedro* with Rojas, Diego de Aguilera, was in no doubt that "the Adelantado pursues all means of impeding that assistance get to Pizarro." Aguilera is also recorded as having heard "from marines and other people" in Alvarado's company their belief that, when all was over, "in these parts he would be king of the land."[19]

The Adelantado's ambitions, literally, knew no bounds.

8. THE ROLL CALL

The number of ships that formed Alvarado's fleet, as Bancroft puts it, "is variably stated."[1] Equally variable are estimates of how many would have been aboard when the armada, "the likes of which has never been seen before," finally set sail, ostensibly for the Spice Islands but with Peru now the intended destination.[2]

Regarding the number of Spaniards who boarded ship, Alvarado himself provides four different tallies. The first, when the fleet was moored at the Gulf of Fonseca, is of "doscientos de caballo y quinientos hombres de pié – two hundred cavalry and five hundred infantry."[3] A second, made five days before departure, is of 450 men, 260 of whom were cavalry and 190 infantry; among the latter were one hundred crossbowmen (*ballesteros*) and shotgunners (*escopeteros*), the remainder foot soldiers with "espada y rodela," carrying swords and shields.[4] Several weeks later, after entering the Bahía de Caráquez in Ecuador and taking stock, he furnishes five hundred, of whom 280 were foot soldiers, 220 horsemen.[5] Six hundred "hombres de mar y tierra" (soldiers and sailors) and 223 horsemen is what Alvarado relays subsequently, the former the same tally invoked by chronicler Gonzalo Fernández de Oviedo (1478–1557), who gives a cavalry count of 240.[6] Writing after Oviedo did, Antonio de Herrera (1549–1626) goes with Alvarado's third reckoning of five hundred men, but with a cavalry count of 227.[7] Prescott also accepts "five hundred followers, of whom half were mounted, and all admirably provided with arms and ammunition."[8] So, too, does Bancroft declare five hundred "the estimate here adopted" in his deliberations concerning the number of Spanish combatants, 230 designated as cavalry.[9]

NAMES AND DESTINIES

Alvarado, we should recall, mentions that a crew of 140 sailors manned the ships, and that two hundred Black slaves accompanied their Spanish masters.[10] An Indigenous contingent numbering in the hundreds if not the thousands, though seldom mentioned, must also be taken into consideration: a precise figure of 1,184 is mentioned in a judicial inquiry conducted years later.[11] The names of these luckless ones have gone unnoticed, if not their fate upon arrival in Peru.[12] However, thanks to the bureaucratic bent of imperial Spain – specifically a register made by His Majesty's notary Hernando de Sosa – we have a record of the names of 436 Spaniards who embarked and sallied forth.[13]

On 11 January 1534, a Sunday, so De Sosa indicates, an *alarde* (roll call) of Alvarado's men was conducted on the Isla de los Jagüeyes (Figure 9) downriver from Realejo at the entrance to the port.[14] The notary witnessed the show of force alongside other observers, among them "the most reverent fathers Fray Marcos [de Niza] and Fray Pedro [Bravo], of the Franciscan order; [attorney] Gabriel de Cabrera and don Pedro Portocarrero; and a good many others." Before him, and them, paraded "Spaniards, gentlemen, and members of the nobility, with their weaponry and horses, ready to wage war and outfitted accordingly."[15]

The roll call (Figure 10 and Figure 11) is a remarkable document, brought to the attention of Spanish historian Carmelo Sáenz de Santa María (1913–1993) in the Seville archive by his "buen amigo," the Salvadoran historian Rodolfo Barón Castro (1909–1986).[16] Sáenz de Santa María transcribed the document and made some incisive commentary about its contents, but his transcription has a number of infelicities that called for the original to be looked at again.[17]

Appendix 1 reproduces the names listed in the order in which they appear in the document, rather than alphabetically, as rendered by Sáenz de Santa María. The two-column format of De Sosa is also adhered to. Five folios record "Los de cavallo," those who boarded with a horse, 274 in all; three folios record the "Alarde de gente de pie," those who boarded on foot, a total of 162.[18]

Alvarado, "el dicho señor Adelantado," is first on the roster, followed by Francisco Calderon, *alferez* (ensign or second lieutenant). Two trumpeters, Diego Daça and Gonzalo Diaz, come next, their placement on the list (see Figure 10) imparting a sense of occasion if not ceremony to the proceedings; one imagines their fanfare bugles blowing as the troops filed past. On De Sosa's roll call are some notable names, including ten Alvarados, the Adelantado's brother Gómez and his cousin Diego among them, registered fifth and sixth respectively. A nephew, Luis de Moscoso, is three or four below; another nephew, Alonso de Alvarado, appears farther down.[19] He went on to become a prominent protagonist in the conquest of Peru, ending his military career at the rank of *mariscal* (marshal).[20] Also noteworthy is Garçilaso de la Vega, a captain whose union with an Inca princess bore them a son.[21] Baptized Gómez Suárez de Figueroa, in recognition of paternal relatives, the son was eventually successful in his quest to be called after his father and yet retain his mother's royal identity.[22] He became Garcilaso de la Vega, "El Inca," the celebrated author of the *Comentarios reales* – the *Royal Commentaries of the Incas* ([1609/1616] 1966), in which he would write about Alvarado's invasion of Peru, having heard about it first-hand from his father and his peers, besides reading about it in the works of Agustín de Zárate, Cieza de León, and López de Gómara.[23]

Just as striking as the names of certain individuals recorded in the roll call are those of a few not on it – yet who we know were aboard the armada when it left Realejo. One such absence is the Franciscan friar Marcos de Niza, later the perpetrator of the myth of the Seven Cities of Cíbola.[24] De Sosa acknowledges Fray Marcos, by name, as having been in his company (see Figure 11) when he drafted the register, but the friar does not appear on it.[25] Fray Marcos "and several other friars," Bancroft discloses, "were added to the expedition" before its departure. Their inclusion came about, in Alvarado's own words, "in order that through the influence of these holy men our consciences may be cleared of guilt."[26] Two other conspicuous absences are Alvarado's Tlaxcalan consort Tecuilvaztzin (Luisa) Xicoténcatl and their daughter, Leonor, both of whom were certainly present, "well looked after by the Spanish women and men who served them during the time they were with the Adelantado in Peru."[27] An *hijo bastardo* (illegitimate son) of Alvarado's, Diego, was also taken along, then eight or nine years of age.[28] All told, Bancroft reckons, "the total number was little short of three thousand," including "two thousand natives, male and female."[29] Having that many on board, with premium space taken up also by horses, weaponry, foodstuffs, and supplies, surely meant cramped, crowded, and precarious passage.

In one of his letters post-departure, Alvarado refers to "good people left behind because of a lack of ships" to carry them. Perhaps when they learned the fate of those who did journey to Peru with the Adelantado, the same "good people" were thankful not to have been among them.[30]

PART THREE

–

Arrival

9. LANDFALL AT CARÁQUEZ

After thirty-three days at sea, on 25 February 1534, Alvarado's fleet sought the shelter of a mainland bay and dropped anchor off the shores of Caráquez (Figure 12) in present-day Ecuador.[1] Knowing where he was headed, but having to justify otherwise, Alvarado claimed that, despite "always sailing to the west, in accordance with Your Majesty's instructions, and covering almost four hundred leagues," the elements proved too formidable. "Strong currents" and "contrary winds," which put the fleet at risk, are singled out as the reasons behind his decision to forgo westward navigation and, instead, "make my way, forced to do so, toward the land of Peru."[2] In order to ensure safe passage, Alvarado informs the king that, prior to entering the Bahía de Caráquez, he had been "obliged to throw overboard more than ninety horses," adding pointedly: "Perhaps it would have been necessary to lose all the others, and even some of the expedition because of lack of water, had we not landed without knowing what part of Peru it was."[3] That assertion is negated by his reckoning that "the beach called Curaqua," where he came ashore, lay "more than three hundred leagues" from Pizarro's location.[4]

Alvarado's head pilot, Juan Fernández, had been in these parts some two years and three months before. As master of the *Santiago*, one of two ships that made landfall in Ecuador on 15 November 1531, he arrived from Nicaragua with "a party of about thirty men and twelve horses" then under the command of his associate Sebastián de Belalcázar, on a mission of assistance for Pizarro.[5] Fernández is credited with having steered the Adelantado's fleet "con mucha dificultad – with great difficulty" – to secure harbour in Caráquez rather than, as originally planned, have it pull into a cove at Charapotó, on account of adverse weather.[6] The natives are said to have welcomed Alvarado hospitably, but informed him that some three weeks prior to his arrival another

Spaniard, one Hernán Ponce, "had landed here and laid to waste five towns lying between Puerto Viejo, ten leagues west of Caraque, and the promontory of Santa Elena."[7] Around the same time that Alvarado was in Caráquez, "a ship captained by Cristóbal Rodrigues also arrived, with twenty Spaniards and five horsemen aboard." Having learned of Alvarado's presence, these men had sought him out and volunteered to join his ranks. "Given their willingness," Alvarado states, "I helped them out, taking care of their freight costs and any other debts that they owed."[8]

Rodrigues, it transpired, was one of the men who had accompanied Gabriel de Rojas aboard the *San Pedro* when the brigantine had been dispatched from Realejo by Governor Francisco de Castañeda to alert Pizarro of Alvarado's intention to leave for Peru. From Rodrigues, Alvarado learned that many Spaniards like him had become so disaffected with Pizarro, and the lack of prospects under his leadership, that casting their lot with a rival conquistador was perceived to be advantageous. While Pizarro was off waging war in the interior, and enriching himself from the proceeds, they languished in San Miguel de Piura, as uncared for as others there who felt marooned by the lack of ship traffic. A strategic coastal base from which to orchestrate the movement of people, horses, goods, and services along the Pacific, back and forth from Panama, needed to be established and made operative.[9]

Alvarado proposed as much in a letter to the governor of Panama, Francisco de Barrionuevo. "The residents of San Miguel are desperate," he conveyed on 10 March, two weeks after landfall. "In all the governorship there is no other Spanish town. And with Pizarro himself so far removed, it strikes me that in order to sustain San Miguel, and assist anyone who comes to these parts, it would be a good idea to found a town in this district where I am." He adds: "I don't wish to be the judge of this, and am not myself disposed to undertake such a thing. But His Majesty would be better served in this province were that to prove the case." Meanwhile, lest resourceful people, stranded and aggrieved, give up on Peru and abandon it altogether, Alvarado alleviated their plight by diverting some of his ships from exploratory ventures to embark on a mission of rescue to San Miguel (Figure 13). As with Rodrigues and his alienated insubordinates, he "assumed the arrears of these notable men, bringing them and what they have to offer back into His Majesty's fold," a gesture that included looking after much-prized horses.[10]

THE COASTAL SETTING

The contact period and early colonial geography of where Alvarado landed has been reconstructed with incisive flair by Linda A. Newson, her work drawing on a plethora of sources, among them the pioneering contributions of John Murra and Jacinto Jijón y Camaaño.[11] Newson identifies, from the Río Mira in the north to the Isla Puná in the south, several cultural-linguistic groups along the Ecuadorian coast (Map 3): (1) the Malaba, whose name means "the devil," so designated by their enemies (2) the Cayapa, who, with the Nigua, Campaz, and Caraque, inhabited the Esmeraldas region; (3) the Manta, conspicuous for their tattooed faces and noted for their seafaring expertise, in addition to being accomplished stonemasons; (4) the Chono, the most spatially dispersed and inland of occupants, but with access to the sea; (5) the Huancavilca, whose lands were naturally the most arid but tremendously fertile when irrigated; and (6) the Puná, reputedly the most belligerent of all the groups, their island territory ruled by seven lords, "of whom one was the paramount chief." These peoples, who farmed and fished, hunted and gathered, "comprised tribes or small chiefdoms" that, though "closely related," nonetheless "remained largely independent" – and indeed "often conducted wars against each other." The Huancavilca and the Puná had resisted Inca encroachment from the east, fending off Andean aggression not long before confronting the conquistador might of Pizarro, Almagro, Belalcázar, and Soto.[12] Juan and Judith Villamarín concur with Newson's deft reconstruction. "Coastal societies remained politically independent of the Inka," they assert, adding: "Inka expeditions into the region were unsuccessful in establishing either control or a significant presence."[13]

Prior to Spanish intrusion, Newson reckons that living conditions on the coast may have supported an aboriginal population of more than half a million – between 546,828 and 571,821, to be precise. Most of them, some nine out of ten, thrived as members of socially stratified and politically integrated communities south of the Río Chone, to which Alvarado was drawn or led, and which suffered appallingly as a result of his depredations. Before the Adelantado's arrival, however, native numbers would have fallen and welfare been compromised on account of the ravages of Old World disease, of which smallpox was the first and perhaps the most fatal of hitherto unknown contagions.

By century's end, Newson estimates, epidemic episodes had levelled coastal populations by 95.3 per cent, to a mere 26,491.[14] After the initial eruption of smallpox (1524–27) came three more bouts (1558, 1562, and 1582) along with outbreaks of measles (1531–33), typhus (1546), mumps (1585–91), and illnesses of an unidentified nature.[15] Indigenous demise in the wake of the Spanish invasion was even more precipitous than during the decade that preceded it, when foreign infections spread ahead of the foreigners themselves, the advance guard of destruction.

DELEGATION OF DUTIES

Though the passage from Realejo had taken its toll – the loss of so many horses was a considerable setback, people were weak and weary, and ships clamoured for repairs, large and small – Alvarado wasted no time in addressing his forces, rallying them to the challenge that lay ahead: to make their way to Quito and the treasure that there lay awaiting, its bounty enough for everyone. Before traversing the coast en route to the Inca citadel high in the Andes, bearings had to be established and a division of labour struck that would allow the party to proceed as an organized, coordinated collective toward its goal. Cieza de León, the "prince of chroniclers" who interviewed participants a decade or so later, and wrote up what was relayed to him in a page-turning narrative, words Alvarado's clarion call memorably thus:

> In this place [Caráquez] the Adelantado spoke to the people with the words that governors here used to mislead in order to carry out their deeds. He said that he had plenty for himself [as] he was governor of Guatemala, but so that all could become rich, he wanted to take on the present endeavor.
>
> Because it was expedient to put the field regiment in order, he decided to choose captains and other necessary officers. He then named Diego de Alvarado [his cousin] as his campmaster [*maestro de campo*] and as captains of the cavalry, Gómez de Alvarado, his brother, and Luis de Moscoso [his nephew]. He chose Don Juan Enríquez de Guzmán as captain of the infantry. [Rodrigo de] Benavides [took command] of

> the arquebuses and Mateo Lascano of the crossbowmen. He encharged Francisco Calderón to be general standard bearer [*alferez general*] and ordered Rodrigo de Chaves to be captain of the guard [*capitán de la guarda*]. And he named, as chief justice [*justicia mayor*] of the camp, Licenciate [*Licenciado* Hernando de] Caldera, and Juan de Saavedra as high constable [*alguacil mayor*]. All of these offices were given and announced with the agreement of Licenciate [*Licenciado*] Caldera and the highest leaders.
>
> Alvarado decided that the ships would go to Puerto Viejo [Manta] and that the people should march on land with the horses and the service people, many men and women whom they took from Guatemala and Nicaragua, and many of whom died either because of the sea or from the great hardship they suffered on land.[16]

Having been contemplated for years, though downplayed or denied for just as long, Alvarado's meddling in the conquest of Peru was about to unfold where it mattered most – on the ground, in territory nominally part of Pizarro's governorship but with the governor himself fortuitously absent.

10. RANSACKING THE COAST

Alvarado's landfall at Caráquez coincided with Pizarro's spearheading operations to assert control over the Inca capital, Cuzco, which culminated in a Spanish presence being established there on 23 March 1534.[1] When Pizarro was last in the vicinity of Caráquez is unclear, but that he had been, and indeed is attributed with having subjugated that part of the Ecuadorian coast, was articulated by Almagro when he addressed the king from San Miguel de Piura on 8 May 1534. Almagro states that Pizarro had sent him to San Miguel to attend to the needs of Spaniards arriving from Panama who planned thereafter to join Pizarro's ranks and "in short order populate and pacify those lands where the governor currently is." When he arrived in San Miguel, however, Almagro found the people, "Spaniards and natives alike, much altered," quite alarmingly so. Their state of agitation, he imparts, was the result of actions taken by Alvarado since his arrival "with many foot soldiers and horsemen further up the coast at Puerto Viejo, some two months ago." Despite the fact that Puerto Viejo – and towns nearby – fell within Pizarro's governorship, were administered from San Miguel, and had been "at peace and under the protection of Your Majesty since the time Pizarro himself passed through," Alvarado had gone on the rampage and reversed a stable state of affairs.[2]

Almagro describes Puerto Viejo, today Manta, as a strategic stop on the way farther south, where ships were repaired, supplies replenished, and Spaniards took rest, received in good faith by native leaders whose people "lodged and fed them, attending to their every need before they moved on."[3] Because of his intent to reach and conquer "a province called Quito, rich in gold that lies inland from Puerto Viejo," Alvarado turned on the locals as a means of helping him get there, "casting them in chains and roping them together to serve as carriers" as part of the expedition. The barbarous behaviour of Alvarado had been so extreme, Almagro alleges, that natives fled their communities and resorted to arms to repel the invaders, killing "one or two Spaniards and wounding several others when they raided a town on the Santa Elena headland, which was formerly at peace." Almagro feared a full-scale insurrection and, once Pizarro learned of Alvarado's plundering, which included the seizure of a ship destined to aid the governor, conflict arising between the two. "May God forgive him," he ends, "but never in all his life will Alvarado be able to make amends for the evil he has perpetrated on such a prosperous land" – and on such a peaceful people.[4]

Five months later, Almagro supported his claims of egregious behaviour by having fourteen individuals, in a deposition dated 12 October 1534, furnish sworn testimony to as many as thirty damning allegations.[5] At least five of those who testified – Vicente de Bejar, Pedro Bravo, Antonio Picado, Bernardo Ramirez, and Diego de Vega – had left Nicaragua aboard Alvarado's fleet and had been party to what took place in the immediate aftermath of landfall at Caráquez.[6] Their statements thus constitute veritable eyewitness accounts, which coincide and do not contradict. Testimony given is corroborated further by the disclosures of crew members of *La Concepción*, a ship of Pizzaro's that had arrived in Panama from Peru early in April 1534, having put into Puerto Viejo for supplies a month or so before as it made its way north from San Miguel. "Instead of finding the Indians at peace," friendly and helpful as before, seamaster Bartolomé García reported that, since the Adelantado's arrival, "towns have been levelled, destroyed, and abandoned." Food had been seized and native leaders, "as well as ordinary men and women," taken away. Nothing remained as once it was. "'Why are you killing us?' the Indians are reported to have asked their aggressors, complaining vociferously about the grief Alvarado had caused them."[7]

MURDER AND MAYHEM

Alvarado dispatched almost half of his ships ten leagues along the coast to Manta, two having returned to Nicaragua (by way of Panama) to pick up more men and horses, another two (with Juan Fernández in command) continuing farther south.[8] Alvarado headed overland to Manta via Charapotó, which he had hoped might serve, at least temporarily, as a base of operations (Map 4). After he and his men had been there "only two or three days," well fed and looked after, their conduct became so obnoxious that, according to Pedro Bravo, "the townspeople rose up against them." The Spaniards left in haste for Manta "with many Indian men and women, boys and girls too, chained or tied together," not all of whom survived the journey. Those who greeted the Spaniards at Manta fared no better, "killed afterwards on the road to Quito because they tired along the way, exhausted and unable to carry the loads thrust on them."[9] Among the fatalities was the *cacique* (chief) of Manta, hanged because he allegedly incited "other Indians who lived close by to rebel." How anyone would have known this, Bravo insists, could never be verified, "because no common language facilitated such an understanding."[10] Equally distressing was to have seen another *cacique* thrown to the dogs, one of his subjects burned alive, and others suffer the same fate "for not being able to show the Adelantado and his captains the road they should take to Quito."[11]

Bravo's testimony is echoed by other witnesses, who add gory details to Alvarado's infamy, none more so than his then secretary, Antonio Picado. On the road to Manta, the Spaniards having been driven out of Charapotó, Picado recalls seeing "the bodies of many Indians, male and female, littering the road – some dead from exhaustion, others killed by sword thrusts or their heads hacked off by knives." Children had been taken from their mothers and left behind to die, the women who had given birth to them forced relentlessly ahead. Even newborn babies were snatched and cast aside as their mothers were driven forward, laden down as carriers of camp equipment, not infant offspring. The sacking of towns was such that, having grabbed people from the safety of their homes to serve as pack bearers on the route march to Quito, "hardly a house remains inhabited."[12] Alvarado's onslaught against "anonymous Indigenous masses" is deemed by one Ecuadorian scholar to be among "the greatest of scourges perpetrated by Spaniards in the Americas," but "no different from the methods used by other conquistadors," the names of Almagro, Belalcázar, Cortés, and Pizarro summoned up with that of the Adelantado.[13]

WAYWARD PEREGRINATIONS

Quito may have been his intended destination, but how to get there was to stymie Alvarado for the next several months. Where he had landed was not a desolate stretch of coast like that of Peru proper, south of Túmbez an arid littoral made that way by the desiccating impact of the Humboldt current and its chilly offshore waters. Instead, "the first European to do so," Alvarado would have to traverse what Jijón y Camaaño describes as "magnificent virgin rainforests" covering a "pre-Andean interior" between the sea and the sierra. It was an environment hospitable, well-tended, and kindly for those who lived there – but intractable to outsiders, who "crossed the coast" only to get "lost in the mountains."[14] The expedition's collective strength was sapped, its momentum waylaid time and again on account of Alvarado never receiving accurate and reliable counsel about what route would take him to where he wanted to go.[15]

In Manta, Cieza de León tells us, "an Indian who said that he had seen, with his own eyes, the many riches that were in Quito promised to lead Alvarado on a safe route to the city."[16] A two-day hike, according to Herrera, took the party to Ramadas, which Loor identifies most likely as the present-day Montecristi.[17] From there the next stop was Jipijapa, which the Spaniards named Del Oro, "the place of gold, because of how much they found there."[18] After Jipijapa came Paján (Map 4), referred to by the Spaniards as Las Golondrinas, so called because of its swarms of swirling swallows.[19] It was here that the Indian guide, after barely one week of assistance, "saw an opportunity and fled," much to Alvarado's consternation.[20] The Adelantado's trek toward treasure was about to become a travail of the lost.

To determine how best to get to Quito, Luis de Moscoso was ordered to head out in an easterly direction, reaching Bani or Vacain and then Chonana, in Huancavilca country (Map 4). There he found abundant provisions, rounded up some locals to serve as replacement guides, and sent word to his uncle, Alvarado, to join him.[21] The Adelantado complied, acknowledging, however, that his whereabouts and the road to Quito were still unknown. To allay confusion and ascertain their position, Alvarado organized another two exploratory parties in the hope that at least one of them would elicit information that could be acted on reliably. His brother Gómez, with thirty horsemen and a contingent of foot soldiers, was dispatched to the north, getting as far as Yagual before reaching "the territory of Niza."[22] Rodrigo de Benavides, a trusted captain, struck off "in the easterly direction," his party making it to the Río Daule, also the name of an important settlement.[23] Despite the two missions having reconnoitered in different directions, both their leaders returned to Chonana to inform Alvarado that they had been told that Quito could be approached either way.[24] The Adelantado chose the Benavides option, which he would later regret.[25]

No road awaited the Spaniards at Daule, though a navigable river did, which served the needs of the locals better than any Inca highway. Had Alvarado been better informed, following the river north to its headwaters would have taken him some one hundred kilometres west of Quito. Instead, rafts carried men downstream south before a decision was made to reverse course. Navigating the river was eventually abandoned in favour of an overland march that zig-zagged for weeks and months to the north and east, skirting the lower slopes of mountains without finding any easy way to cross them. González Suárez depicts the expedition as ending up well and truly lost in "the daunting labyrinth of the intertropical forests" of central Ecuador.[26]

The road to Quito was proving considerably more elusive than had been anticipated.

PART FOUR

–

Up, Over, and Down

11. ASCENDING THE ANDES

Cieza de León is by far our best source in documenting Alvarado's ascent of the Andes, his calamitous trek over a pass between two volcanoes, and his descent thereafter to safety if not security on the eastern side of the sierra. Putting pen to paper in the 1540s, Cieza himself was not an eyewitness to what occurred. He makes it clear, however, that what he narrates comes from testimony relayed to him by individuals who themselves were participants, fortunate to survive a debacle that scores and hundreds, if not thousands, did not. "Some honorable gentlemen alive today," he imparts, "from among those who had entered into this kingdom with the Adelantado Don Pedro de Alvarado, reported to me that …" and off he goes, often with nuance, flourish, and attention to detail worthy of any assiduous documentarian.[1]

Alvarado himself, of course, wrote about the episode, in two letters in particular, both addressed to the Crown and discussed in chapter 12. However, since little (if anything) was to his advantage in revealing incriminating particulars that were the expedition's undoing, some of which took innocent lives and unleashed ruination far and wide, silence or fabrication, at times outright lies, served him better. Not so with Cieza. "Believe me that when I write," he asks of his readers, "I would rather leave out much of what I know and pass it over than to include even a single word of what did not happen. This you will comprehend and learn. My only wishes are to relate the truth with sincerity."[2] The discovery by Francesca Cantù of the long-lost part 3 of Cieza's *Crónica del Perú*, which covers Alvarado's Peruvian (mis)adventures in painstaking fashion, is cause for scholarly celebration.[3]

"After [the Spaniards] reached the Daule River," Cieza tells us, "and still could not find any road, Alvarado ordered squads to go out in all directions to see where the highway to Quito was." Juan Enríquez de Guzmán took off with Luis de Moscoso "to explore wherever fortune would lead him," only to fall sick and die "of an affliction that he had," other Spaniards perishing too "in great misery, without any comfort or anything other than the hardship of marching."[4] The party led by Francisco García de Tovar, "a diligent and very capable man, who later became a captain in Popayán" in Colombia, and whom Cieza "knew well," fared better. His northward advance took him to "a village with a large population and with many cultivated fields, maize, and some roots." Alvarado was summoned and ventured forth. But his foray to join Tovar coincided with an explosive volcanic eruption, "so much ash or earth in the air that it seemed the clouds were expelling from within."[5] With great difficulty – for days on end wind-blown ash blinded his men and covered the vegetation that fed their horses – the Adelantado made it to where Tovar was. There he regrouped and once again "ordered the captains to go out in squads in all directions to explore." One delegation arrived at a place called Chongos, beyond which (a four-day trek) was the village of Noa.[6]

A cousin of Alvarado's, Diego, and eighty others – "split between the horsemen and the footmen" – trudged on, "always in the northerly direction." It was agreed that, upon reaching a staging area from which to cross the mountains, notice would be conveyed to the Adelantado, who would then join them. A cautionary measure called for all those sick, infirm, or exhausted to stay put before following suit, Hernando de Caldera entrusted with looking after them. The party under Diego's command traversed a stretch of forest "so somber and frightening that the thickness of the trees almost kept out the sunlight with their branches." They emerged finally onto flat land, where "herds of sheep increased their joy," and proceeded to a village Cieza names Ajo, "where there was a lot of salt for trade between the natives."[7] Mention of copious amounts of salt suggests that where Diego and his entourage now were was Salinas, the present-day Salinas de Guaranda, also known as Salinas de Tomabela, situated at an elevation of 3,550 metres some twenty kilometres north of Guaranda (Map 4).[8] Native inhabitants, the Tomabela, "were warned about the coming of the Spaniards, news that greatly amazed them because they thought they were crazy to suffer such hardship in order to search for gold." Not wishing to meet such men, the locals did what so many others had done – "they fled."[9]

Cieza continues: "Diego de Alvarado and those who arrived with him rested from the hardship and hunger, eating those good rams that they found there. He decided to send notice to the Adelantado, as well as some meat and salt." Melchor de Valdés was charged with this duty, a mission of relief much welcomed by Alvarado, whose men had resorted to eating "lizards, mice, snakes, and anything that they could put into their mouths, even if it were these repugnant things." Hunger prevailed, "so great that every day Spaniards, Indians, and Blacks were dying, which was very distressing."[10] Some of the animals that Melchor de Valdés had brought with him Alvarado made sure were shared with Caldera, whose struggling assembly plodded farther down the trail, the worst-off of a sad, sorry lot.

At this stage in the campaign, Cieza notes, "the camp was divided into three parts: one with Diego de Alvarado, another with the Adelantado, and another with Caldera."[11] Diego's contingent was the avant-garde. Rather than await the arrival of Alvarado, and Caldera behind him, Diego took the initiative and forged ahead, leaving the shelter of Ajo for what would prove to be the most hazardous leg of the expedition.

12. TRAIL THROUGH THE PASS

Chimborazo (Figure 14, elevation 6,268 metres) towers majestically to the east of Salinas (Cieza de León's Ajo). Ten kilometres northeast of it the jagged peaks of Carihuairazo (Figure 15, elevation 5,018 metres) pierce the Andean skyline. A pass between the two volcanoes, identified by Gonzalo Molina as the "puerto de nieve llamado Tomavela," lay between the Spaniards and the Inca highway that would take them to Quito.[1] "Alvarado chose the wrong route to penetrate the Andes," John Hemming states succinctly, "and climbed one of [its] highest passes."[2] The Adelantado also chose the wrong time of the year to make the crossing, it being late July/early August when he did so, a period "when snowfall is at its heaviest and winds at their fiercest."[3]

Alvarado's cousin, Diego, was the first to try his luck.[4] Before leaving Ajo he conferred with his fellow Spaniards – Indians and Blacks pressed into service presumably had no say in the matter – urging them to accompany him in what all knew would be a perilous undertaking. Agreement attained, Cieza assures us, off they went, "along a path [until] they reached some large mountains, as covered by snow as others usually are by forests." A wind from the south "blew so strongly that it was an even greater evil, because the cold was extreme." Was there no other, no better way to forge ahead? "It was impossible to cross in another place," Cieza asserts, "even though they wanted to attempt it by going the long way around. They feared the mountains, but forced by necessity to learn what lay ahead, they plunged into that snow."[5]

Cieza's compassion – for luckless locals, enslaved natives coerced from Guatemala and Nicaragua, and his own countrymen – suffuses his narrative with a poignant air:

> It horrifies one to describe them – that they would go into this snow without knowing when or where they would end up, or without any other information than whatever the natives gave them. Indeed, when they entered the snow-covered passes, huge snowflakes were falling from the clouds, which bothered them so much that they did not dare to raise their eyes to see the sky because the snow would burn their eyelashes. The Indians whom they brought could not move their feet. They took on the horses those whom they could, and because they did not carry great baggage and travelled lightly, they squeezed through as much as they could with such difficulties that they thought they would all be dead. After they had gone more than six leagues, it pleased God that they did cross the peaks, although it was already late; and coming out of so much snow, they arrived in a somewhat large village where they found many sheep and other provisions.[6]

Cieza does not indicate the name of the safe haven arrived at, Herrera neither, but Jijón y Camaaño believes it was Pasa.[7] From there Diego sent word to the Adelantado "advising him how and in what way he should cross the snow and how afterwards all would find provisions to eat."[8]

ALVARADO'S PASSAGE

Alvarado, whose contingent was the largest of the three, got to Ajo before Caldera did, losing some of his followers on the steep climb up. Fearful of what awaited them, they soon found themselves in deep snow. Into its treacherous drifts they went, many more perishing than when Diego passed through. Spaniards were among the casualties but were far outnumbered by hapless Indigenous conscripts, who had never experienced such extreme conditions before. "The falling snow burned their eyes, and many lost their fingers and feet when they walked," Cieza imparts. "Others froze to death, their expressions fixed. It was very cold. The south wind did not cease to blow." Spanish fortitude he attributes to doughty men having "great constitutions and such marvellous courage," traits not so evident in the natives. But even Hispanic resolve fell short when confronting such untoward elements. Upon emerging from their tents one dawn, chilled to the bone after freezing all night long, the Spaniards decided that enough was enough. "Without further discussion or debate, like those who flee from the plague or are escaping a great storm," Cieza discloses, "they returned to where they had started, the village they left behind."[9]

By then, Caldera's party had arrived and set up camp in Ajo, expecting a guide or two to come down and lead them forward, not an entire body in ignominious retreat – albeit from the forces of nature, not human adversaries. Alvarado consulted with Caldera, the two concurring that another ascent should be attempted. If Diego had succeeded, so could they. Cieza recounts:

> Knowing what he had seen, the Adelantado was distressed that the people could not stop dying in those snowdrifts. He longed as if for salvation to be in the territory that Diego had discovered. Hiding his anguish, he tried to animate the Spaniards, speaking encouragingly to them so that they would go on. He knew that they would rather confront an enemy who had an advantage over them in battle than to fight against the elements. They commended themselves to Almighty God, and setting out on the way, they marched, talking about the snow, until they came to about one-half league from it, and they stationed themselves there.[10]

The following morning, Alvarado, Caldera, and company headed off, onward and upward, "without seeing the sun or the sky or anything other than snow, the wind so strong that it penetrated through them and caused them to lose all feeling." It grieved Cieza to learn of "unfortunate Indian men and women who went with them, crying about dying so miserably, lamenting their misfortune, and calling out with dreadful voices to their elders."[11] He paints a grim picture:

> They had no cloaks, and the cold was so terrible that they fell down deprived of all strength, and expiring, they released their souls from their bodies. There were many who, out of

> exhaustion, leaned against some rocks and ledges that were in the snow, and as soon as they rested, they froze to death in such a way that they looked like scarecrows. The Spaniards who had the strength and walked without stopping were lucky; they escaped, as did those who rode horses without taking the reins or turning back their heads. Many Blacks also froze to death. And although Spaniards have a better condition than any nation in the world, some of them began to die, without having any other graves than the snow.[12]

All told, Cieza reports that "fifteen Spaniards and six Spanish women died in these snows, and many Blacks and more than three thousand Indian men and women of those who had gone. Many of the Indians who did not die escaped maimed, some without fingers and others without feet and some completely blind."[13] Of such manifest tragedy, what does Alvarado have to say?

In the first of two letters addressed to Emperor Charles V, the Adelantado puts his passage from shore to sierra as having lasted seven months – at least one month longer than it actually was. He acknowledges, when starting out, "coming across peoples hitherto unknown" and hacking his way through "enormous swamps" inhabited by "savage peoples, one town to the next, all speaking many different languages." Farther on, beyond "unbearably cold, treeless uplands," lay a pass "where the snow that fell on us was so heavy that for a while we were lost." Alvarado admits "not coming out of that situation at all well" – quite the understatement – and of losing "more than six hundred Christian souls and helpers, though few Spaniards were among them."[14] He makes no specific mention of Indigenous deaths.

In a second letter the Adelantado reiterates seven months as the duration of his ordeal, reckoning that he covered 160 leagues traversing "the roughest of country imaginable, without equal in any part of the world," its "mountains, rivers, and swamps dense and unhealthy." Many fell seriously ill with fever and died, "more than eighty men," survivors left demented and disoriented, obliging Alvarado to inquire daily about the condition of his troops before marching on. He himself "fell so sick that I passed out, gravely ill for two days, and in a critical state for ten more. I almost lost my life." Throughout the ordeal, he relays, "my journey was undertaken without us having any idea of exactly where we were," no assistance or guidance afforded by disparate locals, especially regarding queries about Quito and "any Christians they may have seen or heard of." On trudged the Spaniards until they ran into "a huge windstorm of snow and hail, its ice and chill tremendous," taking the lives of "nine Spanish men and women, and nearly all the Blacks and other helpers, some horses too." Again, no mention is made specifically of native casualties, alluded to nebulously as "other helpers – otra gente de servicio." Such was the torment and suffering "we had to endure to get out of there," the Adelantado laments, that "not a single one of us was able to hold on to our clothing, let alone the gold and silver taken from the Indians, left along the wayside pass for anyone who cared to have it." The only thing that mattered "was to save ourselves." Hunger was so great that "we resorted to eating pieces of cooked palm." And if a horse were killed, "its worth as food to eat was valued at 2,000 castellanos."[15]

Alvarado's debilitated party eventually dropped down from the mountain pass of Tomebela "and arrived in the village of Pasa,"[16] where Diego had reached earlier and lay waiting. There, thankful to God for having spared them, those still alive licked their wounds, recuperated as best they could, and moved on to nearby Quizapincha, from where a day's journey at last took them to "the great royal highway of the Incas."[17] Between Ambato and Muliambato, much to his chagrin, the Adelantado found "traces of hoofprints made quite recently," which meant only one thing: Spanish horsemen had already passed through. First right of conquest would be theirs, not Alvarado's.[18]

13. HOOFPRINTS ON THE HIGHWAY

The hoofprints on the highway that Alvarado stumbled on belonged to horses ridden by men in the company of the Mariscal (marshal), Diego de Almagro, and his second in command, Sebastián de Belalcázar.[1] How did they come to be there?

After Gabriel de Rojas made known Alvarado's Peruvian aspirations (see chapter 7), Pizarro took steps to counter them. Even before word reached him of the Adelantado having landed at Caráquez, Pizarro had assigned Belalcázar to serve as his lieutenant governor in San Miguel de Piura.[2] When Alvarado's impending arrival became the talk of San Miguel, Belalcázar wasted little time in rallying a force that he would lead to Quito to occupy it and establish Pizarro's authority – not only over the imperial city but also over the kingdom ruled less than a year before by the murdered monarch, Atahualpa. Using his share of the spoils from Cajamarca, Belalcázar "began to trade in horses and recruit people," writing to Pizarro to let him know of his intentions and "to excuse himself for leaving [San Miguel] without his authorization."[3]

Belalcázar set off in early March, his ranks swollen by Indigenous Cañaris who sided with the Spaniards against hated Inca enemies now under the command of Rumiñahui, Atahualpa's brother and successor – and a proven military tactician. The entourage led by Belalcázar reached Quito in late June, by way of Tomebamba or Tumibamba (modern-day Cuenca), Teojacas, Riobamba, Ambato, Latacunga, and Pancallo, every leg of its march north met with stiff resistance, which would not have been surmounted without Cañari allegiance and the deployment of thousands of Cañari warriors as auxiliaries. Upon entering Quito, a bewildered Belalcázar found it all but deserted, its stately buildings and ordinary dwellings razed by Rumiñahui, who had absconded with the city's treasure and fled with its inhabitants for the refuge of nearby forests.[4]

Almagro, meanwhile, at the bidding of Pizarro, had been urged to get to Quito at all costs ahead of Alvarado, thereby pre-empting its conquest by the renegade intruder. He first went to San Miguel, where he expected to find Belalcázar, whose being a key participant in his mission he was counting on. Angered by Belalcázar's instigating a campaign of conquest without official sanction to do so, Almagro left San Miguel in early May and followed the upstart's footsteps to Quito. He became even more irate when, upon arrival, Belalcázar was again nowhere to be found, on this occasion off "looking for the treasure that they said was in Cayambe."[5] Summoned back to Quito by Almagro, "who reprimanded him for having left San Miguel without the governor's order," Belalcázar defended his actions, "declaring that it was the wish to serve that had motivated him to do what he did."[6] Whether or not Almagro was convinced by Belalcázar's declaration of loyalty, the two put their differences aside and tracked back south. The conquest of Quito was to be unfinished business for some time to come, but its contours had been delineated. Yet to be ascertained, and of crucial importance, were Alvarado's whereabouts.

THE TWO PARTIES MEET

Because of sustained native defiance, Almagro and Belalcázar's return was just as fraught as their advance, the highway to Riobamba the target of repeated attack while they and "little more than 180 between the horsemen and the footmen" traversed it. Three Spaniards were killed at Chambo, the culprits pursued and captured. Their leader caused quite a stir when, during interrogation, he disclosed that, up by Ambato, "many Christians and horses had crossed the snowy mountains and that they were near them."[7] Alvarado no longer approached – he had arrived.

With Lope de Idiáquez placed in charge, Almagro dispatched eight men on horseback to verify what had been reported by the chief of Chambo. Idiáquez carried a letter from Almagro stating who he was and his disposition, worded diplomatically, to assist those encountered by his scouts in any way he could.[8] A little over halfway between Riobamba and

Ambato, at Mocha (Map 4), Almagro's scouts met their rival counterparts – a party headed by Diego de Alvarado, which had been given the task of tracing where the hoofprints the Adelantado had seen on the highway led to. The two parties faced off but did not come to blows. Being larger and better armed, the Alvarado contingent relieved Almagro's men of their weapons and escorted them to where the Adelantado was camped, at Panzaleo, some twenty kilometres north of Ambato.[9]

When Idiáquez and companions were brought before Alvarado, "he spoke to them courteously, telling them that he did not come to cause offence or to provoke war, but to discover new lands whereby the emperor would be served." They responded, prudently, that "no other thing had been presumed of his lordship, especially because it would be evident to him that that land [he was on at present] fell within the boundaries of Don Francisco Pizarro."[10] It was now Alvarado's turn to have pen put to paper and explain his position: that his goal was to conquer territory that lay *outside* Pizarro's jurisdiction. The Adelantado's viewpoint was stated in "gracious letters" given to the scouts to deliver to Almagro.[11] Matters would be cleared up to the satisfaction of all concerned, Alvarado insisted, if or when he and Almagro met face to face, man to man, in Riobamba.

PART FIVE

–

Saving Face

14. NEGOTIATIONS WITH ALMAGRO

Almagro was rightly apprehensive about having Alvarado in his midst, knowing only too well what he was capable of. His reputation for ensuring that he got what he wanted, by foul means or fair, preceded him. Actions taken by the Adelantado spoke more decisively than his duplicitous words, evident in the devastation wrought since landfall at Caráquez almost six months earlier. How to deal with such a menacing presence would be quite the challenge, not least because, while Alvarado's exertions slogging up from the coast had diminished his apparatus of war considerably, the horses, weaponry, and manpower at his disposal were still far superior to those of Almagro.

Choosing bureaucracy and paperwork over sabre rattling, Almagro moved strategically to found the Ciudad de Santiago de Quito, the first Spanish city to be established in what is now Ecuadorian territory. Lots were laid out in what was then referred to as Riobamba but which in actual fact was Sicalpa, on a level plain near the Laguna de Colta south of Cajabamba.[1] The founding of Santiago de Quito is enshrined in the *Libro primero de cabildos*, the earliest record we have of formal settlement, dated 15 August 1534. Almagro oversaw the proceedings but did so in Pizarro's name. The notary Gonzalo Díaz registered the presence of ten individuals, who took office and assumed membership of the *cabildo*, all of them (unlike Almagro) literate enough to sign their names.[2] Two days later, on 17 August, the council convened again, on this occasion to enter in its minutes the names of sixty-eight Spaniards who declared themselves to be *vecinos* (residents) of Santiago de Quito.[3] Though the formation of the municipal entity was hasty and improvised, its legality prevailed, serving as indisputable evidence that other Spaniards had arrived in these parts before Alvarado – theirs was the authority to rule and dictate accordingly, not his.

Cabildo Counsel

On 19 August, the third meeting of city council in four days, Almagro sought the advice of *cabildo* members on how to tackle the threat on their doorstep. Minutes record the meeting having been called "on account of the damage and disgrace caused by the blatant disregard of the Adelantado don Pedro de Alvarado for the law of the land." His "being here, intent on passing through, is very much against our will." Almagro posed the dilemma thus: "Is the Crown better served by our impeding passage or by allowing him to move on, thereby excusing damages already committed or ones that might be done in the future?" Another issue raised was whether to maintain the population of Santiago de Quito "at its present level" or induce some of Alvarado's men to settle there, with the city's future growth in mind.[4]

Opinion solicited, the *alcalde* Diego de Tapia was the first to respond. "Mariscal Almagro should not leave this province," he argued, "but stay put with those he can depend on to defend our interests. Were he to depart, then Alvarado could arrive and, finding no one to oppose him, easily take over." Tapia perceived divisions in the Adelantado's ranks that, if exploited, might work to Almagro's advantage. "It is known that many who side with Alvarado right now are sore displeased," he contends, "and have made it plain that, given the right time and place, they would come to this city, where the Mariscal is" – and switch allegiance. Furthermore, alluding to the Cañaris who had fought alongside Almagro to crucial effect, Tapia asserts: "With the assistance of so many Indian allies, the Mariscal, in His Majesty's name, can resist Alvarado's advance, the better to serve His Highness, to the benefit of these lands."[5] Tapia's insights indicate awareness of a dynamic, evolving situation that involved more people than the two main protagonists, whose enmity was mutual, despite the rhetoric of correspondence that implies otherwise.

Gonzalo Farfán was next to respond. The magistrate favoured Almagro returning to San Miguel and "recruiting people who would confront the Adelantado, stopping him in his tracks and preventing further plunder." This measure would also "cut off support that might come from Puerto Viejo or elsewhere."[6] What Farfán suggested was seconded by Cristóbal de Ayala and five other *regidores* (aldermen).[7]

ENVOYS AND DEFECTIONS

As Alvarado moved ever closer to Santiago de Quito, envoys shuttled back and forth between the two camps, their mission to devise a peaceful solution, not one settled by force of arms. Almagro delegated the clergyman Bartolomé de Segovia, the captain Rui Díaz, and the ensign Diego de Agüero, who had been recruited by Pizarro in Extremadura in 1529, "to go to the Adelantado to congratulate him and to assure him that he [Almagro] was much distressed by the great hardships and dangers that his lordship had suffered in the snow and since his departure from Guatemala." Alvarado chose as one of his ambassadors the notary Martín de Estete, dispatched "to ask Almagro to provide him with some interpreters and to safeguard his way for going ahead to explore what was not in Pizarro's governance."

At this juncture lines of communication became strained. Almagro responded to the Adelantado's overture "with protractions and excuses," stating that he could not possibly comply – "nor could it be allowed that such a sizeable army should pass through what [already] had been won." Besides, he was simply "unable to furnish provisions for so many people."[8] The situation deteriorated after Alvarado followed up his request for interpreters by taking matters into his own hands. Spies infiltrated Almagro's redoubt and convinced Felipillo, a native go-between who had assisted Pizarro in his dealings with Atahualpa at Cajamarca, "to run away and cross over to [Alvarado's] camp, where he was well received."[9] Almagro retaliated in kind, luring none other than the Adelantado's secretary, Antonio Picado, to his side.[10] The tit-for-tat, of which Felipillo and Picado were but two exemplars, now looked likely to result in violent confrontation.

An incensed Alvarado told four hundred of his men to prepare for action. The squadron left Mocha, marching "in perfect order until [it] reached Riobamba [Santiago de Quito]," where the Adelantado demanded that the traitor Picado be handed over. Almagro held firm, replying that "Picado was free to come and go," that "he could not force him to do anything." Just when an outbreak of fighting seemed inevitable, two of Almagro's delegates, the notary Domingo de la Presa and the *regidor* Cristóbal de Ayala, succeeded in making contact with Alvarado, whom they beseeched "on God's and the Emperor's behalf not to cause any turmoil or enter the city." They further implored "that he should return to his governance of Guatemala" and abandon altogether the territory "that the King had granted to Francisco Pizarro." Somehow, the entreaties of Ayala and de la Presa managed to convince Alvarado, hovering on the brink, not to attack – a resourceful feat of diplomacy.[11]

It might have been the case, however, that the Adelantado was more concerned with the loyalty of his followers, worried whether or not they would stand by him or defect, as had Picado and others, to the enemy. Alvarado would later admit that, while Almagro received his envoys and heard them out, the Mariscal sent with his own messengers "secret letters containing many offers and promises to my captains and soldiers in order that they might leave me and serve him." The Adelantado's men "were so exhausted from our recent experiences" that the temptation proved "too much for some of my people," who "murmured among themselves" and "departed secretly from my camp to go to his." Almagro's largesse, the Adelantado notes, was "so great, giving all of my people gifts and offers, that they were overcome and, talking among themselves, said that if I wished to continue my conquest not more than thirty men would follow me of the 150 horsemen and 250 foot-soldiers under my command." Alvarado was in a parlous if not untenable position. "To put an end to all these things, I determined to interview Almagro, who it seemed to me was somewhat afraid of me, and did not wish to see me." But he did, finally, consent. "I assured him that my arrival would be only to interview him and Pizarro," the Adelantado insisted. "And that I was [only] following the instructions [that] Your Majesty had given me."[12]

Not wishing "to do disservice to the king," Alvarado ordered his chief justice, Hernando de Caldera, to accompany Almagro's two delegates back to their commander and there (along with Luis de Moscoso) arrange for the Adelantado and the Mariscal to meet in person.[13]

FACE TO FACE

Alvarado believed himself, socially, a station or more above Almagro, whose physical appearance – short of stature, skinny and scrawny, worn, haggard looking, and *tuerto* or one-eyed – was somewhat unprepossessing, and visibly enhanced the marked differences between the two men. Though he had been lame in one leg for ten years, and walked with a noticeable limp, the Adelantado's handsome aura as "Tunatiuh," the "son of the sun," exuded still, making him distinctive and drawing admiration. To "show any regard for Almagro" was, if not beneath him, hardly to Alvarado's inclination, so intermediaries acting on his behalf were crucial.[14] Estete, Caldera, and Moscoso played their part, but it was perhaps Fray Marcos de Niza who was most instrumental in brokering a deal.[15] Alvarado assisted the friar at the negotiating table by suddenly conceding that "events had taken a very different course from what he had hoped," above all that "God had permitted that he find the land already settled and taken possession of." The Adelantado now considered it prudent to acknowledge Almagro's and Pizarro's prior claims and not press his own. On the designated day, 26 August 1534, "accompanied by several knights, all armed with hidden weapons," Alvarado "went to the city of Riobamba [Santiago de Quito] to meet with the Marshal," extending him an unctuous embrace before holding forth on his past achievements in the king's name. Almagro was as succinct as his guest was verbose, reiterating "that no other thing had been presumed about him than that he always would do what would be of service to God and the King."[16]

As face-to-face discussions were underway, other protagonists came and went, including Belalcázar, "received with great courtesy" after he kissed Alvarado's hand. Belalcázar's deference was replicated by "those who had come with the Adelantado," who "bowed to the Marshal, talking to the knights who were with him." So too did Picado present himself before Alvarado, "who pardoned him without showing any displeasure." Amends were made on both sides after "Felipillo was returned to Almagro, who also did not reprimand or punish him for what he had done."[17]

Before they signed an accord drawn up in meticulous detail, the Adelantado afforded Almagro a final, fawning gesture: Why not let bygones be bygones and – instead of money and matériel changing hands – "may a partnerhip be forged between us," cemented by "your son marrying my daughter."[18] The Mariscal, however, wanted no part of such a proposal, insisting that the agreement now down on paper be signed, sealed, and acted upon.[19]

Almagro, as Jijón y Camaaño shrewdly observed, was in many regards more Alvarado's "true rival" than Pizarro.[20] Never one to be outdone, least of all when the stakes were so high, the Adelantado found himself in a situation that must have rankled in the extreme. Little did he realize that ever further ignominy awaited.

15. THE PRICE OF PEACE

The accord awaiting the signatures of Alvarado and Almagro was drawn up in Santiago de Quito in three parts. Rights granted the Adelantado by Emperor Charles V to explore and conquer in the Pacific were transferred in a first letter dated 26 August 1534, naming Pizarro and Almagro as the new beneficiaries. A second letter, dated that same day, is a bill of sale between Alvarado and Almagro in which Pizarro's name does not appear, even though it was he who would pay for what was to be purchased – the Adelantado's fleet and all attendant accoutrements. Dated a day later, 27 August, a third missive is a letter of attorney in which Alvarado acknowledges the right, once again, of both Almagro and Pizarro "to take possession of the ships of the aforementioned fleet with everything pertaining to them."[1]

The bill of sale lays down details of the transaction. Alvarado's declaration comes first, the names and types of six vessels spelled out, soon no longer to be his:

> Know all persons who see this bill of sale that I, Adelantado Don Pedro de Alvarado, declare that I admit and acknowledge that I sell to you, Marshal Don Diego de Almagro, the entire armada of ships and all else accessory thereto which I now have and possess – that is, to wit, a galleon named *San Cristóbal*, a *nao* named *Santa Clara*, another *nao* named *La Buenaventura*, another *nao* named *La Concepción*, and two other *navios* named *San Pedro* and *Santiago*, which I sell to you as aforesaid with all their tackle, rigging, boats, sails, arms, artillery, anchors, and ammunition and everything else annexed or appertaining to the said ships and armada, so that

> you may have and hold it as your own property. Which said armada I declare that I sell you in the form aforesaid for the price and sum of one hundred thousand pesos of good gold, of four hundred and fifty maravedis each peso.[2]

Almagro's declaration follows, with mention made of two locations farther south in Peru, where money was to change hands:

> And I, the said Marshal Don Diego de Almagro, declare that I admit and acknowledge that I am bound to give and pay you, the said Adelantado Don Pedro de Alvarado, the said one hundred thousand pesos of gold as above contained, which I shall give and pay to you as soon as they are asked or demanded of me in your name by anyone holding sufficient authority in the province of Jauja, or the town of San Miguel, or in either of these two places which you, the said Adelantado, shall prefer. Provided that, if the payment is to be made in the said town of San Miguel, you shall wait for the time and space of three months, till the said hundred thousand castellanos shall be brought from the said province of Jauja, within which time I bind myself to give and pay you the said hundred thousand pesos of gold in the said town of San Miguel. And it is a stipulation that if one or more of the six ships aforementioned be lost at sea before their delivery (which God forbid), such chance and risk is now assumed by me, the said Marshal, and whether they be lost henceforth after the day of the date of this instrument or were lost up to the present time, that I shall still be obliged to give and pay you the said hundred thousand pesos of gold. And it is likewise a stipulation that everything which the said ships have hitherto had a share in or acquired up to the day of the date of this instrument or shall henceforth have a share in or acquire in any manner whatever, is, and I am to have, as my own property.[3]

Witnesses recorded as having been present during deliberations include Sebastián de Belalcázar, Hernando de Caldera, Rui Díaz, and Juan de Espinosa. After Alvarado and Almagro swore "that we bind ourselves to keep, observe, and fulfill the instrument drawn up in [this] city of Santiago de Quito," both signed the bill of sale – at least Alvarado did, Espinosa putting pen to paper on Almagro's behalf.[4]

Given the stakes, and the temperament of the two men involved, would the agreement last? Fray Marcos, who also witnessed the proceedings, refers to a previous one that did not, testifying "that he saw the Adelantado and Diego de Almagro celebrate contracts proclaimed and read in such a manner that those about heard it and rejoiced." The friar himself "heard the trumpets sound," alerting people of the good news. Then, "within four days," Almagro "broke everything that had been agreed to," on account of his feeling that "under his hand and banner he had all the force of the Adelantado." Thus empowered, "not willing to keep his word nor comply with anything [that] he had sworn and concerted to," Almagro told Alvarado "to sell his fleet and go away and leave the country." Fray Marcos implies that this is exactly what transpired. "The Adelantado, on seeing himself in such necessitous state, alone and without any force, because Almagro had it all under his command and at his orders, sold his ships for 100,000 *pesos de oro*."[5]

Alvarado had serious misgivings about the whole business. The previous arrangement, he tells us, "Almagro did not wish to sign" because discord and desertion in his ranks had weakened the Adelantado's position – which Almagro was keen to exploit, and knew how to. An air of regret is palpable when Alvarado writes: "I therefore made him many concessions, to my prejudice and to his advantage. I lost greatly. Since I could do nothing else, I sold him my ships with all they contained, and my slaves and horses and my own belongings, [for] the sum of one hundred thousand pesos – according to a calculation of their worth which we made there, although this scarcely paid for the cost of the ships themselves. This I did because I did not want to lose everything. The ships alone – with the arms, artillery, and supplies, and the advances which I made to my soldiers – cost me more in Guatemala than I received from Almagro."[6] Alvarado emphasizes that it was against his will – "contra mi voluntad" – that he accepted Almagro's proposition.[7] For his part, Almagro makes it clear that, having ships of his own, six more were of no interest to him. What the 100,000 pesos represented – he valued the vessels at no more than 25,000 to 30,000 pesos – was the price of peace.[8]

BETRAYAL AND RECOMPENSE

No fanfare of trumpets is recorded as having resounded in the wake of this second accord being struck, Alvarado's men divided in opinion as to whether or not their leader had betrayed them. "With the most loving words possible," Cieza de León affirms, "the Adelantado gave his people to understand that he had made that pact in order not to be of disservice to the King and so remain in such a prosperous land." His cousin Diego was having none of it, in no two minds about what he thought. "What a great disgrace this has been for the Alvarados!" Cieza describes him as "exclaiming angrily," arms flung upward in disbelief. The Adelantado "tried to appease him, saying that he would meet with Franciso Pizarro and would make sure" that Diego and company "would be given food and as much respect as they deserved, and that they should go and speak to the Marshal." Another relation, Vítores de Alvarado, retorted: "I will go and see him to get to know him, and to have him as lord, but not in fulfilment of your lordship's command." Others wondered aloud "whether they were Blacks that had been sold for money."[9]

While, Cieza continues, "many were upset by this decision," there were those who felt otherwise, believing it a better option to stay and align with Almagro than "to return and explore again," especially if that meant retracing their footsteps in the snow and once again traversing the mountains to get back to the coast. "These and other things happened in Alvarado's camp," we are told, "but because it was already concluded and sworn, the most principal men went to speak with Almagro and to become acquainted with him." The marshal "received them very well, giving great hope that shortly they all would be rich and prosperous in Peru." Meanwhile, as "they came and went from Riobamba to the camp, and from the camp to Riobamba," Almagro sent word to Pizarro that he and the Adelantado would leave to join him – and have their negotiations paid for.[10]

16. PIZARRO PAYS OUT

Three hundred leagues are said to have been the distance between Riobamba (Santiago de Quito) and where Pizarro was thought to be, in Jauja, some 450 kilometres northwest of Cuzco.[1] Before Almagro and Alvarado left on their journey south, they first headed "thirty leagues or so" north to the freshly founded "Villa de San Francisco," Belalcázar delegated to serve there as lieutenant governor and captain general, some 450 men drawn from both sides under his command.[2] The Villa de San Francisco became the new Quito, during colonial times the seat of the Audiencia jurisdiction of the same name and the capital of Ecuador following independence from Spain in 1822, a status that the city enjoys and benefits from to this day.[3]

While Belalcázar recommenced his campaign to locate and capture Rumiñahui, Almagro and Alvarado ran into resistance mounted by another of Atahualpa's generals, Quizquiz, after they had made it as far as Tumibamba. Quizquiz's forces, recorded as 12,000 to 20,000 strong, "inflicted considerable damage on the Spaniards, avoided the slaughter of a cavalry charge, and remained intact." Almagro and Alvarado held their course as they pushed on toward San Miguel, managing "to seize a vast herd of over fifteen thousand llamas, together with over four thousand conscripted male and female porters."[4] By mid-October, six weeks of arduous trekking later, they were resting up and taking stock in the city founded by Pizarro near Tangarara on the Río Chira, thirty-five kilometres from the Pacific Ocean.[5]

From San Miguel, according to López de Gómara, "Alvarado sent García Holguín to Puerto Viejo, there to hand over the ships of his armada to Diego de Moya, a sea captain of Almagro's." Almagro, he says, even though the Mariscal makes it clear that it was Pizarro who would settle up with Alvarado, "disbursed great gifts and assistance in the form of money, arms, and horses not only to his own men but also to those of the Adelantado."[6] A number of the latter, rewarded or bought off, depending on how one views their situation, would afterwards accompany Almagro in his campaign to conquer Chile, just as Alvarado "left behind many of his company in Quito with Benalcázar [Belalcázar], taking with him some of the best fighters." Belalcázar is said to "have found himself hard pressed, up against very warlike people."[7]

Despite Almagro and Alvarado having forged an alliance of sorts to get them and their assembly thus far, barely halfway to connecting with Pizarro, it was a consortium that could not erase lingering animosity and the need to account. While in San Miguel, Almagro put together a damning dossier of Alvarado's deeds since his arrival in Caráquez eight months before, its contents the sworn testimony of more than a dozen eyewitnesses.[8] Almagro also heard, as he did when he was in these parts back in May, further reports from Spaniards arriving in San Miguel by way of Puerto Viejo about the continuing hostility of natives there to any Spanish presence or passage, a consequence of Alvarado's assaults and depredations.[9] The Adelantado would document his views later – what mattered most was to be reimbursed, if only partially, for the expenditures lavished in coming to Peru in the first instance.

PAID TO LEAVE

The rendezvous that Almagro and Alvarado believed would take place with Pizarro in Jauja (elevation 3,390 metres) never materialized, the governor instead making his way down from the high Andes to the Pacific coast as the year 1534 came to an end. On the lookout for a prime maritime location that would serve Spanish needs better than Jauja, an interim base, Pizarro found himself in Pachacamac, a sacred pre-Inca site forty kilometres south of where Lima was founded as the City of the Kings on 18 January 1535.[10] With Almagro and Alvarado en route, the governor sent word to them as to his whereabouts. "From San Miguel they went to the Chimú Valley," Cieza de León informs us, "stopping first in the Chicama Valley to punish Indians because they had killed certain Christians who had landed there in a ship." After traversing the desert coastal plain for some 140 leagues, the Inca highway paralleling the Pacific littoral but always inland from it, the two reached Pachacamac – "and there found Pizarro waiting for them."[11]

Almagro had the ear of Pizarro first, reassuring him of his loyalty and dismissing as malicious rumours talk of a pact with Alvarado that ran counter to the governor's interests, let alone threaten his life. The Adelantado's turn came after Mass the next morning, when he sought to justify his presence, saying nothing of his actions. Pizarro heard him out, Alvarado declaring that "so he could depart completely satisfied, it was only necessary that [the governor] would give him his word to accept into his company the many important knights who had accompanied him and to honor and favor them." A promise was made by Pizarro "to treat them as his own brothers and that shortly each one of them would have *repartimientos*" – allocations of native workers who would furnish labour and pay tribute in goods and services.[12] A visit to inspect the ruins of the temple at Pachacamac, its gold-plated walls long since stripped, was followed by a social gathering, which included high-stake card games as part of the camaraderie. Alvarado's show of good fellowship was dimmed by gambling losses to Almagro amounting to 13,500 pesos, paid in kind by his giving the Mariscal "certain Black slaves, horses, items of clothing, and hunting equipment, worth much more than what was owed."[13] He likewise forfeited "sable furs valued at 2,000 ducados to Governor Pizarro, without his giving me anything for them."[14] The Adelantado would have to be on the alert when it came time to receive payment for his armada, which is what his being in Pachacamac boiled down to.

Prior to Alvarado's arrival, Pizarro had ordered Hernando de Soto to collect the sum in question from coffers in Cuzco as well as the from the estates of deceased Spaniards.[15] Soto either brought the money to Pachacamac or arranged for it to be taken there, thus allowing the governor to expedite the matter. In a letter to Emperor Charles V, Pizarro praised Almagro for negotiating the deal and expressed his satisfaction at being able "to rid the kingdom of disturbance and commotion, and prevent the loss of life and injuries to Spaniards." The Adelantado's "greed for money" was a small price to pay "for tranquility in the land." And, even though the armada "wasn't worth 30,000 castellanos," Pizarro so wanted Alvarado gone that he paid him not only the 100,000 *pesos de oro* agreed upon but an additional 20,000 in the form of "jewels and very valuable stones."[16]

Pizarro's letter, in which he alludes to Alvarado's marauding behaviour and Almagro's documenting it at length in the deposition he made in San Miguel two months before, has none of the respectful tone that Cieza de León lends to his depiction of the three men's encounter. Neither does Alvarado when he informed the king, from his point of view, of his being shamefully treated and taken advantage of. He accuses Pizarro of refusing to pay all that had been agreed to, "and Your Majesty knows that this was not deserved."[17] To add insult to injury, however, was his finding out, after having accepted delivery of the payment, that he had been "greatly deceived." It turned out that the coins that the contract stipulated were to be "of good gold, of four hundred and fifty maravedis each peso" had actually been struck "using the silver that jewels and crockery are made with in Peru." And not only that – the silver itself had been liberally cut with copper. "By this sleight of hand," the Adelantado reckons, "I lost almost half the value of what I thought I was carrying back to Guatemala with me."[18]

One can only imagine how enraged Alvarado must have been when he realized the trick played on him, about which nothing could be done.

17. BACK TO GUATEMALA

In January or February 1535 Alvarado left Peru to return to where he had sailed from a year or so before. The expectations and high hopes of his outbound journey had been replaced by a mood quite the opposite. What to impart to those who would be surprised to see him, after such a heralded departure, the Adelantado had time to ponder as Central America, not the far shores of South America or those of the Spice Islands, loomed on the horizon. Guatemala would never be home, but home base it was destined to be once more, at least for an interim period during which he dreamed up yet another scheme of exploration to make amends for the debacle that his invasion of Peru had proven to be.

The sources at hand make it difficult to verify precisely when Alvarado took leave. Pizarro implies that, "as a matter of urgency, and in Your Majesty's best interests," he had already sent him packing when he wrote to the king from Pachacamac on 1 January 1535.[1] Writing in the late eighteenth century, but referencing López de Gómara, who wrote in the mid-sixteenth, Juan de Velasco states that the Adelantado "left, at the very latest, early on in 1535."[2] French historian Bernard Lavallé states that the Adelantado "re-embarked for Central America on 5 January, from a deep water anchorage slightly to the north [of Pachacamac] that came to be called El Callao," the seaport of soon-to-be founded Lima.[3] We have a record of Alvarado communicating directly with Emperor Charles V from San Miguel on 15 January 1535, indicating that he was then still in Peru.[4] A subsequent missive to the king mentions that he was back in Guatemala, to reassume its governorship in situ, by 20 April.[5] What else does the Adelantado have to say about his departure and return?

CONSTRAINTS AND CONDITIONS

Though he would change his mind when hard-pressed the following year, Pizarro wanted Alvarado gone – and the sooner, the better.[6] The Adelantado acknowledges that Pizarro "ordered a ship be put at my disposal to take me to Guatemala, along with what I had received for the payment of my armada." To that end, "the Governor gave me a ship, one of those that I had sold him, so that I might come here." Alvarado does not name which vessel it was, only that Pizarro "would not permit the ship to stop midway in Panama, because he knew that I left with the intention of going afterwards to kiss Your Majesty's Royal Hands, seeking justice and punishment for those who had perpetrated such grave disservice and damage." He also reveals that Pizarro "stated beforehand that he would not grant me passage for anywhere other than this governance." Furthermore, "a secret command was issued ordering that I be dropped off in the province of León in Nicaragua." Neither did Pizarro "consent to a single Spaniard of those who came with me being allowed to accompany me," thereby eliminating witnesses who could provide testimony in a legal deposition as to Pizarro's actions and conduct.[7]

To ensure no untoward behaviour on the part of the Adelantado, his transit took place under armed guard, its vigilant members made up of Pizzaro loyalists, among them Diego de Trujillo, whom the governor had recruited in their home town in Extremadura when he was in Spain in 1529.[8] Aboard ship, too, were other Spaniards who, like Trujillo, had done well for themselves in Peru and saw "a good opportunity to leave the kingdom" after Pizarro gave them permission to do so. "They went with the Adelantado to the coast," Cieza de León tells us, and then "embarked and left."[9] The historical record is unforthcoming as to who else, apart from his Tlaxcalan consort, Doña Luisa Xicoténcatl, and their daughter, Leonor, would have accompanied Alvarado.[10] A roll call like the one taken in Realejo on the eve of departure has yet to come to light. In all likelihood, given the circumstances, none was ever drawn up.

RECEPTION AND RECRIMINATION

No hero's welcome awaited Alvarado upon his arrival in Santiago de Guatemala, which he dates as 20 April. His presence is not registered in city council minutes until 2 June, when he presided over a meeting whose primary item of business had to do with the price of goods that merchants posted for sale.[11] Such mundane municipal matters, after the life-and-death dramas of the year before, he must have found tedious if not beneath him, certainly not where he would prefer to channel his energies and ambitions. Even following his prolonged absence, the governor of Guatemala took exception at being urged to stay put, notifying the king that "the city fathers and royal officials are of the opinion that I should not plan on leaving these parts, indeed have given me to understand that if I do not remain here of my own accord, they will complain to Your Majesty." This rebuke was not the least to his liking, though he acknowledges that his return coincided with a bout of native unrest – "a few days ago some Spaniards were killed" – and who better to deal with that situation than himself? Once "unruly Indians were punished and brought to heel," Alvarado wanted "to depart right away for Spain, there to kiss Your Majesty's hands and furnish a detailed account of all that happened to me, imploring that justice be done for the grievances caused me in Peru." Bowing to pressure, however, the Adelantado agreed to delay his departure "until Your Majesty sends me formal licence to come thither," anticipating that what he has to say "will bear fruit and thereby serve Your Highness."[12] Transatlantic passage would have to wait.[13]

In his letter, Alvarado vents vitriolic rage at Almagro in particular. His dealings with him in Santiago de Quito he repents, insisting that the arrangement settled on – payment of 100,000 pesos – was the price of peace, paltry but necessary to avoid conflict between Spaniard and Spaniard. Though the two sides concurred that "a third party arbitrate" and as a result "signed an agreement before a notary," Almagro opposed Alvarado "calling upon witnesses to testify about the proceedings, and the requirements I asked of him." Consequently, "no written record was made, which would have allowed me to show Your Majesty what he did to me, a very bad decision on my part and one that I regret." The Adelantado's honour, standing, and reputation, not to mention his loyal service to the Crown, had been irreversibly slighted – "although in the eyes of Almagro, and those with him, no harm has been done."[14]

Alvarado is disdainful in the extreme about Almagro's capabilities as a military campaigner. "I know that the Mariscal has written to Your Majesty, requesting he be given those parts that I was on my way to conquer and populate," the Adelantado states. "If this request of his has not yet been granted, I beseech Your Majesty that it not be, for he lacks the necessary experience to carry it out. I do not know how he will fare or what will become of his expedition." Prior to Alvarado's arrival, Almagro had under his command "only a small number of Spaniards, both foot soldiers and infantry," which put him in a precarious position, "indeed in danger of having his men perish in such a clamorous land." That risk, the Adelantado asserts, was averted with the swelling of Almagro's ranks "by the people who I put there," so much so that the Mariscal's forces now matched those of Pizarro. Alvarado reckoned, and in the end was proven correct, "that this may trigger great discord between them, in which all might be lost."[15]

His contempt for Pizarro is no less vehement. After "contrary currents and winds" on his inbound voyage had veered the armada off course and into the Bahía de Caráquez, the Adelantado ordered "two of my best ships, both well provisioned and equipped, to continue along the coast of Peru, in order to find out about its ports and the lay of the land in general, without in any way violating Pizarro's governance." He claims that the vessels, sailing south, hugged the coastline, their crews always on the alert. When they reached a port or anchorage where Pizarro's followers were, "no consent was given them to come ashore, not even to buy food or necessary supplies." Relations deteriorated further after Pizarro "secretly lavished gold and jewels on, and made promises to, captain and crew alike, enticing them to jump ship." Many from one vessel did. "Because of too few hands on deck, that ship could not continue its voyage," heading back north at considerable risk on account of its skeleton crew. "The other ship kept on going, seven leagues beyond Chincha, reaching a point where no other ship had sailed to before." Pizarro targeted the vessel and, with a mix of intimidation and bribery, appropriated it. "Thus was I unable, as intended," Alvarado rues, "to explore and discover as far down the coast as Cape Horn."[16]

While condemning the actions of Almagro and Pizarro, the Adelantado lets the king know that he is aware that they, too, are levelling equally vicious accusations against him. Confident in royal authority to discern who is telling the truth, Alvarado declares himself "satisfied that Your Majesty believes in me and in my desire to aggrandize His Estate. He will credit what I have to say, realizing I was not party to their refusal to allow testimony to be taken or evidence drawn up, knowing that such proceedings would reflect badly on them and show the damage done to me, and the sternest complaints I would lodge."[17] The Adelantado continues:

> I am given to understand that Almagro and Pizarro have drafted charges, calling as witnesses people who came with me to Peru, the very persons I was moved to punish for their unworthiness. There being those who wish always to do evil, prominent among them deserters lured by gifts and promises, they now wish to cast blame on me, and thereby have their own conduct pardoned. In view of all this, I beg Your Majesty not to judge me guilty without my being heard. Indeed, I expect to present my case in such a way that Your Majesty will order detractors to be punished for the damage done to me, and give back what was taken from me by force. I anticipate this outcome because Your Majesty knows that I have acted in His Royal Service accordingly, avoiding all scandals in the conquest of the land. In so doing, instead of profiting from serving Your Majesty, I have lost much of my fortune.[18]

Considerably in arrears and deep in debt, Alvarado claims to have to his name but "seventy thousand ducados in gold and silver, which I wish to hold on to until Your Majesty decides how best to proceed."[19]

CHAMPION OF REPRISE

As he contemplated his lot from the confines of Santiago de Guatemala, the Adelantado was in no doubt about how to rectify matters: mount another expedition that would succeed where the Peruvian one had failed, not only signalling a reversal in his finances but also restoring to good standing his personal reputation, in the Crown's eyes at any rate. The proposal he makes is one "I have thought about often, given the great wealth there has to be, dense populations too, on the many islands and stretches of mainland in the South Sea." Regarding how best to undertake such exploration, Alvarado now believed departure from Spanish shores to be less of a risk than setting off "from New Spain or adjoining provinces because of the adverse currents and contrary winds that prevail, as I have learned from experience – and Cortés too," his ships also having been thwarted by the elements when he organized Pacific expeditions.[20] Furthermore, "the flimsy vessels that can be built here are not as seaworthy as those of Castile," which leads him to suggest that "six or seven sturdy ships be constructed in Your Kingdoms over there, with up to seven hundred men aboard, the fleet passing through the Strait of Magellan and on to the Spice Islands or the mainland beyond." Upon arrival, ships should be sent back east across the Pacific to Mexico to tell of what has been discovered, "returning with a quantity of horses, since by that time there will be no shortage of them, and two thousand men," who would reinforce those already in place and continue exploring – and conquering.[21]

Having laid out his scheme, the Adelantado then makes his proposition. "If Your Majesty deigns to consider what I have said, and thinks well of it, trusting me capable of its execution, I beg permission to come to Spain to discuss the matter, as this is something I believe will enhance Your Royal Service immeasurably. Upon receiving licence to do so, I could leave forthwith, making sure the government of Guatemala is in safe hands and that nothing amiss happens in my absence."[22]

Less than a year after his return from Peru, Alvarado left Guatemala for Spain, absconding before being detained by the proceedings of the judicial inquiry into his governorship headed by Alonso de Maldonado.[23] In mid-August 1536 he departed from Puerto Caballos (Honduras) with the intention of presenting his new Pacific plan to Emperor Charles V in person. His proposal for a second exploration of the Mar del Sur and voyage to the Spice Islands was viewed favourably, royal provisions to that effect granted on 9 August 1538.[24] The Adelantado, however, had no better luck in this venture than in his first. While the ships he had built lay at anchor, awaiting him in the port of Navidad on the Colima coast of Mexico, Alvarado succumbed to wounds suffered on 24 June 1541 when waging war in the mountains above Tequaltiche in Nueva Galicia.[25] His planned voyage to the Spice Islands, like his goal of conquering Peru, ended as a delusion.

18. CODA: THE CONQUISTADOR WHO NEVER WAS

And though you came with sword held high,
You did not conquer, only die ...
Keith Reid/Procol Harum, "Conquistador"

After a year of abject failure that all but ruined him, Pedro de Alvarado departed Peru to return to Guatemala and then on to Spain. In what today is Ecuador, from Pacific shores to mountain passes high in the Andes, he left behind not only a record of grievous harm but also men who were party to it, among them relatives and family members who stayed on in Peru in the wake of the Adelantado's ouster. His brother Gómez died in Vilcas after the Battle of Chupas in September 1542, in the end fighting against the Almagro faction he had formerly aligned with during previous intra-Spanish confrontations.[1] A cousin, Diego de Alvarado, became such a trusted ally of Almagro that the Mariscal made him the executor of his estate, Diego's death in Spain in 1540 said to have been caused by his being poisoned by associates of Pizarro.[2] Another Diego, one of Alvarado's offspring with Luisa Xicoténcatl, died at the Battle of Chuquinga in May 1554, when forces loyal to the Crown, led by Alonso de Alvarado, were defeated by insurgents headed by Francisco Hernández Girón.[3] Alonso, who died in Lima in 1555, was a nephew of the Adelantado, his being routed at Chuquinga and an earlier reversal at Abancay (July 1537) compensated for by his successful involvement in the Battle of Las Salinas (April 1538). He led campaigns of conquest into the interior as far as Chachapoyas, on the eastern slopes of the Andes at the edge of the Amazon rainforest.[4] Following his uncle's removal, another nephew, Luis de Moscoso Alvarado, was able to mediate between Almagro and Pizarro before becoming a confidant of Hernando de Soto. He followed Soto to Spain (1536) and afterward to Florida and an epic journey beyond (1538–43) before finding his way back to Peru, where he died in 1551.[5] In present-day Peru, and Ecuador, the surname Alvarado is not uncommon, and resonates.[6]

Of the more than four hundred Spaniards recorded as having gone with Alvarado to Peru (see appendix 1), the majority remained there, afforded scant choice in the matter given how the episode unfolded. The Adelantado "returned to Guatemala almost completely on his own," López de Gómara relays, "leaving his men behind in Peru. Given the high social standing and bravado of those among them, some went on to be key players in that land."[7] Many who sided with Almagro after the agreement reached at Santiago de Quito, like Alvarado's brother Gómez, took part in the Mariscal's expedition to Chile, returning to Peru with as little to show for their loyalty and efforts as earlier they had with the Adelantado.[8] Others were with Belalcázar when he founded San Francisco de Quito and rooted out Rumiñahui from his hiding place, after the Inca leader had levelled pre-Hispanic Quito and left only a burnt-out shell upon which Spaniards could erect a city to serve their needs, not those of the people they had come to depose.[9] Alvarado's men – his nephew Alonso, in aligning with Pizarro, was an exception – for the most part became Almagrists, casting their lot with the Mariscal to the bitter end, as did the Adelantado's cousin, Diego.[10] His fate, if poison indeed was the cause of his death, must literally have been a bitter one.

Of rank-and-file conscripts, we know next to nothing: the depositions of any inclined to register merits and services they considered worthy of Crown recognition and recompense await archival disclosure.[11] Lockhart states that "while many of Alvarado's men were no different from the Spaniards already in Peru, they included a new social stratum, closer to the high nobility than anything seen previously," some of whom "began to receive encomiendas in the years 1535–38." Among the most enterprising of the Adelantado's entourage was the pilot Juan Fernández, but "not many of his colleagues followed him" on the upward trajectory that was his post-Alvarado lot.[12] The *residencia* that Alonso de Maldonado undertook into Alvarado's tenure as governor of Guatemala, albeit an habitually absent one, was carried out in the province over which the Adelantado had official charge.[13] Had Maldonado been able to draw on the testimony of erstwhile followers of Alvarado soldiering on in Peru, what they would have had to say surely would shed more light on the expedition they had been part of, and its inexorable undoing.

As is often the case in situating Indigenous peoples in the overall scheme of events, we know even less about the fate of those involved in the Adelantado's invasion other than their demise in the cold and snow of the Andes. Of the 1,184 recorded in the Alvarado *residencia* as having been forcibly recruited, made to board ship in Realejo and taken to Peru, it is reported summarily that "many died" and that those who survived "remained there, never to return,"[14] bought and sold as the slaves they were.[15] Guillermo Paz Cárcomo claims that Kaqchikel descendants still live in Ecuador in the Otavalo area, their surnames indicating their Guatemalan origin.[16]

Alvarado longed for the recognition given to his one-time mentor and role model, Hernando Cortés, and considered himself at least as deserving as Pizarro, certainly a cut above Almagro. He strove to the utmost, but fell short, the conquistador who never was. Beyond violence and vainglory, greed and gore, a dark aura haunts the very thought of him. In Badajoz, his place of birth, Alvarado is conjured and featured very differently from his counterparts in their hometowns. In nearby Medellín, a statue of Cortés presides, proud and prominent, in a public space close to where his family house was (Figure 16).[17] Not much farther away in the Plaza Mayor of Trujillo, Pizarro is mounted on a grand stallion, sword in hand, the church of San Martín behind him (Figure 17).[18] On the main square of his namesake birthplace in Castilla–La Mancha, Almagro commands similar equestrian poise and exudes an imposing presence (Figure 18).[19] A bust of Belalcázar in his hometown is less conspicuous but nonetheless centrally located (Figure 19). The work of compatriot Francisco Núñez García, it was erected adjacent to the parish church of Santiago El Mayor on 12 October 1976, Spain's Día de la Hispanidad.

Unlike the four contemporaries with whom he contested fame and fortune, Alvarado is conspicuously marginalized, pushed to the side. "Posterity has not been kind," Recinos reflects, "to the most audacious of sixteenth-century Spanish conquistadors."[20] In Badajoz, a statue of his imagined likeness may be found on the banks of the Río Guadiana along the Paseo Fluvial, between the Puente Real and the Puente de la

Constitución (Figure 20). The bronze effigy is the inspiration of sculptor Estanislao García Olivares.[21] When the bus I am riding on drives past, halfway between Seville and Lisbon, I point him out to colleagues and students from the Universidad Pablo de Olavide, and croon for them Procol Harum's emblematic song. Its lyrics embody the statue's despondent air. No stallion stands, and no sword is held high, but a reek of purity prevails:

> Conquistador, your stallion stands
> in need of company
> and like some angel's haloed brow
> you reek of purity.
> I see your armour-plated breast
> has long since lost its sheen
> and in your death-mask face
> there are no signs which can be seen.
>
> Conquistador, there is no time,
> I must pay my respects,
> and though I came to jeer at you
> I leave now with regrets.
> And as the gloom begins to fall
> I see there is no aureole
> and though you came with sword held high
> you did not conquer, only die.[22]

In his solitude, the conquistador leans to one side, the Pipil arrow that wounded him while he waged war in El Salvador convincing the sculptor to cast him with a tilted posture, left leg favoured for support over the right.[23] The Adelantado looks forlorn and dejected, eyes downcast, gaze vacant. There is nothing triumphant about his demeanour – quite the contrary, it intimates loss and defeat. With helmet in one hand, the open palm of his other dangles over the side that was injured. A valedictory figure, Alvarado bids farewell to any illusion that Peru might have been his. He did not meet his death in the snow: fate decreed otherwise.[24] Andean blizzards, however, took the lives of untold Indigenous betrodden, victims of a doomed venture and the man responsible for it.

APPENDIX

Roll call (*alarde*) of men who accompanied Pedro de Alvarado on his expedition to Peru, recorded 11 January 1534 on the Ysla de los Xagueyes (Puerto de la Posesión/Realejo) in Nicaragua by the notary Hernando de Sosa. Source: AGI, Guatemala 41, N.1.

AGI, GUATEMALA 41, N.1, FOLIO 32 RECTO

Los de cavallo

El dicho señor Adelantado
Francisco Calderon alferez
Diego Daça trompeta
Gonzalo Diaz trompeta
Gomez Dalvarado
Diego de Alvarado
El liçenciado Caldera
El padre Francisco Caldera
Juan Denpudia [de Ampudia]
Luys de Moscoso
Don Juan Enriquez
Juan del Valle
Martyn Estete
Don Gomez de Luna
El padre Francisco Hernández
Pedro de Puelles
El comendador Santiago
Francisco Garçia de Tovar
Juan Ordoñez
Hernando de Contreras
Savastian de Sanabria
Garçia Holguin
Melchor de Valades
Juan Ordoñes
Baltasar Mexia
Bernardo Ramirez
Alonso de Mendoça
Jeronimo del Espinar
Vasco Grova
Cristoval Ramyrez
Pero Gutierrez
Marco Marquez
Francisco Montero
Francisco Muñiz
Hernan Sanches
Suero de Gangas
Antonio de Carrança
Francisco Rodrigues
Fernando Dalvarado
Juan Dalvarado

AGI, GUATEMALA 41, N.1, FOLIO 32 VERSO

Nuño de Tovar
Nicolao de
Francisco de Herrera
Francisco de Çieça
Diego Perez
Pedro de Añasco
Xines Muñoz
Alonso de Pulgar
Anton Cuadrado
Anton Ruyz
Gomez Destaçio [de Estacio]
Andres Varon
Pero Mansilla
Pedro Davyla
Alonso Sanches
Rodrigo Dalcala [de Alcalá]
Luys Daça
Baltasar Gomes
Rodrigo Gonçales
Pero Diaz
Alonso de Pedroche
Alonso Savoyano
Melchor de Pinedo
Andres Fernandez
Miguel Hernandez
Cristoval de Tovar
Bartolome Cordonero
Pedro de Quiros
Juan Daguilar [de Aguilar]
Francisco Daguilar [de Aguilar]
Alonso Martin
Estevan Pacheco
Francisco Nuñez
Pero Ruyz de Santillan
Gonzalo Gallego
Pedro de Leon
Alonso Collado
Francisco Ruyz Collado
Bartolome de la Rosa
Gaspar de Vesga
Alvar
Hernando de Villanueva Calçetero
Pero Rodriguez
Francisco de Trigueros
Rodrigo Muniel
Francisco de Villarreal
Gonzalo de la Puente
Juan de Rojas
Nuflo de Villalovos
Diego Ponçe
Alonso Alvarez
Maestre Juan
Juan Rodrigues portugues
Juan Dayuso [de Ayuso]
Pedro de Torres
Francisco Martyn
Antonyo de Prado
Francisco Mosquera
Diego de Sandoval
Lorenço Gallego
Juan Fernandez piloto
Martyn de la Calle
Cristoval de Burgos
Alonso Serrano
Diego Serrano

AGI, GUATEMALA 41, N.1, FOLIO 33 RECTO

Pedro de Arévalo
Alonso de Torres
Diego Gomes
Garçilaso de la Vega
Francisco Burgueño
Anton Ruyz de Guyvara [Guevara]
Juan Muniel
Hernando de Chaves
Juan de la Parra
Blas Lopez
Francisco Ruyz
Gaspar Aleman
Rodrigo Gascon
Domyngo Hernandez
Pedro de Villarreal
Juan de Ortega
Anton de Rojas
Pedro de Moscoso
Cristoval Dcscovar [dc Escobar]
Santos de Medellin
Diego Vendala
Juan de Herrada
Juan de Salmeron
Juan de Sayavedra [Saavedra]
Gonzalo de Çayas
Luys Ordoñes de Porras
Anton de Grado
Pedro de Montes
Pedro de Samanyego
Baltasar Gomez
Antonyo de Rivera
Diego Orsorio
Antonyo de Rivas
Alvaro de Morales
Myguel de la Serna
Alonso de Alvarado
Pedro de Sauçedo
Mateo de Lezcano
Gaspar Luys
Alvar Nuñez
Vitores de Alvarado
Diego de Huelga [Huelva]
Hernando de Sosa cançiller jeneral
Hernan Mendez
Juan Lopez
Marcos Coronel
Rodrigo de Venavides
Rodrigo de Angulo
Pero Gomez
Juan Ximenez
Juan Lovato
Juan de Padilla
Diego del Valle
Juan Çorrilla
Alonso Diaz herrador
Hernando Morea
Francisco de Morales
Hernando Vechicato
Cristoval de Varrientos
Pedro Mato
Sancho de la Carrera
El benefiçiado Garçi Sanches
Alonso Ramyrez
Antonyo Ramyrez
Antonyno de Torres
Hernando de Andiano

AGI, GUATEMALA 41, N.1, FOLIO 33 VERSO

Fernando de Orvaneja
Hernando de Oropesa
Pedro de Villanueva
Juan de Peñarruel
Juan Breton
Juan Ochoa de Oryondo
Pedro Diaz
Francisco de Çisneros
Diego de Vega
Hernando Serrano
Bartolome Albez
Diego Martyn de Hutrera [Utrera]
El doctor Luys Çuares
Alonso de Madrid
Castura
Cristoval Martin
Pedro Solano de Quiñones
Valderrama
Cansyno piloto
Antonyo Picado
Hernando Valer
Diego Gomes
Juan Ochoa de Oriondo
Pedro Hidalgo
Tome Hernandez
Domyngo Martyn
Bartolome Alvarez
Pedro de la Peña
Pedro Mosquera
Maestre Pablo
Alexo Nuñez
Alonso Ramyrez
Lope Sanches Agraz
Juan Sanches
Enriquez Hernandez
Francisco de San Roman
Juan Marquez
Lorençio de Hulloa
Bartolome de Aguilar
Cristoval Rodrigues
Luis Ximenes
Alonso de Palma
Alonso Hernandez Aviles
Bautista
Pedro de Contreras
Alonso Gallego
Francisco Barragan
Hernando de Quino
Rodrigo de Vargas
Ferran Raposo
Diego de Sahavedra
Juan de la Puente
Rodrigo de Chaves
Gomez Dalvarado el Moço
Hernando de Villanueva
Fernando de Santistevan
Hernan Gomez
Alonso de Lera
Juan Vaquez de Moguer
Juan Vaquez de Osuna
Cristoval de Velasco
Diego Martyn de Hutrera [Utrera] [*sic*]
Fernando Maldonado
Juan Rodrigues
Juan Tofino
Juan Fernandez

AGI, GUATEMALA 41, N.1, FOLIO 34 RECTO

Bernabé/Bartolomé de Camora [Zamora]
Alonso Gil de Triana
Hernan Lopez
Gregorio Viscayno
Alonso del Valle
Bernaldo de Sedano
Francisco Galdamez
Alexo de Medina
Francisco de Londoño
Pedro de Guzman
Bernaldino
de Santa María
Diego de Urediña
Diego Arias
Graviel Pie de Hierro
Francisco de Salinas
Francisco de Porras Sedano
Diego de Medina
Alonso de Salamanca
Francisco de la Granja
Alonso de Grajeda
Pedro de Arevalo
Juan Lopez Lovo
Francisco de Orellana
Miguel de Truxillo
Pedro Hernandez
Antonyo de Pedrosa
Francisco Lopez
Pere Estevan
Hernando de Valençia
Francisco Gomez
Cristoval de Esquivel
Viçente de Bejar
Juan de Varrientos
Pedro de Triana
Cristoval Sanches
Ximon del Cavo
Alonso Alvarez

Los de pie
Rodrigo de Venavides
Rodrigo Dangulo
[de Angulo] alferez
Bartolome Davila [de Ávila]
Juan Garcia de Lerma
Hernando de Busto
Juan Parrado
Martyn de Guilde
Martyn de Morote
Pedro Requelme
Juan Martyn Talavera
Juan del Salto
Martyn del Salto
Martyn de Bilvao
Myguel de la Chica
Juan de Santiago
Juan de Herrera
Francisco de Jahen
Alonso Perez
Gonçalo de Argüello
Alvar Garçia
Myguel de Velvoso
Juan de Mondragon
Hernando de Veas

AGI, GUATEMALA 41, N.1, FOLIO 34 RECTO (cont.)

Francisco Sanches
Bartolome Rodrigues
Martyn Perez
Pedro Anton
Estevan Ramos

AGI, GUATEMALA 41, N.1, FOLIO 34 VERSO

Francisco Gachon
Alonso Infançon
Anton Nuñez
Francisco de Llerena
Juan de Almaçan
Vasco de Vide
Graviel de Medina
Diego Martyn
Hernando Cordonero
Rodrigo de Bustillo
Cristoval Tenorio
Juan de Lara
Juan Tomas
Cristoval de Aranda
Pedro Hernandez
Pedro Calvo
Juan de Ledesma
Alonso Castaño
Pedro Gutierrez Dovando [de Ovando]
Juan Ruyz
Alonso Gomez
Pedro de Orduña
Cristoval Saravia
Juan Dalva
Francisco Martyn
Alonso de Tiro
Martyn de Melgar
Diego Hernandez Çamarra
Martyn Sanches
Juan Enrriquez
Juan Sarmiento
Alonso Dalmagro [de Almagro]
Diego Quixada
Cristobal Gomes
Garçia de Castro
Alonso Duran
Francisco Beçerra
Diego Vayo
Juan Charra
Luys Carrasco
Diego de Vaca
Pedro Muñoz
Rodrigo Perez
Alonso Martyn
Juan Dargüello [de Argüello]
Domingo Dolagorta [de Olagorta]
Pantaleon de Myravalles
Francisco Cavallero
Andres de Valle
Alonso de Arevalo
Myguel Carrion
Alonso de Villamayor

AGI, GUATEMALA 41, N.1, FOLIO 34 VERSO (cont.)

Bartolome Calvo
Anton Ximenez
Pedro Martynez
Francisco Panyagua
Rodrigo de Cueto
Francisco Pacheco
Gaspar Ruyz
Pedro Vaca
Pero de Yzaçaga [Isazaga]
Gonzalo Pelaceyra
Juan de Tovar
Chaves
Sevastian Gallego
Francisco Velazquez
Juan de Prado
Pedro Navarro
Juan de Orgueta
Bartolome Hernandez [Sanbra?]
Bartolome de Santander
Pedro de Vilbao
Menchor de Alvarado
Juan de Oviedo
Andres de Çaberio
Francisco Parenteso
Juan de la Mira
Juan Gomez Peñaparda
Francisco Pedro Gariño
Hernan Rodrigues

AGI, GUATEMALA 41, N.1, FOLIO 35 RECTO

Jines de Medina
Juan Ochoa
Andres Perez
Francisco de Çisneros
Anton Marques
Diego del Varco
Juan de Toro
Pedro Yañez
Juan Alonso
Juan Gomez
Myguel de las Cuevas
Pedro Gomez
Francisco de Castro
Cristoval de Torres
Myguel de Llestrella
Pedro Duran
Rodrigo Muñoz
Juan Sancho
Juan de Guadalupe
Domyngo
Savastian de Fuentes
Andres Apariçio
Vanegas
Francisco de Linares
Juan Borgoño
Pedro Lopez
Antonyo Davia
Hernan Muñoz
Comes Muñoz
Hernando Muñoz
Juan de Castañeda
Juan Morillo

AGI, GUATEMALA 41, N.1, FOLIO 35 RECTO (cont.)

Estevan Davyla
Cristoval de Medina
Juan de Çepeda
Savastian Ojalvol
Vasco Hernandez
Martyn Monje
Francisco de Nogales
Lorenço Sesstaño
Pedro Gutierrez
Cristoval Martyn
Pedro Çepera
Francisco Sanches Sardina
Juan Ruyz
Pedro Duarte
Gonçalo Gordillo
Francisco de Salazar
Pedro Gonçales
Pascual Hernandez
Juan Davila
Juan Sanches
Juan de Sepulveda
Machin de Veçerra

CHRONOLOGY

1485 Pedro de Alvarado born in Badajoz, with twin sister, Sarra, to Gómez de Alvarado and Leonor de Contreras.

1510 Passage from Spain to the Indies (Isla Española) where Alvarado meets Hernando Cortés.

1511 With Cortés, both under the command of Diego de Velázquez, Alvarado involved in the conquest of Cuba.

MAY 1518 Under the command of Juan de Grijalva, Alvarado's first foray into Mexico.

18 FEBRUARY 1519 Alvarado embarks with Cortés on the conquest of Mexico.

MARCH 1519 On the island of Cozumel, altercation between Cortés and Alvarado about the latter's mistreatment of the native population.

22 APRIL 1519 Arrival of Spanish ships off the coast of mainland Mexico.

23 SEPTEMBER 1519 Cortés enters Tlaxcala, which allies itself with the Spaniards.

SEPTEMBER 1519 Tecuilvaztzin, daughter of Tlaxcalan leader Xicoténcatl, becomes Alvarado's consort, later baptized Luisa and the mother of three of his children.

14–18 OCTOBER 1519 Massacre at Cholula, for which Alvarado may have been responsible.

8 NOVEMBER 1519 Spaniards arrive at the Aztec capital, Tenochtitlán, the future site of Mexico City.

19 MAY 1520 Massacre at Tenochtitlán, for which Alvarado was responsible.

30 JUNE 1520 After an Aztec uprising, the Spaniards flee Tenochtitlán for Tlaxcala.

AUGUST 1521 In the wake of an outbreak of smallpox, Tenochtitlán falls to the Spaniards.

6 DECEMBER 1523 Alvarado departs for Guatemala.

16 FEBRUARY 1524 The defeat of K'iche' Maya forces at Zapotitlán marks the beginning of the conquest of Guatemala.

MARCH 1524 Alliance struck between Alvarado and the Kaqchikel Maya.

22 MARCH 1524 Birth in Guatemala of Alvarado's daughter, Leonor.

11 APRIL 1524 Alvarado writes to Cortés, furnishing details of his exploits to date.

MAY 1524 Alvarado leaves Guatemala for El Salvador.

8 JUNE 1524 Alvarado wounded at Acajutla, an arrow piercing his leg and causing him life-long infirmity.

21 JULY 1524 Alvarado arrives back in Guatemala, having failed to conquer El Salvador.

AUGUST 1524 Demands made by Alvarado foment a Kaqchikel uprising.

AUGUST 1526 Alvarado leaves Guatemala for Mexico.

FEBRUARY 1527 Alvarado sets sail for Spain.

18 DECEMBER 1527 Emperor Charles V names Alvarado governor and *capitán general* of Guatemala.

1528–29 A judicial inquiry (*residencia*) detains Alvarado in Mexico.

APRIL 1530 Alvarado returns to Guatemala.

8 MAY 1530 Surrender to Alvarado of Cahí Ymox and Belehé Qat, leaders of the Kaqchikel uprising.

1531–33 Alvarado arranges for ships to be built at Iztapa in Guatemala, supposedly to explore the Pacific but in fact Peru being the armada's eventual destination.

MARCH and APRIL 1533 Alvarado's fleet moves to the Gulf of Fonseca, offshore from Honduras.

MID-1533 to EARLY 1534 Alvarado puts the finishing touches to his fleet at the Puerto de la Posesión (Realejo) in Nicaragua.

11 JANUARY 1534 Roll call (*alarde*) made of those Spaniards accompanying Alvarado to Peru.

23 JANUARY 1534 Alvarado's armada sails for Peru, territory already ceded for conquest to Francisco Pizarro and Diego de Almagro.

25 FEBRUARY 1534 After thirty-three days at sea, Alvarado makes landfall at Caráquez in Ecuador.

Early MARCH 1534 Having learned of Alvarado's intention to invade the kingdom of Quito, Sebastián de Belalcázar heads there from San Miguel de Piura, in northern Peru, to pre-empt him.

10 MARCH 1534 Alvarado writes to the governor of Panama, Francisco de Barrionuevo, from Puerto Viejo (Manta) in Ecuador.

23 MARCH 1534 Pizarro establishes Spanish Cuzco on the site of an Inca foundation.

8 MAY 1534 Almagro informs the Crown about Alvarado's intrusion and his designs on Quito, where he leaves for, in the footsteps of Belalcázar.

MAY–AUGUST 1534 Alvarado's party treks from coast to sierra, laying Indigenous communities to waste during its onerous march through unknown territory.

Early AUGUST 1534 Crossing the Andes, Alvarado's party succumbs to freezing blizzards, which take a heavy toll on Indigenous conscripts.

MID-AUGUST 1534 At Mocha, on the Inca highway between Riobamba and Ambato, scouts of Almagro's encounter Alvarado's advance guard.

15 AUGUST 1534 Almagro founds Santiago de Quito on the site of present-day Sicalpa.

26 AUGUST 1534 Alvarado meets Almagro face to face in Santiago de Quito and agrees to sell his fleet for 100,000 gold pesos, whereupon he will return to Guatemala.

28 AUGUST 1534 San Francisco de Quito founded, replacing Santiago de Quito as the hub of Spanish subjugation in Ecuador.

SEPTEMBER to EARLY/MID-OCTOBER 1534 Passing through Cuenca, Almagro and Alvarado march south to San Miguel de Piura, their forces embattled but prevailing.

12 OCTOBER 1534 Almagro compiles a lengthy missive to the Crown, documenting Alvarado's excesses and depredations earlier that year.

Late OCTOBER–NOVEMBER 1534 Almagro and Alvarado traverse the Pacific littoral, by way of Chicama and Chimú, en route to a rendezvous with Pizarro.

DECEMBER 1534 Pizarro awaits the arrival of Almagro and Alvarado in Pachacamac, in central Peru.

Late DECEMBER 1534 Almagro and Alvarado meet with Pizarro, who pays Alvarado the agreed-upon sum for his fleet and paraphernalia.

1 JANUARY 1535 Pizarro informs Emperor Charles V of having settled up with Alvarado.

15 JANUARY 1535 Alvarado in San Miguel de Piura on his way back to Guatemala.

18 JANUARY 1535 Founding of Lima, the City of the Kings.

APRIL 1535 Alvarado returns to Guatemala.

AUGUST 1536 Alvarado sets sail a second time for Spain.

AUGUST 1539 Alvarado returns to Guatemala.

SEPTEMBER 1540 Another fleet of Alvarado's leaves Central America ostensibly for the Spice Islands, which it never reaches.

4 JULY 1541 Death of Alvarado in Guadalajara, Mexico, from injuries sustained in a mishap during the Mixtón War ten days before, when the horse of one of his men fell on him.

GLOSSARY

Adelantado. Recipient of a royal licence to explore and conquer territory, which carried with it entitlement to govern with supreme authority. A title associated with Pedro de Alvarado.

Alarde. Literally, a parade, from which a register or roll call could be made of those participating.

Alcalde. Mayor of a city council or *cabildo*.

Alférez. A military rank, that of an officer who could be an ensign or standard bearer.

Alguacil. Constable or officer.

Audiencia. High Court or governing body of a region and, by extension, the name given to the territory of jurisdiction itself.

Cabildo. City council of elected officials.

Cacique. Indigenous leader.

Capitán de la guarda. Literally, captain of the guard.

Capitán general. A high-ranking military officer or governor.

Capitulación. A contract or concession to explore and settle, granted by royal authority.

Carabela. A caravel.

Casa. Literally, a house, in colonial parlance a household.

Casa de Contratación. House of Trade, established in Seville in 1503 to control commerce and monitor other aspects of Spain's imperial ventures.

Castellano. A gold coin worth 480 or 485 *maravedís*.

Caudillo. Political or military leader, a strongman.

Comendador. Commander.

Consejo de la Indias. Council of the Indies, a royal entity established in 1524 to administer Spanish territories in the New World.

Contador. An accountant, a treasury official assigned to look after the fiscal interests of the Crown.

Crónica. A narration of events written either by a lay person or, as often the case, a clergyman.

Ducado/Ducat. Gold coin worth 375 *maravedís.*

Encomendero. Holder of an *encomienda*, a recipient of Indigenous tribute in the form of commodities, goods, labour, and services.

Encomienda. An award of Indigenous tribute.

Fiscal. An attorney.

Galeón. A galleon.

Gobernador. Governor, the title by which Francisco Pizarro was often referred.

Hidalgo. A member of standing in Spanish society, but without a title.

Indio or *yndio.* Literally, "Indian," a designation today considered derogatory but in Spanish colonial times (and parlance) a generic term used to identify Indigenous inhabitants.

Indios or *yndios amigos.* Used to denote Indigenous allies who sided with Spaniards in their campaigns of conquest.

Justicia mayor. Literally, a chief justice or magistrate.

Legua. A distance of 4.2 kilometres.

Libro de cabildo. A log of city council minutes that recorded meetings held by elected members of committee.

Licenciado. Literally, a licenciate, an educated person, a university graduate.

Lugarteniente or *teniente de gobernador.* Lieutenant governor.

Maestro de campo. Field commander.

Macegual. An Indigenous commoner.

Mariscal. Marshal, a high-ranking military officer, a title associated with Diego de Almagro.

Mar del Norte. Literally, the North Sea, what Spaniards called the Atlantic Ocean.

Mar del Sur. Literally, the South Sea, what Spaniards called the Pacific Ocean.

Maravedí. Unit of currency, one thirty-fourth of a *real.*

Mayordomo. An overseer or manager in charge of operations.

Méritos y servicios. Literally, merits and services, usually recorded as a court document detailing a Spaniard's loyalty and dedication to the Crown, corroborated by witnesses testifying on his behalf.

Nao. Carrack, a large sailing vessel.

Oficial real. A royal official.

Oidor. A judge.

Patax. A supply ship, a tender.

Peso. A gold or silver coin divided into eight *reales*, hence "pieces of eight."

Pleito. Formal complaint made by one party against another.

Probanza. Paperwork connected to sworn declarations, a certified statement of particular events and circumstances, proof of deeds done or services rendered.

Procurador. An attorney or legal representative of one party who acts before another.

Provisor. A bishop's deputy.

Puerto. Port.

Quintal or *centena*. A weight of some 100 pounds or 46 kilograms.

Quinto real. The "royal fifth," a Crown entitlement to one-fifth of all business proceeds, especially those pertaining to mining or the melting down of gold and silver objects.

Real. A military encampment.

Real. A coin worth one-eighth of a *peso*.

Real cédula. Royal order or decree.

Regidor. An alderman, an ordinary member of city council.

Relación. Descriptive account or report about a particular subject or occurrence.

Repartimiento de indios. System of draft labour imposed on Indigenous male adults, obliging them to work for their Spanish masters.

Residencia. Judicial review and inquiry into the conduct of a Spanish official. Pedro de Alvarado was subjected to two such proceedings in his lifetime.

Salinas. Salt works.

San Francisco de Quito. Second Spanish and present-day capital of Ecuador, officially founded 6 December 1534.

Santiago de Guatemala. Capital city of Spanish Guatemala, founded 22 November 1527 by Jorge de Alvarado in the valley of Almolonga.

Santiago de Quito. First Spanish capital of what is now Ecuador, officially founded 15 August 1534 in Sicalpa, twenty kilometres west of present-day Riobamba.

Tesorero. Treasurer.

Traslado. A copy of a document.

Tunatiuh. The "Sun" in Náhuatl, the name given to Pedro de Alvarado by the Indigenous inhabitants of Mexico on account of his fair hair and handsome complexion.

Vecino. A Spanish resident of an established settlement.

Veedor. An inspector.

Villa. Town.

NOTES

PREFACE

1 Galeano ([1982] 1985, 91–2). "Captain Benalcázar," first name Sebastián, hailed from Belalcázar, which lies some one hundred kilometres north of Córdoba in southern Spain. Embarking on conquistador exploits, he assumed as his surname his place of birth and so should more properly be known and referred to as Sebastián de Belalcazár, as I have opted to call him. After Belfrage's death in 1990 – Galeano ([1989] 1991, 9) paid him tribute by saying that "a part of me died with him / A part of him lives with me" – the baton of translating one of Latin America's most accomplished writers was passed on to Mark Fried. He, like Belfrage, engages with aplomb what Kate Briggs, influenced by Helen Lowe-Porter, calls *This Little Art* ([2017] 2020), an absorbing read but a tongue-in-cheek title that fails to capture the imperative of translation. Interactions with Fried and Galeano – I struck a bond with the latter, who died in 2015, after we met and began corresponding in 1991 – have been an enduring source of inspiration. Throughout *Death in the Snow*, to afford readers ample scope to judge for themselves how I render any given text, I make note of the original in Spanish as a complement to my English iteration of it.

2 Two sources consulted and drawn upon are the works of American scholars William Hickling Prescott (1796–1859) and Hubert Howe Bancroft (1832–1918). Their approach to history no longer in fashion, both receive little attention from present-day researchers, a great pity. The pair's achievements were attained in no small part by the deployment of teams of assistants who worked in the archives and generated findings for them, a luxury that these days few can afford.

3 Writing halfway through the nineteenth century, Prescott (1847, vol. 2, 180) states the case for more thorough investigation than he was able to expend. He observes: "Such was the terrible passage of the Puertos Nevados, which I have only briefly noticed as an episode to the Peruvian conquest … [I]n all its details [it] would give one a better idea of the difficulties encountered

by the Spanish cavaliers than volumes of ordinary narrative." Prescott (1847, vol. 2, 186) distills Alvarado's Andean intrusion concisely thus: "His expedition to Peru was eminently characteristic of the man. It was founded in injustice, conducted with rashness, and ended in disaster." Woodrow Borah (1954, 134n8) considered the subject "marginal" to what he was then researching, which was trade and navigation between Mexico and Peru in early colonial times, but deemed it "intensely interesting" nonetheless. Linda A. Newson (1995, 247) concurs. "Alvarado's expedition is worthy of extended comment," she writes, "because of the havoc it wreaked on the coast south of the Bahía de Caráquez where he landed."

CHAPTER ONE

1 Taylor (1980, 325), in his review of Sherman (1979). Kelly (1932, 186–201) entitles a chapter of his biography of Alvarado, as apt as Taylor's designation of Central America, "Neighbours' Fields Are Greener."

2 Remesal ([1620] 1964–66, vol. 1, 203), his precise words being "como don Pedro era hombre de ánimo orgulloso y levantado y deseoso de cosas grandes, respondía que aquella gobernación [Guatemala] era poco para él y que quería ir a buscar otra mayor." Like his mentor, fellow Dominican and "Defender of the Indians" Bartolomé de las Casas (1484–1566), Remesal was no admirer of "don Pedro," documenting the conquistador's deeds so negatively that he was accused of defamation of character. His chronicle, *Historia general de las Indias Occidentales* (1620), was impounded, copies of it burned or destroyed, and otherwise withdrawn from circulation soon after it reached Guatemala. The chronicler himself was hounded while there by incensed descendants of the first Spanish colonists, whose animosity at their heroic forebears being so maligned was fierce and sustained. Especially driven to denounce the friar and discredit his work was the powerful Felipe Ruiz del Corral, cathedral dean and settler champion. "Remesal must have seemed like a second Las Casas come to plague them and their way of life," MacLeod (1970, 64) writes. Following a period of imprisonment in Guatemala, Remesal was released and exiled to Mexico in 1623, where "it is thought that he died in 1627, or shortly thereafter." See Valcárcel Martínez (1995) for elaboration.

3 See Lovell and Lutz (2018) and Lovell, Lutz, and Kramer (2020, 34–6, 42–64, and 79–93) for extended discussion of Kaqchikel resistance to the Spanish invasion.

4 The findings of Asselbergs (2004, 2008, [2010] 2018), her meticulous analysis of the "conquest narrative" known as the *Lienzo de Quauhquechollan* above all, point to Jorge, more than Pedro de Alvarado, as having brought Spanish might to prevail. See also Lovell, Lutz, and Kramer (2020, 64–9 and 111–15). Between Alvarado's initial intrusion in February 1524 and his death in July 1541, a period of some seventeen years and five months, we reckon him to have been physically present in Guatemala less than one-third that time, absent almost eleven years.

5 Recinos (1952, 16). His precise words are: "A corta distancia de la ciudad de Santo Domingo, en el pequeño pueblo de Azúa, vivía desde cinco años atrás un caballero, extremeño como Alvarado, llamado Hernán Cortés, que ejercía el cargo de escribano público y especulaba con el trabajo de los indios en tierras que el Gobernador Ovando y don Diego Colón le habían concedido." Vallejo García-Hevia (2008, vol. 1, 125) records 1512, not 1510, as the "probable" year of Alvarado's passage to the Indies. Haiti lies on the western side of Española/Hispaniola, the Dominican Republic to its east.

6 "One can easily imagine," Recinos (1952, 16) writes, "how Alvarado and his brothers, new to the Indies, poor and without friends, found in Cortés a source of counsel and protection," his precise words being: "Es fácil suponer que los Alvarados, recién llegados a las Indias, pobres y sin amigos, encontraron en Cortés consejo y protección."

7 Recinos (1952, 16–17). His precise words are "prosperó en varios años de labor como hacendado … y persona de confianza del desconfiado gobernador Velázquez." Recinos states categorically: "En Cuba ha de saber seguido floreciendo la amistad de los dos," which is to suppose that "friendship between the two continued to flourish in Cuba."

8 Recinos (1952, 19–20). The "navío muy bueno que se decía San Sebastián" sailed up "un anchuroso río que los indios llamaban Papaloapan," which Recinos translates as "río de las mariposas" – the "river of butterflies." On account of Alvarado's actions, Spaniards henceforth referred to the river not by that name but as the "Río de Alvarado."

9 Recinos (1952, 19–20). He emphasizes his point by recourse to the words of Díaz del Castillo ([1632] 1963, 34–5 and 39), who records: "We were waiting with the three other ships at the mouth of the river for him to sail down, and the General [Grijalva] was very angry with him for having gone up without his permission. He ordered him never to go ahead of the other ships, in case he should meet with some accident, in which we could not

come to his assistance … It was therefore decided that Pedro de Alvarado should take the good ship *San Sebastián* and [return] to Cuba." Díaz del Castillo ([1632] 1963, 39) indicates that Alvarado was ordered to return not only because "Grijalva and the other captains were annoyed [with him] for having sailed up the Río Papaloapan" but also because "he had come on the expedition against his will, as he was not in good health." He adds: "It was agreed that all the wounded men, and all the cloth and gold that had been obtained by barter, should be sent back with him." Somewhat more flippantly, López de Gómara ([1552] 1966, 14) claims that Alvarado's returning to Cuba was because he was "madly in love with an island girl."

10 Recinos (1952, 20). His precise words are: "Entró nuestro capitán al puerto de Santiago triunfalmente, llevando el oro, mantas y demás objetos recogidos durante la expedición. El gobernador escuchó con intenso júbilo el relato que le hizo de las tierras descubiertas y decidió al instante enviar otra expedición más fuerte y numerosa para explorar las riquezas de tan extenso territorio." Díaz del Castillo ([1632] 1963, 40) words things thus: "Pedro de Alvarado arrived with the gold and cloth and the wounded men, and told the whole story of our discoveries. Everyone was astonished at the riches of the lands we had discovered. Alvarado was a good storyteller, and they say that Diego Velázquez could do nothing but embrace him, and there were great rejoicings for the next eight days. There had been rumours enough already about the existence of rich lands, but now, with the arrival of this gold, they were exaggerated still further throughout the islands and in Castile."

11 Recinos (1952, 21) records Díaz del Castillo as having stated: "De aquella villa salieron cinco hermanos que se decían Pedro de Alvarado y Jorge y Gonzalo y Gómez y Juan de Alvarado el viejo, bastardo," adding: "Se agregaron también allí a la expedición Alonso de Ávila, Cristóbal de Olid y otros hidalgos."

12 Recinos (1952, 22). His precise words are: "Alvarado aspiraba al mando de la armada, y parece ser lastimado porque no lo consiguió; pero seguro se conformó con desempañar en ella un papel importante, como segundo de su amigo Cortés."

13 Vallejo García-Hevia (2008, vol. 1, 125).

14 Díaz del Castillo ([1632] 1963, 58). His precise words (Díaz del Castillo [1632] 1970, 41) are: "[L]a primera cosa que hizo fue mandar hecho preso en grillos al piloto Camacho, porque no aguardó en la mar como le fue

mandado. Y reprendióle gravemente a Pedro de Alvarado, mostró tener mucho enojo de ello, y le dijo que no se habían de apaciguar las tierras de aquella manera, tomando a los naturales su hacienda."

15 See Schwaller (2014) for a full account of the founding of Veracruz, including a transcription (and translation into English) of a "lost petition of Cortés and his company" dated 20 June 1519, which Schwaller considers "the first letter from New Spain."

16 For a biographical sketch of Doña Luisa "Tecuilvaztzin" or "Teohquilhuastzin" – the name translates as "fire that sings" – see Meade de Ángulo (1992).

17 Bancroft (1883, 212).

18 MacLeod (1998, 33) points out that Alvarado "did not treat Luisa as an occasional concubine but rather respected her, appeared in public with her regularly, and demonstrated that he considered her to be of noble lineage and his constant companion." In documentation that MacLeod cites, witnesses were called upon to testify as such, it being noted too that "Luisa was a baptized and observant Christian and that Pedro fully acknowledged and recognized his bastard children by her."

19 Cabezas Carcache (2019, 5), his precise words being "un matrimonio religioso en toda ley, *in facie Ecclesiae*," the term in italics meaning "in the face of the Church" or "in the presence of the congregation."

20 Cabezas Carcache (2019, 5). His precise words are: "Agradecido por tan especial obsequio, Pedro de Alvarado recomendó a Cortés castigar de modo ejemplar a los de Cholula, aliados de los aztecas, lo que al ejecutarse terminó en una cruenta masacre." Restall (2018, 209–10) is not so sure that any Spaniard, let alone Alvarado, can be held responsible for the Cholula massacre. "Cortés later claimed that he had marched to Cholollan for supplies," he discloses. "But Chololan was neither on the way to Tenochtitlan, nor any closer to it than Tlaxcallan itself – it was a detour to the south. The fact is [that] neither Cortés nor his fellow captains were in control: the Tlaxcalteca led the Spaniards to Chololan for their own political purposes, telling the Spanish captains that it was on the way [to Tenochtitlán] and rich in supplies." Restall argues that "the march to Chololan and the sacking of the city constituted a well-executed Tlaxcalteca plan to test the new alliance with the [Spanish] invaders, to punish the Chololteca for switching sides, and to restore in Chololan a leadership loyal to the Tlaxcallan Triple Alliance." In his treatise on the conquest of Mexico, Thomas (1993) draws on many

of the same sources as Restall but interprets them quite differently, in the end offering a view of events, occurrences, and circumstances that may be considered a more traditional narrative than the revisionist thrust of Restall.

21 Restall (2018, 209). Díaz del Castillo ([1632] 1963, 192–9) records Cortés, before he summoned the Tlaxcalans into action, as being ill at ease as the mood in Cholula turned increasingly hostile. He writes: "Our Captain called us together and said: 'I see that these people are greatly disturbed. We must keep very much on the alert, for they are up to some mischief.' He was well aware, he said, that they had many companies of warriors lying in wait for us in some ravines near by, ready to carry out the treacherous attack they had planned."

22 The character of the two men Bancroft (1883, 209–10) distils thus: "Cortés possessed a certain greatness and nobility of soul: Alvarado was mendacious, treacherous, and dishonest; his frank demeanor cloaked deceit, and favors heaped on him were repaid with ingratitude. To govern by fear was his delight. Cortés was cautious and far-sighted; Alvarado impetuous, never anticipating other than favorable results." Closer to our day, Sherman (1979, 9) opines: "Magnanimous to his friends and ruthless to his enemies, Alvarado was the quintessential *caudillo*, whose charisma derived from his imposing physical presence, exploits on the field of battle, grace, charm, self-assurance, a mercurial character, and an inclination to violence – all of which impressed the Indians as much as his Spanish companions." He evoked "awe more than affection; indeed, the Indians feared him, and it was said that his very presence had the effect of calming – or better put, intimidating – the local populace."

23 Recinos (1952, 38), his precise words being "fué la muerte a manos de los españoles de la flor de la nobleza mexicana y el alzamiento de la población entera de la ciudad contra los extranjeros." Padden (1967, 192–202) describes the attack and its repercussions vividly, portraying Alvarado as "a capable officer and a good leader of men" but a psychopath who "did not possess the genius of his commander." According to Padden's reading of the sources, "only those who feigned death survived," with Cortés considering the carnage wrought by Alvarado "ill done and an error of tragic proportion." Restall (2018, 434n48) considers "the blame assigned to Alvarado for the Toxcatl massacre universal; the only split is between those arguing that he imagined an Aztec plot (gaining confirmation through torturing seized Aztecs) and those asserting it was real." Restall adds, invoking Torquemada, that "the Aztecs had set up huge cauldrons in which to cook the Spaniards."

24 Díaz del Castillo, as quoted in Recinos (1952, 39), his precise words describing the act being "era muy mal hecho e gran desatino."

25 López de Gómara ([1552] 1964, 208), his precise words being: "Cortés, quien debió haberse sentido mal con respecto al incidente, enmascaró sus sentimientos para no irritar a los perpetradores, ya que sucedió en un momento en que los necesitaba, ya sea en contra de los indios, o para sofocar problemas entre sus propios hombres."

26 Díaz del Castillo, as quoted in Recinos (1952, 43), his precise words being: "eramos pocos, no quedábamos sino cuatrocientos y cuarenta, con veinte caballos y doce ballesteros y siete escopeteros, y no teníamos pólvora, y todos heridos y cojos y mancos."

27 See Lovell, Lutz, and Kramer (2020, 43–5 and 136–8), who note a legend below a battle scene from the "Historia de Tlaxcala" recording "[l]a guerra que hubo por todas las calles de Tacuba y calçada por las puentes quebradas que avian quebradas los mexicanos y el salto grande que hizo don Pedro de Alvarado que hoy día se llama el salto de Alvarado."

28 The fall of Tenochtitlán was also due, in no small measure, to an outbreak of smallpox, which not only caused high mortality but also reduced the effectiveness of mounting a war of resistance, exacting a psychological as well as physical cost. Drawing on testimony recorded by the Franciscan friar Bernardino de Sahagún (1499–1590), Anderson and Dibble ([1555] 1978, 64) write: "About the time that the Spaniards had fled [to Tlaxcala], there came a great sickness, a pestilence, the smallpox. It spread over the people with great destruction, causing great misery. Some people it covered with pustules, everywhere, the face, the head, the breast. Many indeed perished from it. They could not walk; they could only lie at home in their beds, unable to move. If they stirred they cried out with great pain. Like a covering over them were the pustules. Indeed many died of them. But many just died of hunger. There were so many deaths that there was often no one to care for the sick; they could not be attended to."

29 As rendered by Mackie (1924, 89–90). Alvarado's precise words are: "[Suplico] a Vuestra Merced le haga relación [a Su Majestad] quién yo soy, y lo que a Su Majestad he servido en estas partes, y … cómo en su servicio me han lisiado en una pierna, y cuán poco sueldo hasta ahora he ganado yo y estos hidalgos que en mi compañía andan, y el poco provecho que hasta ahora se nos ha seguido … De mí no tiene noticia [Su Magestad] – que no me maravillo – y de esto nadie tiene la culpa sino Vuestra Merced."

30 A Pipil arrow that pierced his leg in a fierce battle that took place in Acajutla, El Salvador, left Alvarado crippled for the rest of his life. The arrow went clean through his leg and struck his horse's saddle. His precise words – see Recinos (1952, 90) for a transcription of the original – are: "[Q]ue me dieron un flechazo que me pasaron la pierna y entró la flecha por la silla, de la cual herida quedo lisiado que me quedó la una pierna más corta que la otra bien cuatro dedos."

31 Kaqchikel resistance to Spanish rule is best read in their own words, translated into English by Recinos and Goetz (1953, 123–34). The uprising is featured at length in Lovell, Lutz, and Kramer (2020, 30–69 and 79–93).

32 As rendered by Kramer (1994, 44), drawn from her reading of Ramírez ([1847] 1930–33, 7 (1): 117–18). See also Lovell, Lutz, and Kramer (2020, 59). Alvarado's precise words, articulated before the Cabildo of Santiago de Guatemala on 30 January 1526, are recorded as being that "Hernando Cortés le avia dado quanto tenia e con el queria morir."

33 Cortés to Emperor Charles V, as rendered by Mackie (1924, 19–20).

34 Cortés to Emperor Charles V, 3 September 1526, as rendered by Mackie (1924, 20).

CHAPTER TWO

1 Szászdi (1978, 525 and 554) dates the encounter as having occurred on 1 October 1526. Murphy (1941, 17 and 24) reckons the end of February the following year, considering it "the first tangible indications of the rich empire of the Incas." Both consult the same sources, described by Murphy (1941, 3) as "few, sketchy, and filled with disagreements," which helps explain (if not reconcile) divergent readings of them. "Dates cited," he adds, "differ not only by months but in several instances by as much as a year." MacCormack (1999, 122) registers the raft as being sighted in 1525, for example, Villamarín and Villamarín (1999, 609) one year later, 1526. In his day, too, Prescott (1847, vol. 1, 235) lamented the difficulty of establishing a definitive timeline for the conquest of Peru. "I regret," he writes, "not to be able to give precise dates of the events of these early expeditions. But chronology is a thing beneath the notice of these ancient chroniclers, who seem to think that the date of events, so fresh in their own memory, must be so in that of every one else." Developments in the field since the time of Prescott have been noteworthy, but problems of chronology remain. Hemming ([1970] 1972, 501–5) distils the facts most

commendably, as does Lockhart (1972, 3–16). Both mark the conquest of Peru as beginning with the sighting of the Pacific, the Mar del Sur or Southern Sea, by the party led by Vasco Núñez de Balboa on 25 September 1513, after it had traversed the Isthmus of Panama, guided across it from the Mar del Norte, the Atlantic, by native assistants.

2 Smith et al. (2008, 47) take pains in establishing the nature and carrying capacity of the vessel piloted by Ruiz, an inquiry whose findings apply also to the native *balsa*, or raft, on account of an observation made by one of Ruiz's crew. "The raft had masts of very fine wood, and cotton sails of the same style as on our ships – traye sus masteles y antenas de muy fina madera y velas de algodon del mismo talle de manera que los nuestros navios." The crew member's description comes from the "Relación Sámano-Xerez," an eyewitness rendering also consulted by Edwards (1967, 67 and 133). Smith et al. (2008, 47) conclude that "the native vessel was fore-and-aft rigged" with triangular-shaped sails, as was Ruiz's caravel. Edwards (1967, 155–7, plates 15, 16, and 17) has contemporary illustrations of what Ecuadorian and Peruvian sailing rafts are thought to have looked like. Figure 1, plate 16a from Edwards (1967, 156), reproduces a drawing (Spilbergen [1619] 1943) that most closely resembles the description of the raft encountered by Ruiz. Figure 2, from a display in the Museo Nacional del Ecuador of pre-Columbian Indigenous seacraft, depicts a single-masted, ocean-going *balsa*.

3 Lockhart (1972, 5). His evocation of Pizarro (Lockhart 1972, 135–57) is incisive, his conjuring of Almagro (passim) likewise. Regarding the actions and deeds of Pizarro, Varón Gabai (1997) and Lavallé ([2003] 2007) are also notable contributions. For Almagro, see Busto Duthurburu (1986, vol. 1, 61–6), Ballesteros Gaibrois (1987), and Larraín Valdés (1996).

4 For his role in expediting the conquest of Peru, Ruiz has yet to receive the attention and recognition he deserves. Medina (1919, v–xxiv) furnishes a biographical sketch before presenting transcriptions (1–28) of eight documents pertaining to his life and times. Ruiz was born in Moguer in southern Spain in 1485 and died while accompanying Almagro to rendezvous with Pizarro in Cajamarca in Peru in 1533. The deeds of the "pilot of the Southern Sea" are engaged most insightfully by Jijón y Caamaño (1941, 87–92) and also noted by Bravo Guerreira (1976), Currie (1995), Smith et al. (2008), and Szászdi (1978). His exploits and their import are perhaps best handled by Loor (1956, 147–91), whose discussion includes a map (153) of Ruiz's voyage along the Ecuadorian coast.

5 Prescott (1847, vol. 1, 240) remarks that, "although the Spaniards had now reached the outer limits of the Peruvian empire, it was not Peru, but Quito, and that portion of it but recently brought under the sceptre of the Incas." South of Atacames, how much of the Manabí coast of Ecuador at that time was Inca controlled, indeed where the raft Ruiz encountered might have come from, is a matter of debate. "In a dry and arid strip extending from the Equator south towards Guayaquil," Saville (1907, 2) claimed over a century ago, "there developed a unique civilization which apparently suffered but little from Incasic influence." Jijón y Camaaño (1936, vol. 1, 58) words the matter thus: "Los Incas habían más explorado que conquistado parte de Manabí – Manabí had been explored more than conquered by the Incas." León Borja de Szászdi (1964, 433) and Newson (1995, 121) concur, the latter stating categorically "there is little evidence for Inka conquest of the coast." Szászdi (1978, 507) is equally emphatic: "There is documentary and archaeological evidence from the Ecuadorian coast," he asserts, "to prove that the Incas never conquered that region." Rowe (1946, 207) takes care not to invoke conquest but notes: "In the course of fighting in Quito, Topa Inca" – who ruled from 1471 to 1493 – "pushed his way down to the Ecuadorean Coast in the neighborhood of Manta." His son, Huayna Capac, "widened the frontiers of the Empire in the north and also conquered the hot Coast around the Gulf of Guayaquil and the large Island of Puná." According to Murra (1948, 808–9), under the rule of Huayna Capac (1493–1525) the Incas reached Esmeraldas. "But there was not much here to attract the conqueror," he states, "the tropical lowland dwellers regarded as naked uncivilized savages hardly worth the bother of enforced civilization. On the Coast the Empire ended at Túmbez." Porras Barrenechea (1937, 67–8) and Murphy (1941, 24–6) read available sources to indicate Túmbez as the raft's port of origin, their designation echoing – see note 6 below – that of Cieza de León ([1555] 1998, 75–6). Jijón y Caamaño (1941, 91), León Borja de Szászdi (1964, 427), Szászdi (1978, 527–54), Newson (1995, 65–71), and Topic (2013, 348) favour Salango, from where Manteño (Manta) culture thrived on the Manabí shores of Ecuador. "The sailing raft seems to have been more directly associated with the people of coastal Ecuador," Edwards (1965, 114) concludes, "than with the Inca-dominated Peruvians." His view is supported by the findings of Currie (1995) and Smith et al. (2008). The Museo Arqueológico in Salango certainly celebrates and showcases the Manta region's pre-Inca prowess of ocean-faring trade and commerce as

well as its Pacific littoral connections. Jijón y Caamaño (1941, 92) goes so far as to consider the "confederation of merchants" engaged in these activities "akin to a pre-Columbian Hanseatic League – una confederación de mercaderes, especie de Liga Hanseática precolombina." Murra (1948, 804 and 811) observes that "the large raft met by Bartolomé Ruiz gives an idea of the extent and magnitude of coastwise traffic. There is no reason to doubt Jijón y Caamaño's suggestion that the headquarters of these people can be located in Manabí … but it seems fairly obvious that the flourescence of such commerce must have received its impetetus from the south." He sums up astutely: "On the Coast, which the Incas never actually controlled, imperial influence was weak and indirect, but, nevertheless, gave a terrific impetus to the development of native coastwise commerce."

6 Hemming ([1970] 1972, 25). Prescott (1847, vol. 1, 233–4) reads the sources differently. "Ruiz found several Indians, both men and women, on board," he writes, "some with rich ornaments on their persons … Two of them had come from Túmbez, a Peruvian port, some degrees to the south … Ruiz resolved to detain some of the Indians, including the natives of Túmbez, that they might repeat the wondrous tale to his commander and, at the same time, by learning the Castilian [language] might hereafter serve as interpreters with their countrymen. The rest of the party he suffered to proceed without further interruption on their voyage. Then, holding on his course, the prudent pilot, without touching at any other point of the coast, advanced as far as the Punta de Pasado, about half a degree south, having the glory of being the first European who, sailing in this direction on the Pacific, had crossed the equinoctial line. This was the limit of his discoveries; on reaching which he tacked about, and, standing away to the north, succeeded, after an absence of several weeks, in regaining the spot where he had left Pizarro and his comrades." Cieza de León ([1555] 1998, 75–6) puts the number of natives aboard the raft at ten – "five Indian men, two boys, and three women, who became prisoners on the ship." Ruiz, Cieza says, "treated them well." When, "using signs," those captured were asked "where they were from and what land lay ahead," the Spaniards understood them to say "that they were natives of Túmbez." And when taken before Pizarro, Cieza records a cordial reception: "It was a joy to see and hear them."

7 Porras Barrenechea (1962, 54). The document describing the raft is housed in the Imperial Library in Vienna, catalogued there as Codex CXX.

Bravo Guerreira (1976, 38) questions Porras Barrenechea's attribution of authorship, as does Szászdi (1978, 553). The latter credits Ruiz himself with providing information to the chronicler Gonzalo Fernández de Oviedo y Valdés, who then put pen to paper. "Los datos acerca el viaje de Bartolomé Ruiz en 1526," Szászdi asserts, "proceden del mismo Ruiz." For indications of pre-Columbian contact between the peoples of Ecuador and Central America and Mexico, see León Borja de Szászdi (1964, 390–9), Currie (1995), Salomon ([1986] 2007, 92), Smith et al. (2008, 57–8), Moreno Yánez ([2008] 2015, 35), and West (1961). Wright ([1992] 2003, 64) states that "the great balsa raft ... was one of a fleet heading north," carrying "thirty tons of freight – close to what a caravel could hold." León Borja de Szászdi (1964, 396) reckons that the largest of rafts would have had room aboard for as many as "cinquenta hombres y animales – fifty men and animals."

8 The description is that of Hemming (1974, 25). Prescott (1847, vol. 1, 233) transcribes an extract from the manuscript in the Imperial Library of Vienna that describes "what most attracted [Ruiz's] attention" as follows: "Espejos guarnecidos de la dicha plata, y tasas y otras vasijas para beber, trahian muchas mantas de lana y de algodon, y camisas y aljubas y alcaçeres y alaremes, y otras muchas ropas, todo lo mas en ellos muy labrado de labores muy ricas de colores de grana y carmisi y azul y amarillo, y de todos otras colores de diversas maneras de labores y figuras de aves y animales, y Pescados, y arbolesas y trahian unos pesos chiquitos de pesar oro como hechura de Romana, y otras muchas cosas." See Jijón y Caamaño (1941, 89–90) for an alternate rendering in Spanish, MacCormack (1999, 122) and Villamarín and Villamarín (1999, 609) for translations into English. "The people sponsoring the raft were efficient tradesmen," Murra (1948, 804) notes, "who knew how to assay metals and who used a steelyard to weigh their goods. Merchandise such as wool cloth and the use of the steelyard indicate that the Incas were involved in these trading operations."

9 Cieza de León ([1555] 1998, 85–8). See also Prescott (1847, vol. 1, 238–47), who makes good use of documents composed early on, ones again located for consultation in the Imperial Library in Vienna.

10 Murphy (1941, 25). In his view, the departure of the ship would have meant that some "eighty-five Spaniards" remained with Pizarro.

11 "There were not many provisions on the island," Cieza de León ([1555] 1998, 89) says, "and almost nothing to eat."

12 Prescott (1847, vol. 1, 250). His source is the seventeenth-century chronicler Fernando de Montesinos, who transcribed a manuscript dated 1527 as follows: "Pizarro sacó un Puñal, y con notable animo hizo la punta una raya de Oriente á Poniente; y señalando al medio dia, que era la parte de su noticia, y derrotero dijo: 'Camaradas y amigos, esta parte es de la muerte, de los trabajos, de las hambres, de la desnudez, de los aguaceros, y desamparos; la otra la del gusto. Por aquí se ba á Panama á ser pobres, por allá al Peru á ser ricos. Escoja el que fuere bien Castellano lo que mas bien le estuviere.' Diciendo esto pasó la raya." Lockhart (1972, 5) imagines that choices were made "[not] so theatrically as is often thought," believing instead that "Pizarro spoke for continuing, in a way simpler, more matter of fact, and at the same time more moving than is usually reported." Cook and Cook (Cieza de León [1555] 1998, 95n2) concur. "This event," they write, "was told and retold by subsequent authors, with much embellishment." According to Cieza, Tafur's first name was "Juan." Murphy (1941, 25) records it as having been "Pedro Alonzo." The "cavalier" Tafur – the designation is that of Prescott (1847, vol. 1, 248) – is identified by him as "a native of Cordova."

13 Lockhart (1972, 5–6). "But this was not the case with all," he adds. "Some were wounded, or ill, and did not intend to abandon the venture permanently, as they later showed by their actions. Others were on specific missions for Pizarro, including pilot Ruiz himself."

14 Cieza de León ([1555] 1998, 100) records Governor Ríos as being "distressed when he learned that Pizarro had remained with so few Spaniards. He said that if they should die or if the Indians came to kill them, it would be their own fault since they refused to come on the ships with Juan Tafur."

15 Prescott (1847, vol. 1, 252). Ruiz's securing a ship to return with to Pizarro was achieved in remarkably short time.

16 Cieza de León ([1555] 1998, 97). He reinforces his bleak depiction by stating that the Isla Gorgona's "many forests are as thick as they are frightening" and "the hardships [the Spaniards] suffered there were in the extreme." Prescott (1847, vol. 1, 253) is more sanguine in assessing the island's attributes. Lockhart (1972, 5) is too, indicating that it "was better provisioned" than the Isla del Gallo, hence Pizarro's decision to relocate. Covey (2020, 183) points out that Isla Gorgona not only "offered safety from the coastal natives, who had been attacking the Spaniards on the Isla del Gallo," but

also that "its rocky terrain would provide a conspicuous landmark for returning ships."

17 Cieza de León ([1555] 1998, 101) has a warm description of Ruiz's return, part of which reads: "The captain [Pizarro] and the Spaniards who had stayed [awaited] the ship as if it were the salvation of their souls. One day, well at sea, they saw the ship approaching. Some thought it was a log, others that it was something else. Because they had yearned for it so long, even when they recognized a sail, they did not believe it. But as [the ship] came closer, the sails whitened, and they realized that it was what they had longed for. They became ecstatic and could not speak from the excitement. Ruiz then disembarked with some sailors, and they all embraced one another with delight." How Ruiz knew to head for Isla Gorgona and not Isla del Gallo is not made clear.

18 Hemming ([1970] 1972, 24) attributes the corruption to the explorer Pascual de Andagoya. He writes: "In 1522, Andagoya sailed some two hundred miles along the coast of Colombia and ascended the river San Juan (Map 1). He was seeking a tribe called Virú or Pirú; and the name of this tribe, altered to 'Perú,' came to be applied to a country lying far to the south." Covey (2020, 177) states that Andagoya "returned from exploring the southeastern coast of Panama, bringing the rumor of a rich land ruled by a native *cacique* (leader) called Peruquete, which lay just beyond where he had been." Murphy (1941, 10) observes that, while "Birú became a symbol of a land rich in treasure," the name was not one known to the Incas themselves. "As a matter of fact," he points out with geographical precision, "while the Spanish adventurers of 1524–1526 were supposed to be searching for Birú, they had already left it far behind."

19 Hemming ([1970] 1972, 24). He refers to Pizarro and Almagro as "citizens of Panama and holders of quotas of Indians there," and to Luque as "a priest who was apparently acting as an agent of the trio's financial backer," the judge Gaspar de Espinosa. The "memorable contract between three adventurers" is reproduced by Prescott (1847, vol. 3, 274–8) "from the manuscript history of Montesinos," whose rendering Prescott claims, rather unflatteringly, "derives more value from the insertion in it of this and other original documents than from any merit of its own."

20 Prescott (1847, vol. 1, 276). Luque, he writes, "was chained by his professional duties to Panamá." Almagro, "now much disfigured by the loss of an eye, was not so well qualified for the mission as his companion in arms,

who, possessing a good person and altogether a commanding presence, was plausible, and, with all his defects of education, could, where deeply interested, be even eloquent in discourse … No one," Almagro maintained, "could tell the stories of their adventures with such effect as the man who had been the chief actor in them. No one could so well paint the unparalleled sufferings and sacrifices which they had encountered; no other could tell so forcibly what had been done, what yet remained to do, and what assistance would be necessary to carry it into execution." See also Covey (2020, 182), who sums up succinctly thus: "On his return to Panama, Pizarro and his partners unsuccessfully sought permission from Pedro de los Ríos to mount yet another expedition. When it was denied, they combined their resources so that Pizarro could return to Spain to make their case at court."

21 Prescott (1847, vol. 3, 279–86) reproduces the *Capitulación de Toledo* in its entirety, a document formerly part of the holdings of the Archivo de Simancas now housed in the Archivo General de Indias (hereafter AGI) in Seville. From "the original that I had in my power in this City of the Kings" Cieza de León ([1555] 1998, 136–40) also reproduces "here verbatim some clauses taken from the agreement," the transcription he made in Lima rendered from Spanish into English by Alexandra Parma Cook and Noble David Cook. Bancroft (1883, 13) erroneously records the contract between Pizarro and the Crown as having been signed in Toledo on 26 July 1528. Hemming ([1970] 1972, 26) concurs with Prescott that the date indeed was 26 July but the year in question 1529, not 1528. Covey (2020, 185) agrees, citing AGI, Indiferente General 415 (Libro 1, folios 119 recto to 124 recto) as his source. Cook and Cook (Cieza de León [1555] 1998, 140n7) state that "documents were issued at Toledo from 15 May 1529 to 24 August of the same year."

22 Prescott (1847, vol. 3, 280). The original is worded: "[P]odais continuar el dicho descubrimiento, conquista y población de la dicha provincia del Perú, fasta duscientas leguas de tierra por la misma costa, las cuales dichas duscientas leguas comienzan desde el pueblo que en lengua de Indios se dice Tenumpuela, e despues le llamásteis Santiago, hasta llegar al pueblo Chincha, que puede haber las dichas duscientas leguas de costa, poco mas o menos." Described by DeBoer (1996, 171) as a "major coastal center" in pre-Columbian times, the former Tenumpuela lay some seventy kilometres east of Esmeraldas in present-day Ecuador. Chincha lies approximately two

hundred kilometres south of Lima, its people of the same name conquered by the Incas in the mid-fifteenth century.

23 "The 1529 contract built upon an incredibly optimistic representation of Peru," Covey (2020, 189) contends. "Pizarro and his partners clearly played up the significance of their earlier voyage, treating the Pacific coast as a place 250 Spanish colonists could occupy and hold. For someone who had lost more men than that on his first two expeditions, Pizarro must have known better than to expect that he could settle and govern the colony in the manner stipulated in his contract." Covey continues: "Because Charles V believed the Inca world to be civilized, he expected unprecedented success in establishing a colonial kingdom in Peru," meaning that (as the king informed his Council of the Indies) "there will be no need to conquer them and subject them militarily, but rather to treat them with love and good works." For this reason, 250 men were deemed a sufficient number to deploy.

24 Hemming ([1970] 1972, 26–7). "Pizarro sailed from Seville in January 1530 with a flotilla full of would-be conquerors," he writes, but Prescott (1847, vol. 1, 298) makes it clear that, six months after the *Capitulación de Toledo* was drawn up, "Pizarro had assembled somewhat less than his stipulated complement." He departed for La Gomera, one of the Canary Islands, before officers of the Crown arrived in port to inspect and verify that the stipulation had been met, which it had not. Bancroft (1883, 14) concurs with Prescott, stating: "Small as was the force required by his capitulation with the Crown, Pizarro was unable to raise it. With the assistance of Cortés, he managed to make ready the three small vessels, in one of which, by eluding the authorities, he embarked, and awaited his brothers at the Canary Islands. By liberal bribery and the solemn assurance of Fernando that all requirements of the King had been complied with, and that the specified number of men were with his brother who had gone before, the other two ships were allowed to depart."

25 The wording of the *Capitulación de Toledo* – see Prescott (1847, vol. 3, 282) – runs: "A suplicacion vuestra hacemos nuestro piloto mayor de la Mar del Sur a Bartolomé Ruiz, con setenta y cinco mill maravedís de salario en cada un año, pagados de la renta de la dicha tierra." A *maravedí* was a gold or silver and subsequently copper coin, by 1537 the smallest unit of account in Spain, a thirty-fourth of a *real*. Eight *reales* made up one *peso*, hence the term "a piece of eight." Medina (1919, 9–10) transcribes a *real cédula* (royal

order) to that effect, which he located in the Seville archive (AGI, 109–7–1, Libro 1, folio 37) and dates as being drawn up on 26 July 1529.

26 Prescott (1847, vol. 1, 298). He adds: "No one was in a better condition to hold out a helping hand to a brother adventurer, and probably no one felt greater sympathy in Pizarro's fortunes, or greater confidence in his eventual success, than the man who had lately trod the same career with renown." Of Pizarro's financial situation and the Crown's position, Prescott (1847, vol. 1, 293) remarks: "It was careful to reap the fruits of his toil, but not to pay the cost of them." From the standpoint of present-day sensibilities, Covey (2020, 187) words the arrangement thus: "The royal strategy would make sense in today's business world as a franchising venture – the conquistadores put up most of the capital for new conquests, and the Spanish monarchs stood to receive 20 percent of the profits."

CHAPTER THREE

1 Remesal ([1619] 1964–66, vol. 1, 93) states that Alvarado arranged for the friar Tomás Ortiz, and other members of the Dominican order, many of whom were very sick or in poor health, to accompany him. The chronicler records that Alvarado and Ortiz, the latter described as a "caballero liberal," agreed to travel together "y así se concentraron los dos y se hicieron a la vela por el mes de febrero de mil y quinientos y veinte y siete" – the "congenial gentleman" accompanying Alvarado "when they set sail in February 1527."

2 Hemming ([1970] 1972, 26), who also records Pizarro returning from Spain in January 1530.

3 García Añoveros (1987a, 247). According to Remesal ([1619] 1964–66, vol. 1, 120), upon landing in Palos de la Frontera, the port from which Columbus first departed in August 1492, Cortés made his way directly to Madrid, not passing through Seville, where he knew Alvarado would be. See also Bancroft (1883, 102–3).

4 Remesal ([1619] 1964–66, vol. 1, 94) furnishes a litany of wrongdoing, culled from a document drawn up by Gonzalo de Mejía, *procurador* (attorney) and *tesorero real* (royal treasurer) of Mexico, who lobbied the Casa de la Contratación (House of Trade) in Seville to press charges, which it did. See Barón Castro (1943, 128), Recinos (1952, 122), García Añoveros (1987b, 84), and Cabezas Carcache (2019, 26–7) for confirmation. Bancroft (1883, 100) puts a value of 15,000 ducats on Alvarado's gold alone, "seized as security for any fine in which he might be mulcted."

5 Bancroft (1883, 102) words things thus: "It was true that [Alvarado] was already betrothed to Cecilia Vázquez, a cousin of Cortés, but a mere vow could not be allowed to stand between him and high connection. Cortés had been a true friend; but Alvarado could now win stronger support than [even] the conqueror of Mexico could bestow on him, and what mattered friendship when help was no longer needed?"

6 Recinos (1952, 123). His precise words are: "La boda de Alvarado y doña Francisca debe haberse celebrado a fines de 1527 o enero de 1528, pues el 19 de dicho mes, en la ciudad de Burgos, donde a la sazón residía la Corte, el Adelantado [Alvarado] ortogó carta de dote a favor de su esposa. En dicha carta reconocía haber recibido siete mil pesos de oro." Recinos (1952, 123) also observes: "El gallardo capitán probablemente no consideraba estar casado en forma regular con la princesa de Tlaxcala, doña Luisa Xicoténcatl, y se sentía en libertad para contraer una nueva unión," meaning "the gallant captain probably did not consider himself married in any formal sense to the Tlaxcalan princess doña Luisa Xicoténcatl, and so felt at liberty to enter into a new union." Cabezas Carcache (2019, 5) notes that López de Gómara, a man of the cloth well versed in ecclesiastical law, considered Alvarado to have received dispensation to marry twice – "se casó por dispensación en dos ocasiones" – thereby avoiding prosecution (see Cook and Cook 1991) as a transatlantic bigamist.

7 Recinos (1952, 123). His precise words are: "[A]l unirse con doña Francisca de la Cueva, ganó en posición social y política y alcanzó el favor del Secretario del Consejo de Indias, Comendador Mayor de Castilla, Francisco de los Cobos, privado del Emperador y amigo, pariente y protector de la familia de la Cueva." According to García Añoveros (1987b, 86), Francisca was a "pariente lejana" (distant relative) of De los Cobos. Alvarado in due course struck a business deal with De los Cobos, in partnership with another eminent figure, Beltrán de la Cueva y Toledo. He states in a letter dated 15 December 1527 that he "would undertake to procure and place six hundred slaves in the mines of Guatemala, or whatever other parts," it being agreed by all three parties that "the gold extracted by the said slaves be shared equally between us." The letter – see Cabezas Carcache (2019, 27) for further details – was penned in Burgos three days before Alvarado was officially named governor and captain general of Guatemala. In the original, the wording runs: "[Y]o fuese obligado poner 600 esclavos

en las minas de esta provincia e mi gobernación o en otras cualesquier partes, para que el oro que se sacasen los dichos esclavos lo heredásamos por iguales partes." Cabezas Carcache believes that the slaves referred to would have been Black, but Wendy Kramer (personal communication, 21 January 2022, in the wake of research on the matter conducted by Esther González Pérez) concludes that the slaves were Indigenous, not African. Whether or not the contract between the three men came to fruition – see also García Añoveros (1987b, 86) – we don't know.

8 Chancing one day to see Alvarado strolling by in his royal gardens in Aranjuez, Emperor Charles V inquired as to who he was. Upon being told, and struck by Alvarado's demeanour, the king – see Bancroft (1883, 101) and García Añoveros (1987b, 85) – is reputed to have declared: "No tiene este hombre talle de haber hecho lo que de él me han dicho – this man does not have the look of someone who has done what they have told me." He then ordered all charges against Alvarado to be dropped.

9 Recinos (1952, 123–4). His precise words are: "[P]or Real Cédula firmada en Burgos el 18 de diciembre de 1527 fué nombrado Gobernador y Capitán General de la provincia de Guatemala y de las demás tierras a ella pertenecientes con el salario de costa de 562,500 maravedises en cada año que ejerciere dicho oficio … y a agregar a sus títulos el de Adelantado." See also García Añoveros (1987b, 85–6).

10 Remesal ([1619] 1964, vol. 1, 120), the chronicler asserting that Alvarado, "en llegando a su gobernación enviaría navíos a su costa por la mar del Sur a descubrir las islas de la Especiería, cosa que en Castilla se deseaba mucho." Kelly (1932, 186) states that the proposal "to discover and conquer the legendary Isles of Spice in the East Indies" was "made to [Alvarado] by the Emperor," not the other way around. Rahn Phillips (2019) dates a *capitulación* being drawn up between Alvarado and the Crown as early as 17 November 1526 in the city of Granada – which would pre-date Alvarado's actual arrival in Spain by several months. Her source is a *traslado* (copy) of the original, the duplicate in this instance housed in the AGI as Indiferente General 417 (Libro 1, folios 3 recto–14 recto). Ortuño Sánchez Pedreño (2005, 253), accessing a similar document (AGI, Indiferente General 415, Libro 1, folios 133–9 verso) that Vas Mingo (1986, 278–80) transcribed, dates the act as having been agreed to in Medina del Campo on 5 August 1532, the Crown represented by the Empress Juana. Citing Ortuño Sánchez Pedreño

(2005), Cabezas Carcache (2019, 38) dates the *capitulación* 5 January 1532. Covey (2020, 187) indicates only the year, 1532, citing yet another source in the Seville archive (AGI, Patronato 21 N.3 R.1).

CHAPTER FOUR

1 Remesal ([1619] 1964–66, vol. 1, 120) informs us that Zurrilla and Castellanos each received a salary of 100,000 *maravedís*, Ronquillo half that. Also promised, according to Recinos (1952, 127), "honores y ventajas materiales – honours and material benefits" were Luis de Vivar, Antonio de Salazar, and Pedro de Camino, the three chosen to serve as members of the city council of Santiago, the capital of Guatemala. All went aboard ship "a principios de julio de 1528," early in July, Recinos citing "el historiador Fr. Francisco Ximénez" as his source for that information. "Before he embraced God," Recinos observes, "Marroquín was married and fathered a son, one Alonso Marroquín, who remained a resident of Spain and himself had offspring." Alonso's residency in Spain appears not to have been life-long, the "hijo del licenciado Marroquín y de Francisca de Palacios" recorded as having come to the Indies, from Berlanga in Extremadura, in 1538 (Wendy Kramer, personal communication, 6 March 2022). In tribute assessments made by President Alonso López de Cerrato in 1549 (AGI, Guatemala 128, folios 64 verso and 122 verso), he is listed as the *encomendero* of Cacaotlán and Tecpán Guatemala. After his death (17 March 1567) the rights to both towns were pass to his son, Francisco, named after his grandfather.

2 In his biography of Alvarado, Recinos (1952, 127–8) states that "la muerte de su esposa doña Francisca" was "ocasionada por el tormentoso viaje de mar o por los efectos del clima tropical." However, among his papers for the published work, housed in the Archivo Histórico of the Centro de Investigaciones Regionales de Mesoamérica in Antigua Guatemala, are notes Recinos took after consulting the *Boletín de la Real Academia de la Historia*, volume 107 of which (1935, 133) records: "Doña Francisca fallecío joven y de parto en Veracruz, sin haber logrado sucesión," meaning that Alvarado's young wife died while giving birth, no child surviving her. The funeral service held for her there took place (Recinos 1952, 128) "con mucha pompa – with much pomp and ceremony." Barón Castro (1943, 130) registers a different cause of death, believing "she succumbed to fevers – acometida a fiebres." Díaz del Castillo ([1632] 1970, 534) simply states that she died "upon arrival in Veracruz."

3 Zúmarraga's pithy remark, "tanto aparato y cosas ricas," is invoked by Barón Castro (1943, 130).

4 Cabezas Carcache (2019, 29–30) furnishes a long list of charges, drawn from the *residencia*, or judicial inquiry, Alvarado was subjected to in 1529, admirably transcribed by Ramírez ([1847] 1930–33). Bancroft (1883, 103–4) distils matters as follows: "The celebrated trial … was protracted as long as party faction, envy, and personal enmity could make it last. The more important accusations were three – embezzlement of royal fifths and soldiers' booty, cruelty, and illegal warfare; but any act of Alvarado's previous life that could be used against him was pertinent. The total number of charges preferred was thirty-four, and there were ten witnesses for the prosecution. On the 6th of April, 1529, the examination commenced; on the 4th of June Alvarado presented his reply; and on the 10th began the examination of his witnesses, who numbered thirty-two … Eighty-four questions were submitted, and in addition to verbal evidence twelve documents were filed for the defence. On the 5th of July the defence was closed and the case submitted, but all efforts to obtain a speedy decision were unavailing."

5 García Añoveros (1986, 90). From the transcription of a letter penned by Bishop Zúmarraga on 27 August 1529, Cabezas Carcache (2019, 31–2) renders items that Alvarado paid as bribes to Núno de Guzmán, the governor of Mexico who presided over the tribunal. These were made, in the end successfully, so as to have all charges dropped and in effect have Alvarado buy his way out of prison. Zúmarraga estimated the value of the objects offered as bribes as at least 4,000 to 5,000 pesos.

6 Recinos (1952, 132), his precise words being "privado de sus bienes, pero llena la cabeza aventurera de proyectos para el cercano porvenir."

7 Remesal ([1619] 1964–66, vol. 1, 201). His precise words are: "Estando el Adelantado en Valladolid año de mil y quinientos y veinte y siete que fue para él tan próspero y dichoso, en agradecimiento de las grandes mercedes que del César había recebido, prometió de hacer una armada y enviarla o ir él con ella por el mar del Sur, a descubrir grandes tierras de que se esperaban muchas riquezas. Y para hallar paso para las islas de la Especiería, cosa muy deseada del Emperador y de todos los reinos de Castilla."

8 Recinos (1952, 133), Rubio Sánchez (1956, 24–5), and Gall (1978, vol. 2, 367).

9 Writing to the king on 1 September 1532, Alvarado states plainly that "mi

intención es sea en lo que es – servir a V[uestra] M[agestad] [y] no tener compañero," his intention being to serve His Majesty, not an associate. He goes so far as to describe the meddling of Cortés as an "importunación" – a "molestation" (*Libro viejo*, 283). Based on his reading of Herrera ([1615] 1728), Borah (1971) depicts the situation differently – that it was Cortés who had vehemently rejected ("el capitán general había rehusado terminantemente") Alvarado's attempts to strike a partnership. Recinos (1952, 135) is of the opposite opinion: his reading of the documents indicates that it was Alvarado who saw no part in the enterprise for Cortés. Ayón ([1882] 1977, 197), Kelly (1932, 186), Schottelius (1938–39, 38), and Cabezas Carcache (2019, 36) concur, as does Bancroft (1883, 102n5), who says of the accord between Alvarado and the Crown that "Cortés was much displeased with this agreement, as he considered the search for the Spice Islands and the navigation of the South Sea to be his exclusive right."

10 Gall (1978, vol. 2, 367–71). Kelsey (1986, 65–8) describes Iztapa as a "miserable town" but records Álvaro de Paz, a loyal supporter of Alvarado and a *mayordomo* (foreman) charged with overseeing ship construction, as considering its waterways "a larger and better locatíon for a shipyard than anywhere else in the Indies," somewhat of an exaggeration given Diego García de Palacio's negative assessment – see Rubio Sánchez (1956, 27) – of the port's potential when reporting to Philip II in 1574. "For any number of reasons," García de Palacio told the king, "Iztapa is unsuitable for trade with Peru," furnishing a list of disadvantages related to coastal geomorphology and sea conditions. The positive appraisal of Paz comes from a document consulted by Kelsey (1986, 65–8) at the AGI (Guatemala 41), notice of Paz's close ties to Alvarado – as an attorney he testified on the Adelantado's behalf in court proceedings – from Recinos (1952, 162). Alvarado favoured Iztapa on two occasions, the first for what became his ill-fated expedition to Peru in 1534–35, the second for an equally ill-fated expedition to the Spice Islands in 1540–41. After Alvarado's two ventures, Iztapa figures only minimally in Pacific navigation and commerce, the "gran dificultad – great difficulty" that ships had in clearing the sand bar at the mouth of its estuary mentioned in a report penned by Juan Bautista Antonelli and Diego López de Quintanilla on 7 October 1590 (AGI, Patronato 183–1–16).

11 Bancroft (1883, 127) and *Libro viejo*, 283. Kelly (1932, 186) also records the number of vessels built at Iztapa as three.

12 *Libro viejo*, 282–3, Alvarado's precise words being: "Procuraré que me tuxesen mucha copia de carpinteros, calafates i maestros. He hecho en pocos días estos navios: un galeón, San Cristóbal, de 300 toneles, la más hermosa pieza que se pudiera hacer en Vizcaya. Otra nao, Santa Clara, de 160 toneles, mui buena pieza. Otra, la Buena-Ventura, de 150 toneles. Otra … también de 150 toneles. Una carabela de 60 toneles y un patax de 50 e otras dos carabelas más medianas. Por todas ocho … Irán pez, hierro, jarcia, velas … de respeto para repararlas en caso de necesidad." A *galeón* was a large, multi-decked and multi-masted sailing ship deployed as an armed cargo carrier with a capacity for as many as five hundred aboard. Before the *galeón* was designed and built, the *nao* plied the seas, a three- or four-masted trading vessel of Portuguese renown with two storage holds and room for some ninety people. A *carabela* was a small, easily manoeuvred craft again pioneered by the Portuguese to explore the west coast of Africa and out into the Atlantic. It could carry as many as fifty crew and passengers. On ship construction and design, see Castro (2008) and Meide (2002). Instructions as to how to make the boats at Iztapa, and thereafter navigate them, would for the most part have been relayed by experienced word of mouth. Despite the antiquity of shipbuilding in the Old World, it was in the New World that one of the earliest works about it was published, the *Instrucción náutica* (1587) of Diego García de Palacio, which appeared as an imprint of Pedro Ocharte in Mexico City. See Laanella (2008) for an incisive critique of García de Palacio's treatise, in addition to insightful discussion of his spell as *fiscal* (royal attorney) for the Audiencia (High Court) of Guatemala between 1572 and 1580. In April 1579 he was charged to serve as *capitán general* (fleet commander) of an expedition to confront the marauding Francis Drake, which called for him to marshal Spanish forces at Iztapa and determine how best to combat the English pirate's incursions along the Pacific coast.

13 *Libro viejo*, 283, Alvarado's precise words being: "He gastado más de 50,000 castellanos en hacer la más hermosa armada que se podrá ver en estas partes, llegada la mejor gente que se pudiera buscar." According to the *Diccionario de Autoridades* (1726), a "castellano" was a valuable gold coin worth 480 or 485 *maravedí*.

14 Alonso de Maldonado, 11 December 1537, "sentencia dictada en la residencia secreta tomada al Adelantado Pedro de Alvarado," in Vallejo García-Hevia (2008, vol. 2, 910). The judge's precise words are: "[A] causa de la dicha

armada, el pueblo de Iztapa, donde la dicha armada se hacía, y otros pueblos de la costa Sur, quedaron muy fatigados y perdidos." Rubio Sánchez (1956, 25) also reckons armada construction the cause of "depopulation and demise – la despoblación y decadencia" – in Iztapa and environs. Running counter to these views is contemporary testimony that attributes ruination – see Vallejo García-Hevia (2008, vol. 1, 284) – to "outbreaks of great pestilence – las grandes pestilencias que por ellos vienen."

15 See Lovell and Lutz (2018) and Lovell, Lutz, and Kramer (2020, 34–6, 42–64, and 79–93) for details of an Indigenous-Spanish relationship, the dynamics of which are still not fully appreciated.

16 Las Casas, *Destrucción de la Indias* (1552), as cited in Recinos (1952, 137). The original runs: "Mató infinitas gentes con hacer navíos; llevaba de la mar del norte a la del sur, ciento y treinta leguas, los indios cargados con anclas de tres y cuatro quintales que se les metían las más dellas por las espaldas y lomos; y llevó de esta manera mucha artillería en los hombros de los tristes desnudos; y yo vi muchos cargados de artillería por los caminos angustiados." Recinos (1952, 136) imagines "thousands of Indians forced to toil under the blistering sun on the shipyard shores – en la empresa de la fábrica de la flota, millares de indios obligados a estos trabajos bajo el rigor del ardiente sol." He singles out two pieces of artillery in particular, weaponry given by Cortés to Diego de Mazariegos for the conquest of Chiapas, hauled to Iztapa from San Cristóbal de los Llanos, six hundred kilometres away – "Desde lugares tan lejos como San Cristóbal de los Llanos, hizo llevar Alvarado dos piezas de artillería que Cortés proporcionado a Diego de Mazariegos para la conquista de Chiapas." In Spanish units of measure, a *quintal* (or *centena*) is a weight of one hundred pounds, some forty-six kilograms.

17 Ximénez, *Historia de la provincia de San Vicente de Chiapa y Guatemala* (1715–20), as cited in Recinos (1952, 137). The original runs: "Empezó a descubrir astilleros, sacar maderas, fabricar jarcías, acarrear fierro, sacar brea, conducir piezas de artillería, todo a costa de los pobres indios, sacándoles de su patria y llevándolos a partes muy remotas. Mató muchos indios con hacer navíos." Culling from the contents of AGI, Justicia 295, Sherman (1979, 59) concurs: "In preparing his ambitious expedition to Peru," he writes, "Alvarado made liberal use of available Indians, both free and slave. Many of them were used to carry equipment down to León [in Nicaragua], and on their way back [to Guatemala] a number

were killed by warlike natives." Contemporary testimony – see Vallejo García-Hevia (2008, vol. 1, 284) – notes "nothing extraordinary" about such deployment, considering it "customary – nada extraordinario, sino algo muy acostumbrado."

CHAPTER FIVE

1 The *capitulación* drafted in Medina del Campo on 5 August 1532 – see chapter 3, note 10, for archival provenance and textual authenticity – has been transcribed and may be perused in several sources, including the *Libro viejo*, 284–5, and Ortuño Sánchez Pedreño (2005, 253–5).

2 *Libro viejo*, 284–5, and Ortuño Sánchez Pedreño (2005, 253–4). As transcribed by the latter, in its entirety the preamble to the *capitulación* in the original runs: "Por quanto vos, don Pedro de Alvarado, Adelantado y Gobernador de la provincia de Guatemala, nos hezistes relación que por los buenos y leales servicios que nos heçistes en la conquista de la ysla de Cuva y Nueva España y dessa provincia, la qual diz que abeis poblado de cristianos y fecho hazer iglesias, y descubierto minas, e hase paçificado toda la tierra de que los yndios están en paz, y de su voluntad bienen a servir a los cristianos, e que agora con deseo de Nos servir y del bien y acrecentamiento de nuestra Corona Real, como siempre lo abeis fecho, abeis començado a hazer una armada en el puerto questá çerca de la çiudad de Santiago, desa dicha provincia, para descubrir los secretos del mar del Sur porque teneis notiçia de muy rricas yslas e de otras tierras en la costa de aquella mar, de que entre ellas se nos seguirá mucho serviçio y provecho, y porque para una cosa tan principal teniades neçesidad de llevar suficiente armada y bien proveída de todo lo neçesario, os ofreçeis de hazer hasta cumplimiento de doze navíos con los que agora teneis, y que metereis en ellos quatroçientos hombres cristianos, de pie y cavallo. Y porque la costa dello según paresçia por espiriençia de lo que teniades hecho os llegaría a más de cuarenta mil castellanos, y para lo cumplir y acavar os aviades de poner en neçesidad, me suplicastes y pediste por merced vos mandase dar liçencia para hazer la conquista de las dichas tierras y vos conçediese y otorgase las mercedes y con las condiciones que de yuso serán contenidas, sobre lo qual yo mandé tomar con vos el asiento y capitulación siguiente."

3 *Libro viejo*, 285, and Ortuño Sánchez Pedreño (2005, 253–4). As transcribed by the latter, the wording of the *capitulación* in the original runs:

"Primeramente, vos damos liçencia, poder y facultad para que por Nos e en nuestro nombre, y de la Corona Real de Castilla, podais descubrir, poblar y conquistar cualesquier yslas que ay en la mar del Sur de la Nueva España, questá en su paraje, y todas las demás que hallardes hazia el poniente della no siendo en el paraje de las tierras en que oy ay proveídos gobernadores. Y ansímismo vos damos la liçencia y facultad para que podais descubrir cualquier parte de tierra firme que hallardes por la dicha costa del Sur hazia el poniente que no se aya hasta agora descubierto ni entre en los límites y paraje norte-sur de la tierra questá dada en gobernación a otras personas."

4 See chapter 2, note 21.

5 Francisco Marroquín to the Crown, 17 August 1545, in Marroquín ([1545] 1949, 344), noted also by Recinos (1952, 141) and Sáenz de Santa María (1964, 207). The bishop's precise words are: "[F]ue en tiempo que sonó el Pirú y, como fue tan grande el sonido, capitán y soldados toda la desampararon; y después acá como el adelantado … tenía puesto los pensamientos en cosa mayor, olvidóse este rincón."

6 The Audiencia's strictures and contrary position, noted by Francisco del Paso y Troncoso in his *Epistolario de la Nueva España* (1939–40), are incorporated by Recinos (1952, 135–6) in his depiction of affairs. Wording in the original runs: "[Q]ue entendiese en su gobernación y no en hacer armada ni descubrimiento sin tener licencia para ello."

7 AGI, Guatemala 45. See also chapter 4, note 1. Ayón ([1882] 1977, 197) describes the opposition of Zurrilla, Castellanos, and Ronquillo as "pertinaz – pertinacious."

8 Unless stated otherwise, the information that follows is drawn from AGI, Guatemala 45 (Zurrilla, Castellanos, and Ronquillo to the Crown, 28 September 1531), translated into English by the author.

9 AGI, Guatemala 45 (Zurrilla, Castellanos, and Ronquillo to the Crown, 28 September 1531).

10 The *ducado* was a gold coin, which replaced the *dobla* as a unit of currency in June 1497, worth 375 *maravedís*.

11 Regarding native demise, writing to the king on 1 September 1532, Alvarado himself acknowledges (*Libro viejo*, 284) an outbreak of "sarampión" (measles) among the Indigenous population, "the pestilence having arrived in this province three months ago from Mexico." He claims, however, that "not many died" on account of his preventative actions,

which included his ordering that "all Indian slaves be relieved from working in the mines" so as to be "cured" as best one can from such a dreadful scourge. The Adelantado's sanguine reckoning notwithstanding, measles was but one of several contagions of Old World origin – see Cook and Lovell ([1992] 2001) – to have had a devastating impact on Native American populations in the early sixteenth century. Of this particular outbreak of disease, Alvarado's precise words are: "En toda la Nueva España vino una pestilencia por los naturales que dicen sarampión, y llegó a esta provincia hará tres meses, y por mucha diligencia que puse en curallos no ha podido lograse que no muriesen muchos."

12 Zurrilla, Castellanos, and Ronquillo to the Crown, 28 September 1531 (AGI, Guatemala 45).

13 Though this was alleged to be the case – see Vallejo-García Hevia (2008, vol. 1, 284, and vol. 2, 783) – it was adamantly denied by one of Alvarado's staunchest supporters, attorney Álvaro de Paz, at least in relation to San Miguel in El Salvador. "The Adelantado has no need to entice the residents of San Miguel to be on the armada," he declared. "He already has more than enough people." Paz went on to note that, come embarkation time, "many were left behind on the seashore, on account of too few ships to carry them." His words in the oringinal run: "[E]l dicho Adelantado tenía poca necesidad de llevar en su armada vecinos de la dicha villa de San Miguel, por tener, como tenía consigo, gente demasiada, y aún, al tiempo que se fue a embarcar, dejó mucha gente por la plaza de la mar, por no tener navíos en que la llevar."

14 Zurrilla, Castellanos, and Ronquillo to the Crown, 28 September 1531 (AGI, Guatemala 45). The precise words calling for copies of the document to be made and dispatched are: "Que se duplique la provisión que en esto hay y se envie a Guatemala y otra a Pizarro."

CHAPTER SIX

1 For a detailed history of Realejo, see Rubio Sánchez (1977). His 843-page monograph is replete with lengthy transcriptions of documents housed in the AGI in Seville, culled for inclusion in the massive, seventeen-volume *Colección Somoza: Documentos para la historia de Nicaragua* (1954–57) compiled by Andrés Vega Bolaños. The indefatigable Patrick S. Werner, with whom I travelled to Realejo in December 2018, my late friend and erudite colleague pointing out the slips where ships were built as we

coasted its waters, himself compiled a guide to the archival foraging of Vega Bolaños (Werner 2004) that makes working with the *Colección Somoza* less intractable. An incisive distillation of Realejo's storied past is the collaborative effort of Radell and Parsons (1971). See also León Sáenz (2009, 54–5 and 72–5), who notes that Realejo (as its name intimates) enjoyed royal patronage, one of the two most important shipyards (the other was Guayaquil) of the twenty-three recorded as operative during colonial times along the Pacific littoral.

2 Of Realejo, Squier (1852, vol. 1, 366) writes: "It is a small town, situated upon a tide-water stream, full five miles from the harbor proper. It is said that the town was originally built nearer the harbor, and that the present site was afterwards adopted in consequence of the frequent attacks of pirates, who infested this coast." He quotes Dunlap (*sic* Dunlop, 1847, 26) as declaring: "I may confidently say that Realejo is as good a port as any in the world. It is a salt-water creek, into which several small streams of water enter themselves. The entrance is protected by an island about two miles long, which leaves at each end a channel where ships can enter the harbor, forming the port in such a manner as to protect it entirely from any wind that can possibly blow, and also entirely breaking the swell which enters the outer bay." Radell and Parsons (1971, 301–2) observe that Realejo's hinterland "provided abundant raw materials suited to ship construction. Indeed, it was claimed that few places in the New World were so well endowed with the resources required for the development of a shipbuilding industry. From the upland pine forests of the Central Highlands of Nicaragua" – see Denevan (1961) for elaboration – "lumber, pitch, and resins were carried to … Realejo by Indian porters. The amount of pine lumber transported overland for shipbuilding was so great that Las Casas ranked the rigors of hauling timbers as one of the chief causes of death and misery among the Indians of Nicaragua." Tall stands of pine were coveted for the masts of ships. Other sources of local wood available for maritime use were "*cedro* (Cedrela), *caoba* (Swietenia), *guacimo* (Guazumo), *madero negro* (Gliricidia sepium), which was a durable 'underwater' timber, *palo cuadrado* (Macrocnemum glabresceus), a very hard wood for levers and rudders, and *sapodilla* (Achras sapota)." The last wood listed by Radell and Parsons (1971, 298) was famed for its resistance to the invasive *teredo*, "the shipworm which feasted on wooden sailing ships and which often caused their hulls to be riddled with holes."

3 Bancroft (1883, 126), Altoaguirre y Duvale (1927, 184), and Recinos (1952, 139–40). Antonelli and Quintanilla (AGI, Patronato 183-1-16) reckon the sailing time from Iztapa to the Gulf of Fonseca, the latter also indicated on maps as the Golfo de Amapal, as being "navegación de cuatro días – four days' navigation." Two letters that Alvarado penned in Puerto Fonseca – see Schottelius (1938–39, 26) – are dated 23 March and 25 April 1533. A transcription of the latter, the original of which is in AGI, Patronato 192-1-1, forms part of the Obadiah Rich Collection (roll 82), housed at the New York Public Library. That letter is also transcribed in Medina (1889, 172–4), and the version there is the one consulted for this study. In it, Alvarado complains about naysayers bad-mouthing him ("cosas contrarias á la verdad") and asserts that in His Majesty's service he will achieve great things ("acometer gran cosa") first by reaching the Strait of Magellan and from there navigating across the Pacific to China ("el Estrecho de Magallanes hasta la [*sic*] clima [China]"). Writing to the governor of Panama, Francisco de Barrionuevo, on 10 March 1534, Alvarado (*Libro viejo*, 291) alludes to "the calm waters of Realejo and the danger of those of Puerto Fonseca – la bonanza de aquel puerto, y peligro del de Fonseca." Today, El Salvador lies on the western shores of the Gulf of Fonseca, Honduras on its north, and Nicaragua on its east. It remains an enticing but little-frequented body of water.

4 Ayón ([1882] 1977, 245) attributes Realejo being named as such by Alvarado himself, its "royal" connotation also indicating a military encampment. An acclaimed scholar and diplomat, considered Nicaragua's first official historian, Ayón (1820–87) believed that "beautiful natural conditions made Realejo one of the best ports on the Pacific coast – considerada por sus bellisimas condiciones naturales como uno de los mejores puertos que hay en la costa del Pacífico."

5 Alvarado to the Crown, 1 September 1532, in *Libro viejo* (1934, 282). The Adelantado's precise words are: "Viendo la poca posibilidad que el Gobernador Pizarro para lo conquistar … tiene, pense con mi armada poder proveer en darle a él socorro y conquistar todo lo demás que por aquella parte huviese. Y en este tiempo se me ofreció que vinieron dos portugueses a esta provincia para pilotos, hombres de mucha experiencia i habilidad en la navegacion, los cuales a fama del armada fue su venida, de los quales informándome muchas i diversas veces de la especería i de toda la tierra e islas, della han dado mui gran relación, por saber la tierra a cabsa que ha mas de treinta años que han navegado por ella i saben la

lengua de algunas gentes que en ella hai … Por hacer este servicio mudé la voluntad de ir al Perú, y pues el pensamiento creció en mayores cosas … de nuevo comencé a hacer naos gruesas con muchas espensas." Bancroft (1883, 125) summarizes thus: "Alvarado addressed a letter to Charles, asking permission to go to the assistance of Pizarro, assuring him that, from what he had learned of the difficulties encountered by that conqueror, he was convinced of his inability to complete unaided the conquest of Peru. In a previous despatch, wherein he had asked for his final instructions, he prayed that they be granted as speedily as possible. 'For,' he says, 'after exhausting my private means, I have contracted heavy debts in order to save Your Majesty all expense.' The fleet, he informs him, is well provided with stores and provisions, the force of men almost complete, and, the better to insure the success of the expedition, he declares that he will take command of it in person, leaving a sufficient number of Spaniards in the province to guard against any possible uprising of the natives." See also Kelly (1932, 188) and Recinos (1943, 62, and 1952, 138). Indication of Alvarado biding his time in León as well as Realejo comes from Vallejo García-Hevia (2008, vol. 1, 284), who notes the Adelantado "residing there while he attended to preparations underway in the Puerto de la Posesión concerning the expedition – donde residía mientras entendía en los preparativos de la expedición en el puerto de la Posesión."

6 Alvarado to the Crown, 18 January 1534, in *Libro viejo* (1934, 286). The Adelantado's precise words are: "Que teniendo concluida el armada e para me poder partir muchos dias antes, no saber la orden que Vuestra Magestad, hera servido tobiese en este descobrimiento y derrota, para mejor satisfacer Vuestro Real Deseo y mi voluntad, porque mis trabaxos se conformasen con ella para recebir el premio e merced que merece. Y como tanto tiempo se dilatase el mandato de Vuestra Magestad, fueme forzado para sostener la gente y naos, otro tanto gasto como lo prencipal de la flota. Y por esta razon, si en los primeros gasté, me convino adebdar para esto, en quarenta mil pesos de oro; porque pasan de cxxx los que hasta hoy he gastado, lo qual constará por las ynformaciones que con esta ymbío e téngolo por bien gastado, considerada la cantidad del hecho y la esperanza del fruto." The letter is introduced as having been written on 8 January 1534, even though the transcription of it (*Libro viejo*, 288) indicates 7 January – as noted by Recinos (1952, 141). Kelly (1932, 253) dates the letter 18 January 1534, as does a transcription of it copied for J.E. [Ephraim George] Squier and published in the *Revista Peruana* (1880, vol.

4, 191–4). Saville (1917, 3) makes note of this in his transcription of another letter of Alvarado's written two days later, a facsimile of which clearly indicates 20 January 1534 as its date of composition. I have consulted an English translation made by Kelly (1932, 249–53) of the 18 January letter but choose to render the original in many instances differently. Kelly's translation comes either from the handwritten transcription copied for Squier or the version of it published in the *Revista Peruana*.

7 Alvarado to the Crown, 18 January 1534, in *Libro viejo* (286–7). The Adelantado's precise words are: "Vista la Provision e Capitulacion, hallé que Vuestra Magestad me obligaba, a que en el descobrimiento y conquista presente, sacara partido; y puesto que como cosa imposible se pudiera encarecer que el dicho capitulo se compliese por estar en tierra, nuevamente, y tan aptado, do podiere proveerse, tóbelo por favor alzado, pues en mi se experimentó lo que nadie podiera en estas partes. Y como mi deseo es qual debe complir con lo que Vuestra Magestad manda en los dichos capítulos, antes creciendo en la conclusión que falleciendo en lo preferido, porque su magestad, yo me parto, mediante Dios, el dia desta fecha con doze velas de ccc toneladas hasta xl, en que las ocho dellas no vaxan de ciento, proveidas en municiones y bastimentos, no menos cumplidamente que en Sevilla, otros quatrocientos y cincuenta españoles, los doscientos y sesenta de cavallo y los ciento ballesteros y escopeteros, y el resto de espada y rrodella [sin ciento y cuarenta] que llevo de la Mar con que van amarinadas las naos, y otros cc negros esclavos de los españoles. Tenga Vuestra Magestad por cierto, que nunca hasta oy se ha visto en estas partes, ansi gente qual la demanda requería, porque van muchos hidalgos gente noble; usados a la tierra, y trabaxos de la guerra, lo qual en estas partes se estima mucho, por la esperiencia que hay del menoscabo que se hace. De la gente venida nuevamente a España, lleve ansi mesmo muy buenos pilotos, expertos en la navegacion, sabios en su arte, a quien dan salarios muy crecidos." See also Alvarado to the Crown, 18 January 1534, in *Revista Peruana* (1880, vol. 4, 191–2).

8 Zurrilla, Castellanos, and Ronquillo to the Crown, 28 September 1531 (AGI, Guatemala 45). See chapter 5, note 8, for elaboration and Sherman (1979, 384n73) for Indigenous origins.

9 Numbers for native fatalities are those given, respectively, by Herrera ([1615] 1728, 140) and Cieza de León ([1553] 1998, 336). Sherman (1979, 56 and 382n54) alludes to Francisco de Barrionuevo, governor of Panama, stating that Alvarado "took four thousand Indians, leaving both Guatemala

and Nicaragua very depopulated." The statement, made on 19 January 1534, Sherman qualifies by adding: "However, this estimate is probably exaggerated; other accounts say the Adelantado took about one thousand Indians." His sources for these figures include Alvarado's *residencia* (AGI, Justicia 295 and 296) and the *Cartas del Perú* (1524–34), edited by Porras Barrenechea (1959, 96).

10 Alvarado to the Crown, 18 January 1534, in *Revista Peruana* (1880, vol. 4, 193), his precise words being: "Mi derrota será conforme á la merced de Vuestra Majestad, y desde los trece hasta los viente grados de la otra parte de la linea descubriré todos los secretos de esta mar y las Islas, y tierra firme, y donde mas convenga conquistaré y poblaré." Bancroft observes pertinently (1883, 129n14) that "Cuzco lies slightly to the south of the thirteenth parallel, and was therefore in the territory assigned to [Alvarado]; but it is not probable that he was aware of this fact."

11 Alvarado to the Crown, 18 January 1534, in *Revista Peruana* (1880, vol. 4, 193), his precise words being: "Que en los bienaventurados días de Vuestra Magestad seré tan venturoso, que haga á vuestra corona Real los mas señalados servicios que en estas tierras se le han hecho, porque además de lo preferido enviaré dos naos para este efecto hechas á navegar, y calar el estrecho, para que por esta derrota provea las cosas destas partes, y de acá tenga ordinarias relaciones, que es la cosa mas importante á estos Reinos."

12 Belalcázar's role in the conquest of Peru is detailed by Lockhart (1972, 122–9), who describes him as "plebian to the core" yet "a senior and formidable figure," albeit one considered "a bit disreputable." He is the subject of an extended study by Jijón y Caamaño (1936) and the centrepiece of a collection of documents compiled by Garcés (1936). According to Jijón y Caamaño (1936, 8–10), who attributes the designation to the "Inca Cronista" Garcilaso de la Vega, Belalcázar's family surname was Moyano. The conquistador assumed that of his homeland "por ser más famoso – in order to be more famous" – upon embarking for the Indies in 1507, when he was "still a young lad – era muy mozo." Following the Spanish poet Juan de Castellanos (1522-1606), whose epic *Elegías de varones ilustres de Indias* (1588) has some memorable stanzas about him, Jijón y Caamaño and Garcés both opt for Benalcázar as the conquistador's surname, not Belalcázar, as I have. His involvement in the conquest of Ecuador is scrutinized by Loor (1956, 215–44). According to Lockhart (1972, 359), the pilot Fernández – a shipmaster and sea captain too – eventually became "a great encomendero of Lima."

13 Sherman (1979, 56). Fernández was "condemned to death" by the governor of Nicaragua, Francisco de Castañeda, for flouting the law that prohibited such trafficking but pardoned "allegedly because Diego de Almagro sent from Peru a gold Crown worth one thousand to two thousand pesos to Castañeda in exchange for the life of the captain." Three chapters of Sherman's magnum opus deal with the slave trade in comprehensive detail, the subject also addressed by Radell ([1976] 1992) and Newson (1987, 101–6).

14 Loor (1956, 199). "Not even the treasures of Montezuma had yielded such a harvest," Bancroft (1883, 126) comments, how it was collected and divvied up vividly described by Cieza de León ([1553] 1998, 238–51). Hemming ([1970] 1972, 74, 85, and 556n74) draws on Loredo (1958, 72–4) to place a value on the treasures Pizarro exacted at 1,326,539 gold pesos and 51,610 marks of silver. "The total gold and silver, spoils and ransom together," Lockhart (1972, 13) states, "turned out to be worth over 1.5 million pesos, beyond anything seen or dreamed of in the Indies to that date. All but the King's fifth went to the more than 160 men of Cajamarca. Even lowly footmen now had fortunes exceeding what captains had been able to get in Mexico, Guatemala, or Nicaragua." Following his capture on 16 November 1532, Atahualpa had negotiated his liberty, he hoped within two months, by offering to fill with golden objects – see Hemming ([1970] 1972, 48) – a room measuring "22 feet long by 17 feet wide … to a white line half way up its height, over eight feet high." Atahualpa kept his side of the ransom deal only to be accused by Pizarro of plotting to be rescued by force after what he amassed had been melted down and dispersed among his captors. The Inca was executed in a public garrotting on 26 July 1533, his death considered by Cieza de León ([1553] 1998, 252) "the most ignoble act the Spaniards have ever done in all this empire of the Indies."

15 Bancroft (1883, 126).

16 Bancroft (1883, 125–6). See also Cieza de León ([1553] 1998, 293).

CHAPTER SEVEN

1 Alvarado to the Cabildo de Guatemala, 20 January 1534, as transcribed by Saville (1917, 5–6), the Adelantado's precise words being: "Yo me hago la vela mañana, placiendo á Nuestro Señor … de este puerto de la Possession – God willing, I set sail from Realejo tomorrow."

2 Zurrilla, Castellanos, and Ronquillo to the Crown, 28 September 1531 (AGI, Guatemala 45).

3 Alvarado to the Cabildo de Guatemala, 20 January 1534, as transcribed by Saville (1917, 5), the Adelantado's precise words being: "Os suplico que en esa provincia haya toda concordia y amor y buen zelo al servicio de Su Magestad … y que á Jorge de Alvarado mi hermano y lugarteniente se le tenga el respeto y voluntad que es razon y se conformen con él, por manera que la tierra se conserve."

4 Alvarado to the Cabildo de Guatemala, 20 January 1534, as transcribed by Saville (1917, 5–6), the Adelantado's precise words being: "Muy grande Merced me harian las vuestras Señores se lo supliqueis por vuestra parte que mi buen suceso será para vuestro servicio. De la tierra [donde] Dios me encamináre [*sic*] escribiré a Vuestras Mercedes larga relación … y que siempre os halláredes y de salud de vuestras muy nobles personas."

5 Stoddard's poem, "Pedro de Alvarado," was read on 27 April 1881 at the Grand Annual of the Philhistorian Society, Santa Clara College, California. A first edition of it may be perused in the Bancroft Library on the campus of the University of California at Berkeley. After the three lines quoted comes pertinently the following: "And to conquer and blazon his name above Cortez!" Stoddard also notes, of Alvarado's desire to avail himself of the treasures of Inca Atahualpa, that "ambition lured him on / Perchance to drag from out his golden house / Another Montezuma." In a letter to the governor of Panama, Francisco de Barrionuevo, dated 10 March 1534, from Puerto Viejo in Ecuador, Alvarado records his departure from Realejo as 23 January (*Libro viejo*, 291). While confirming that date, Vallejo García-Hevia (2008, vol. 1, 155) mistakenly registers the Adelantado's port of departure as "Iztapa (hoy, puerto de Corinto)" when he meant to indicate that it was Realejo – "El Realejo," as he correctly identifies the Nicaraguan port to be elsewhere in the transcription made of Alvarado's *residencia*.

6 Recinos (1952, 142), with reference to Bishop Francisco Marroquín having been instructed on 30 June 1542 to draw up what would be Alvarado's last will and testament. Remesal ([1619] 1932, vol. 1, 261 et seq.) renders extracts from the will in detail, which Wagner (1946, 309) combed through for his distillation, translating one provision thus: "Inasmuch as the said adelantado took for his fleet from Juan Rodriguéz [Cabrillo], a citizen of this city [Santiago de Guatemala], a ship which he had on the South Sea and did not pay for it, I [Marroquín] order that there shall be paid to the said Juan Rodríguez from the effects of the adelantado the value of the ship when the adelantado took it, to be ascertained from persons who saw it and who shall assess the

value of it. Besides, he shall be paid for his personal services according to proofs which he may present." Wagner implies that the unnamed ship was part of a second fleet of Alvarado's that set sail for Mexico, destination the Spice Islands, in 1540, but Recinos links its seizure to the first armada – erroneously so, according to Wendy Kramer (personal communication, 8 March 2022). Of a ship of Rodríguez's called the *Santiago*, constructed in Acajutla at a cost of 3,000 *castellanos de oro*, Kelsey (1958, 60) suggests that "perhaps for a trial run [in March 1533] Rodríguez sailed down to the Gulf of Fonseca, taking important messages to the Adelantado" before Alvarado left for Peru, which Kramer (personal communication, 8 March 2022) also believes to be erroneous. It was on his return from Peru in 1535, she elucidates, that Alvarado appropriated the *Santiago*, after it caught his eye docked in Acajutla. The vessel, Kramer (2019, 55) states, subsequently was given back to Rodríguez "in a deplorable state." Alvarado eventually agreed to buy the *Santiago* "for very little," refitting and upgrading it for his second expedition.

7 Leaning on Remesal ([1619] 1932, vol. 1, 270), Wagner (1946, 309–10) words the eventual reparation thus: "I [Marroquín] also say that inasmuch as at the time that the adelantado formed a fleet for the discoveries in the South Sea, Antonio Diosdado, a citizen of this city [Santiago de Guatemala] now deceased, gave to the adelantado a galleon of his for which he did not pay, I order that two people who saw the said galleon at the time the adelantado took it shall be called and what they swear it was worth at the time shall be paid from the effects of the adelantado."

8 Again leaning on Remesal ([1619] 1932, vol. 1, 270), Wagner (1946, 309–10) words this instance as follows: "I [Marroquín] also say that at that time Santos de Figueroa gave to the adelantado the part which he had in a ship in company with Cisneros and Álvaro de Paz, and he paid no part of it." Remesal has the bishop making amends thus: "Mando que se pongan dos personas que vieron el dicho navío y lo que juraren que valía la parte que en el tenía el dicho Santos de Figueroa al tiempo que se dio al dicho Adelantado, aquello se lo pague al dicho Figueroa de los bienes del dicho Adelantado – I order that two people be called who saw the said ship, that they swear as to how much it was worth at the time Figueroa handed it over, and that such a sum be paid him from the effects of the Adelantado." No mention is made of a settlement in favour of Paz and Cisneros.

9 Alvarado asserts that he purchased the ships in his letter to the governor of Panama – see note 5 above – the original of which is housed in AGI,

Guatemala 39. The letter arrived in Seville from the Archivo General de Simancas in 1785, among the contents of *legajo* 11 of the "Relaciones y descripciones" in the holdings designated *Consejo de Indias*, the papers of the Council of the Indies that are the foundation of the Archivo General de Indias. Transcriptions of it appear in *Revista Peruana* (1880, vol. 4, 194–6); *Libro viejo*, 290–2; and the *Colección Somoza*, vol. 3, 308–11 (Vega Bolaños 1954). Alvarado's words in the original are: "Y estando por mías, queriendo entregarme en ellas, las tomaron por el tanto el licenciado Castañeda y otros amigos suyos, y como me faltaron fuéme forzado comprar y fletar dos Naos que en el puerto de la Posesion estaban, una de Hernán Ponce, y el otro del bachiller Pedro Bravo y Cristóbal de Burgos: y hecho ya contrato con las partes." He declares that he sent proof of purchase to the Crown via the services of Domingo de Solaluz. His claim of purchase is also asserted in statements made on 13 May 1535, the original depositions part of AGI, Guatemala 965, transcribed and published in the *Colección Somoza*, vol. 3 (Vega Bolaños 1954, 351–8). Quality gold worth 2,500 pesos – "dos mill e quinientos pesos de buen oro" – is said to have changed hands for one of the ships, the *Victoria*. The two vessels alleged to have been taken from Alvarado by "Castañeda and friends of his" formerly belonged to Pedrarias Dávila (1440–1531). They were auctioned in Nicaragua after Dávila died there, which Alvarado learned of from Luis Farfan, whom he insinuates knew full well that "I would purchase them for my armada at the high price being asked, no one else being the least bit interested – sabiendo que yo los compraría para mi armada á subidos precios, porque ya en Nicaragua anduvieron en almoneda, y no se halló quien los comprase." Bancroft (1883, 127) reckons that more than two ships – "several," he says – were purchased by Alvarado "from the estate of Pedrarias Dávila," the amount of the "high price" he paid for them not divulged.

10 "Alvarado is charged with the seizure of two vessels in Nicaragua," Bancroft (1883, 128n10) writes, but he considers the Adelantado's actions "most likely in the form of an appropriation with the consent of the owners." Denying the charge, Alvarado "forwards vouchers to prove, as he says, that they were bought at the request of the owners and paid for to their entire satisfaction," adding that "even had they been seized, such an act was justified by the importance of the undertaking." Jijón y Camaaño (1936, vol.1, 49) concurs with Bancroft. "Taking possession of

the ships was not an act of piracy," he states, "but a deal in which whoever was richest emerged victorious – La toma de los navíos no es un acto de piratería, sino, un negocio en que el más rico triunfa." The contents of the *Colección Somoza*, vol. 3 (Vega Bolaños 1954, 283–304) suggest otherwise – appropriation *without* consent of the owners (see note 11 below). Jijón y Camaaño makes it clear, however, that Alvarado "was not in Nicaragua, by surprise, merely overnight." On the contrary, "he spent a long time in Realejo with the full knowledge of the authorities – no estuvo en Nicaragua sorpresivamente una noche, sino que pasó largos días en el Puerto de la Posesión, con pleno conocimiento de las autoridades."

11 The documentation in question is suffused with intrigue and innuendo, making it difficult if not impossible to verify what actually took place. Study of records yet to materialize from archival vaults, and further perusal of those at hand, may shed more light on the matter. What follows is culled for the most part from AGI, Justicia 1051, as transcribed in the *Colección Somoza*, vol. 3 (Vega Bolaños 1954, 283–304). The Soto alluded to as co-owner of the *Concepción* was almost certainly Hernando de Soto, a leading figure in the conquest of Peru and a business partner of Ponce de León. Their association is noted by Lockhart (1972, 73 and 190–201), who considers arrangements made between them "remarkably similar to that between Pizarro and Almagro," though always perceived of mutual benefit, not in the end cause for intrigue, suspicion, and murder. The *compania* they struck "was a long-standing universal partnership in which Soto was the more active captain and Ponce the business manager; Soto came to Peru while Ponce stayed in Nicaragua to see to their affairs, then followed much later."

12 Sebastián de Saavedra, 23 October 1533 (AGI, Justicia 1051), in *Colección Somoza*, vol. 3 (Vega Bolaños 1954, 284). The notary's precise words are: "Entro en esta dicha çibdad el capitan Gabriel de Rojas con diez compañeros el qual dixo que venia de la governacion e probinçias de Nicaragua por mandado del gobernador Francisco de Castañeda a ynformar al señor gobernador don Francisco Piçarro de algunas cosas que an pasado en la governaçion de Nicaragua, las quales an ido cabsa que no aya venido a estas partes la gente e socorro que de aquella governaçion se esperaba." Saavedra records Sebastián de Belalcázar as having been present in San Miguel when Rojas and his companions bore witness. Belalcázar wrote directly about the matter to His Majesty on 11 November 1533 – see AGI, Patronato 27–11,

in *Colección Somoza,* vol. 3 (Vega Bolaños 1954, 306–7) – echoing what Saavedra duly recorded.

13 Saavedra to the Crown, 23 October 1533 (AGI, Justicia 1051), in *Colección Somoza,* vol. 3 (Vega Bolaños 1954, 290–303).

14 Testimony of Gabriel de Rojas, 23 October 1533 (AGI, Justicia 1051), in *Colección Somoza,* vol. 3 (Vega Bolaños 1954, 286–7). The pilot's precise words, invoking those of Castañeda and as recorded by Saavedra, are: "[L]a venida de Moscoso a sido a negoçiar conmigo que no salga desta naçion ningun navio ni gente para Francisco Piçarro governador del Perú hasta quel adelantado se despache y sea partido a aquellas partes ... Se supo como un galeon quel adelantado tiene, que dize ques de porte de tresyentos toneles, le avia echado al agua seys dias avia que le tenia artillado y se le tenia por çierto e se desya publicamente que ... avia de poner el galeon a la boca del puerto para no pudiese salir ningun navio de Nicaragua para ninguna parte."

15 Testimony of Juan Rodrigues, 23 October 1533 (AGI, Justicia 1051), in *Colección Somoza,* vol. 3 (Vega Bolaños 1954, 291). The words of the *marino* (marine) are recorded by Saavedra thus: "Luys de Moscoso avia venido a comprar çiertos caballos e negros quel dicho governador Castañeda alli tenia, y le dava cuatro mill pesos por ello con tan condiçion que no saliese navio ninguno del dicho puerto." Some witnesses put the offer of payment that Moscoso made Castãneda at three thousand pesos.

16 Testimony of Gabriel de Rojas, 23 October 1533 (AGI, Justicia 1051), in *Colección Somoza,* vol. 3 (Vega Bolaños 1954, 289). His precise words, as recorded by Saavedra, run: "[S]ecretamente ... el dicho vergantin [*San Pedro*] ... abaxo por estero abaxo y con el baxaron dos barcos de los otros navios con gente armada ... a faboresçer el dicho vergantin hasta que saliese del puerto [Realejo] porque se tenia sospecha que avia de aver navio en la boca questorbase la salida del vergantin ... y que a tardado que llegar hasta el puerto desta dicha çibdad [San Miguel] treynta e çinco o treinta e seis dias y questa a sydo la cabsa de su venida, y dixo que en la governaçion de Nicaragua hay algunas personas questan para yr con el dicho adelantado [Alvarado] a su harmada ... que tiene honze o doce navios ... [Y] la gente que con el estavan platicaban [dicen] quel dicho gobernador Francisco Piçarro andava fuera de los limites de su governaçion y en los limites de su governaçion que Su Magestad avia dado al dicho adelantado

en estas partes, e que a ynformar de todo esto es su venida para quel dicho governador Francico Piçarro lo sepa."

17 Testimony of Cristóbal Rodrigues, 23 October 1533 (AGI, Justicia 1051), in *Colección Somoza,* vol. 3 (Vega Bolaños 1954, 301–3). His precise words, as recorded by Saavedra, are: "[Q]ue a dicho el dicho adelantado [Alvarado] quel dicho governador don Francisco Piçarro no esta en su governaçion quel emperador le dio e questa dosyentos leguas adelante en su governaçion y que sy viene a estas partes que a de tomar el oro al dicho governador … e que si se tardara en venir que llevaran al dicho *Santiago* e los otros navios que alli estavan [como] avia llevado dos navios de çinco que alli avia, que heran los mayores, e los tres dexo porque no los pudo sacar pero que les llevo la velas, anclas e cables e los bateles. "

18 Declaration of Francisco de Castañeda, 30 September 1533 (AGI, Justicia 293), in *Colección Somoza,* vol. 4 (Vega Bolaños 1955, 493). The precise words of Castañeda, excerpted from the *residencia* (judicial inquiry) into his term in office undertaken by Rodrigo de Contreras, who succeeded him as governor, are: "Mando que ninguna persona vesyno ni morador estante ni abitante en esta governaçion de Nicaragua de ni venda al adelantado don Pedro de Alvarado ningund bastimento de mahiz ni carne ni otro bastimento ninguno ni a las personas que por ello vinieren ni ninguna persona le vaya a ver ni comunicar ni le embie bastimento ninguna ni le embie mensajero ni escriva carta so pena que el que lo contrario hiziere carga e yncurra en pena de muerte e perdimiento de todos sus bienes para la camara e fisco de su magestad por quanto el dicho adelantado quebranto el puerto de la posesyon y saco y llevo del dos navios los mayores que en el estavan e agora ha tornado y esta surto con vna nao armada y con gente a la boca del dicho puerto de la posesyon para tomar los demas navios que estan en el dicho puerto y estorvar que el governador Francisco Piçarro que esta conquistando por su magestad en el Peru no sea socorrido siendo como es vassallo y governador de su magestad en aquella provincia y tener la nescesidad que tiene de gente lo qual mando que sea apregonado publicamente para que ninguno pretenda ynorançia." Altoaguirre y Duvale (1927, 185) depicts Castañeda's dealings with Alvarado quite differently, stating that "ningún daño le resultó – no harm was caused" by the Adelantado's conduct. He goes so far as to say that "not only did Castañeda stop being hostile to Alvarado" but that the

governor "invited him and his flotilla to Puerto de la Posesión [Realejo] because it was safer than Puerto Fonseca." For the time that Alvarado's armada was anchored at Realejo, "everything required was attended to," Altoaguirre y Duvale's precise words being: "[N]o sólo dejó Castañeda serle hostil, sino que le invitó a que llevara su escuadra al Puerto de la Posesión, por ser más seguro que el de Fonseca, y la atendió con todo lo necesario el tiempo que estuvo allí anclada." Upon what basis Altoaguirre y Duvale makes his assertion is, alas, not indicated.

19 Testimony of Diego de Aguilera, 23 October 1533 (AGI, Justicia 1051), in *Colección Somoza*, vol. 3 (Vega Bolaños 1954, 295). His precise words, as recorded by Saavedra, are: "[E]l dicho adelantado busca todas las maneras que pueda para estobar que al dicho governador don Franciso Piçarro no le venga socorro alguno e que asymismo a oydo desyr a los dichos marinos e a otras personas que an venido de donde esta el dicho adelantado que pasado en estas partes el seria rey de la tierra."

CHAPTER EIGHT

1 Bancroft (1883, 127n9) words the matter thus: "Herrera mentions 11; Remesal, 10; Juarros, 8; Oviedo, 11; and Prescott, 12." He himself acknowledges a dozen: "The fleet now numbered twelve sail, eight being vessels of one hundred tons or more." In a letter dated 18 January 1534 (*Libro viejo*, 287), Alvarado states that "doze velas" (Bancroft's "twelve sail") were in his armada, the same number referred to in a letter dated 10 March 1534 (*Libro viejo*, 291). In another letter dated 15 January 1535 (*Libro viejo*, 294), he states that the ships were ten in number ("diez naos").

2 Of the spectacle of his ships about to take to the high seas, Alvarado's precise words (*Libro viejo*, 287) are: "Tenga Vuestra Magestad por cierto que nunca hasta oy se ha visto en estas partes." He was addressing the king, from his moorings in Realejo, in the letter dated 18 January 1534, cited in note 1 above.

3 Alvarado to the Crown, 25 April 1533, in Medina (1889, 172).

4 Alvarado to the Crown, 18 January 1534, in *Revista Peruana* (1880, vol. 4, 192).

5 Alvarado to the governor of Panama, Francisco de Barrionuevo, 10 March 1534 (*Libro viejo*, 291).

6 See *Libro viejo*, 294 – Alvarado's letter is dated 5 January 1535 – and Bancroft (1883, 128n11).

7 As recorded by Bancroft (1883, 128n11).

8 Prescott (1847, vol. 2, 176).

9 Bancroft (1883, 128n11).

10 See chapter 6, note 7, drawing on Alvarado's letter to the Crown dated 18 January 1534, in *Revista Peruana* (1880, vol. 4, 192). See also *Libro viejo*, 287.

11 The *residencia* into Alvarado's affairs, including his expedition to Peru, was conducted by the *oidor* (judge) Alonso de Maldonado, charged to do so by royal order on 27 October 1535 (AGI, Justicia 295 and 296). A transcription of this massive document by Julio Martín Blasco – see Vallejo García-Hevia (2008, vol. 2, 655–1132) – details all sorts of iniquities alleged to have been perpetrated by Alvarado, which the Adelantado and his sympathizers refuted. The number given for abducted natives comes from Vallejo García-Hevia (2008, vol. 2, 758), as recorded in AGI, Justicia 295, folio 197 verso – "mil y ciento y ochenta y cuatro indios, hombres y mujeres, libres y esclavos." When he perused the *residencia* in the Seville archive, Sherman (1979, 59) also noted the precise figure of 1,184. "Full of slaves and *maceguales* (commoners)," one witness testified when the ships sailed off.

12 "Most of the slaves who survived," Sherman (1979, 59) writes, "were sold in Peru."

13 Hernando de Sosa to the Crown, 11 January 1534 (AGI, Guatemala 41, N.1, folios 32 recto to 35 recto). The name Diego Martyn de Hutrera [Utrera] appears twice on folio 33 verso. Assuming this is the same man, then the total number of Spaniards on the roll call should be reduced by one, to 435.

14 In Figure 7, the Isla de los Jagüeyes is identified as the "Carenero de Jagüey." A *carenero* is where ships could be careened for repair. The word *jagüey* may be translated either as a pond or vegetation known as a strangler fig, the latter an invasive species whose roots grow around trees, cutting off water and nutrients and eventually killing them.

15 Hernando de Sosa to the Crown, 11 January 1534 (AGA, Guatemala 41, N.1, folios 32 recto and 35 recto. De Sosa's opening words (folio 32 recto) are: "Yo Hernando de Sosa escrivano de su majestad doy fee a los señores que la presente vieren en como el señor adelantado don Pedro de Alvarado governador e capitan general de la provincia de Guatimala por su magestad hizo alarde general por ante my e los testigos yuso escriptos en la ysla de

los Xagueyes en domingo honze dias del mes de enero año del señor de myll e quynyentos e treynta e quatro años e que asy al dicho alarde como despues dél paresco e pareçieron ante my e muchos testigos los españoles cavalleros e hijosdalgo e personas yuso contenydas con sus armas e cavallos a punto de guerra e con los adereços neçesarios." His closing remarks (folio 35 recto) run: "E yo Fernando de Sosa … fuy presente a lo que dicho es con los dichos testigos los quales fueron los muy reverendos padres fray Marcos e fray Pedro de la Orden de San Francisco, Gabriel de Cabrera e don Pedro de Portocarrero y otros muchos."

16 Sáenz de Santa María (1983, 318n3).

17 The experienced paleographer Esther González Pérez undertook the transcription, assisted by José Manuel Manzano González. They worked together in situ at the AGI in Seville, but the document in question can now be accessed online via the PARES (Portal de Archivos Españoles, www.pares.mcu.es) initiative of the Spanish Ministerio de Cultura y Deporte.

18 Hernando de Sosa to the Crown, 11 January 1534 (AGI, Guatemala 41, N.1, folios 32 recto to 35 recto). From his reading of Alvarado's *residencia* (AGI, Justicia 295), Sherman (1979, 384n73) extracts the following: "Horsemen were allowed [to take with them] three slaves, Black or Indian, though some were permitted only two. If three, one was usually a female. Foot soldiers took one, some of them two. Alvarado took for himself twenty to twenty-five Indian men and women, of whom only seven or eight returned." Vallejo García-Hevia (2008, vol. 1, 268) confirms most of Sherman's tallies, but with some differences.

19 See appendix 1 and Hernando de Sosa to the Crown, 11 January 1534 (AGI, Guatemala 41, N.1, folio 33 recto).

20 For a detailed account of Alonso de Alvarado's exploits in Peru, see Del Busto (1986, vol. 1, 93–101). Of the names listed on his reading of the roll call, Sáenz de Santa María (1983, 325) identifies 190 as having stayed on in Peru after arrival there. His identification is attributed to the chronicler Cieza de León ([1553] 1984–5), from whom he designates fifty-two "de Guatimala" incorporated into the ranks of Diego de Almagro. In the conflict between Spaniards that took place in Peru between 1537 and 1555, forty-three fought in the Guerra de Chupas, forty in the Guerra de Salinas, and fifty-five in the Guerra de Quito.

21 See Recinos (1952, 142), appendix 1, and Hernando de Sosa to the Crown, 11 January 1534 (AGI, Guatemala 41, N.1, folio 33 recto). The captain's full

name was Sebastián Garçilaso de la Vega Vargas, that of the Inca princess Ñusta Chimpu Occlo (Livermore 1966, part 1, xv and xx and part 2, iv, x, and xvii). Their offspring, "one of the first of the new race of mestizos," was born in Cuzco on 12 April 1539, making him a great-grandson of Tupac Yupanqui, the tenth Sapa Inca, who ruled from 1471 to 1493. "During his childhood," Livermore writes, "[the boy] heard the traditions of the Indian rulers from his mother's relatives and tales of the conquest from his father's comrades."

22 "Having surrendered his hopes from Peru," Livermore (1966, part 1, xxiii) states that, upon arrival in Spain in 1561 to lay claim to familial rights there, "the young Inca was attracted by, and began to model himself on, [a] distant kinsman." The "distant kinsman" was another Garcilaso de la Vega, "the great Castilian poet, whose name he now began to assume."

23 For the most part, Garcilaso de la Vega ([1609/1616] 1966, vol. 2, 731–4) depicts Alvarado and his deeds positively, "proofs of his excellent character which I heard in my father's house," distinctly at odds with how López de Gómara and other contemporaries portray him. "We can only suppose that he [López de Gómara] had his information from one of the many jealous rivals Alvarado had," writes El Inca, "who could not conceal [Alvarado's] great deeds since the whole world knew of them, but sought to blacken him by describing his nature and character very differently from what they were." He recalls listening to "gentlemen who had accompanied [Alvarado] to Peru praising his goodness and virtue, and many of them could recount particular instances of his generosity toward each of them."

24 Sauer (1932, 21–32) remains one of our best insights into Fray Marcos – "in any light a most dubious fellow" – and his search in 1538–39 for the "seven cities" whose legend he helped promote. Reputed to be rich in gold, Cíbola was most likely nothing more than a complex of modest Zuni pueblos in present-day New Mexico, a far cry from what the Franciscan friar beheld in Peru.

25 Hernando de Sosa to the Crown, 11 January 1534 (AGI, Guatemala 41, N.1, folio 35 recto). Fray Marcos – see Vallejo García-Hevia (2008, vol. 2, 608, 864, 866, and 869) – is recorded in Alvarado's *residencia* as having been in Peru as a result of the Adelantado's foray there.

26 Bancroft (1883, 128). In the case of Fray Marcos, head of an earlier delegation of Franciscan friars who went to Peru, his being a chaplain in Alvarado's party was for him a return voyage. He stayed on in Peru – see Cook and

Cook (Cieza de León [1553] 1998, 297n14) – until 1536, when he headed back to Central America and then on to New Spain. Wagner (1934) is perhaps our most comprehensive study of the headstrong friar's life and times.

27 Testimony of Gonzalo Ortiz, "Provanza del Adelantado D. Pedro de Alvarado y doña Leonor de Alvarado su hija" ([1563] 1937, 479), his precise words being: "[C]uando el Adelantado fue al Perú llevo a Doña Luisa y a Doña Leonor a las dos muy honradamente con guarda de mugeres españolas y de españoles que las servian."

28 Recinos (1952, 142). Citing AGI, Justicia 295, Vallejo García-Hevia (2008, vol. 1, 546) records Diego as "seis o siete años de edad" in 1532. He would have been a year or two younger than his sister, Leonor. Diego may have been left behind in Peru when his father departed in 1535, Vallejo García-Hevia (2008, vol. 2, 1267) noting his death there in 1554 at the battle of Chuquinga. The Diego de Alvarado who appears on the roll call (see appendix 1, line 6, and Figure 7, line 17) is the Adelantado's cousin, not his son.

29 Bancroft (1883, 128). See chapter 6, note 9, for further discussion.

30 Alvarado to the governor of Panama, Francisco de Barrionuevo, 10 March 1534 (*Libro viejo*, 291), his precise words being: "[P]ersonas de bien detenidas por falta de naos." He also alludes, writing from Puerto Viejo in Ecuador, to sending ships back to Panama "so that they can bring forth those noble folk at my expense, without them having to pay freight for themselves, their horses, and their attendants – para que fuesen a traer esos hidalgos á mi costa sin que paguen fletes de sus personas, caballos y servicio."

CHAPTER NINE

1 Alvarado to the Crown, 15 January 1535, in *Libro viejo*, 294, his precise words being: "a cabo treinta y tres dias que anduve por la mar." Thirty-three days has a historic ring to it, that being the same length of time it took Columbus to cross the Atlantic on his first voyage of discovery in 1492, Sauer (1966, 19–20) noting that the Admiral of the Ocean Sea left the Canary Islands "on the night of September 8" and sighted land in the Bahamas "two hours after midnight on October 12." Herrera ([1615] 1728, 128) says Alvarado's sea journey lasted "treinta Dias – thirty days," his reckoning accepted by González Suárez (1881, 67). Cieza de León ([1553] 1998, 294) states "more than thirty days." Recinos (1952, 144–5) records the Adelantado's departure

from Realejo as 23 January and his landfall at Caráquez as 25 February, as does Jijón y Caamaño (1936, 51); Molina ([1986] 2004, 193–4) indicates the dates, respectively, as 7 January and 10 February, citing AGI, Patronato 118, as his source. Loor (1956, 202) also opts for thirty-three days at sea in his schema, believing that landfall occurred "most likely on 10 March, but in any case not before 27 February 1534 – lo más probable el 10 de marzo de 1534, pero de todos modos no antes del 27 de febrero de este mismo año." Recinos and Jijón y Caamaño had access to more contemporary evidence than either Loor or Molina; their dates are therefore the more persuasive and accord with those of Alvarado himself. The Adelantado embarked at the most propitious of times: Lockhart (1968, 117) maintains that winds from the south make it "nearly impossible to reach Peru from [Central America] except during the months of January and February." He adds: "When the winds were right, a ship could reach [San Miguel de] Piura from Panama in nine or ten days" but that "ordinarily the trip took longer." A return voyage from Peru to Central America "presented little problem, and could be undertaken at most times of the year, the trip between Lima and Panama, even with frequent stops, lasting usually less than a month."

2 Alvarado to the Crown, 12 May 1535, *Libro viejo*, 299, his precise words being: "Despues que me hice a la vela, yo di a los pilotos de mi armada la derrota de rrumbos que habían de seguir, conforme a la comisión que de Vuestra Magestad yo tenia, y a lo capitulado; y ansi siguieron siempre enderezando mi viaxe al Poniente y metidos en la mar casi quatrocientas leguas, las corrientes fueron tan grandes y los tiempos tan contrarios, que aunque se fizo todo lo posible para seguir el viaxe, unos tobimos el reparo a mucho riesgo de la armada fue forzado ir a reconocer la tierra del Perú."

3 Alvarado to the Crown, 12 May 1535, *Libro viejo*, 299, his precise words being: "Aviendo echando al agua más de noventa caballos" and fearing "se echaran todos los demas, y aun la xente, por falta de agua, si no se tomara tierra y seguir en la tierra del Perú sin saber que parte della era." Regarding horses being thrown overboard, Loor (1956, 202) mentions Alvarado having been urged to do so, for safety's sake, by "the pilot Juan Fernández," an action that the Adelantado would not have taken lightly, "horses in those days fetching in Peru between three thousand and four thousand pesos – porque de no hacerlo se acabaría de morir el resto de los caballos, que en aquellos tiempos costaban en el Perú de 3 a 4,000 pesos cada uno." The going price of a horse is confirmed by Cieza de León ([1553] 1998, 305), who records the monetary

worth of one as between "three and four thousand castellanos." Herrera ([1615] 1728, 138) ups the value to between four and five thousand pesos. In settling a debt with the estate of Juan de la Parra, Alvarado himself – see Archivo General de la Nación (AGN, Lima, Peru), Obligación N1 Pac1 0, 717 488 – agreed to pay 4,500 pesos for a horse that belonged to the deceased, "who died on his way to Peru with me – que murio veniendo conmigo a estas partes de Peru." Alvarado's letter is dated 4 January 1535, his acknowledgment witnessed by Fernando de Alvarado, García de Contreras, and Bernaldo Ramires.

4 Alvarado to the Crown, 12 May 1535, *Libro viejo*, 299, his precise words being that landfall was made "en una playa que se llama Caraque, bien mas de trecientas leguas de donde Pizarro estaba."

5 Lockhart (1972, 8), who cites as his source AGI, Contaduría 1825. Belalcázar's men were "well received" by Pizarro, "though there was some grumbling at their small number, not the large party expected." Pizarro's disappointment at the size of Belalcázar's contingent, however, was compensated for two weeks later with the arrival "from Nicaragua and Panama of Hernando de Soto's party: two ships, perhaps a hundred men, and twenty-five horses." See also Varón Gabai (1997, 22–3).

6 Molina ([1986] 2004, 195). Molina's reconstruction of the landfall and its aftermath is drawn from archival documentation in Seville along with perhaps the most consulted printed source regarding Alvarado's Peruvian exploits, the *Historia general* (1601–16) of Antonio de Herrera. His *Década quinta, libro sexto* ([1615] 1728) is based on the access Herrera had – see Cook and Cook (1998, 23) – to the "thick, bound bundles of manuscript pages" (some eight thousand in all) that constituted Pedro de Cieza de León's chronicle of Peru ([1553] 1998). Lockhart (1972, 94) also indicates Herrera's appropriation of Cieza de León, a source upon which Herrera "relied heavily," the "subsequently lost third part of Cieza's work" in particular. While praising renderings he deems to be "faithful," Lockhart laments nonetheless Herrera's "considerable deviation" and "ill-informed attempt to correct apparent mistakes," specifically in relation to the register of men recorded as present with Pizarro at Cajamarca. "Fernández came to claim his share of the profits," Lockhart (1972, 125) states, having witnessed in Cajamarca, according to Loor (1956, 199), the capture of Atahualpa (Atabaliba) on 16 November 1532. Receiving no reward, as did others

who believed that they should have, Fernández returned "unsatisfied to Nicaragua, there, according to Cieza, to incite Pedro de Alvarado to attempt the conquest of the Quito region." Belalcázar was awarded 9,909 gold pesos and 407 and 2/8ths silver marks of Cajamarca spoils, an allocation "not much above that of the standard horseman," which Lockhart (1972, 97 and 125) takes to have signalled that Pizarro by then "no longer considered Benalcázar [Belalcázar] indispensable."

7 Alvarado to Francisco de Barrionuevo, governor of Panama, 10 March 1534, in *Libro viejo*, 292, his precise words being: "Tomada tierra en Caraque, que es a diez leguas de Puerto Viejo, tuve noticias de los indios que había veinte dias que Hernán Ponce pasó por allí y que desde Puerto Viejo hasta la punta de Santa Elena había ya quemado y despoblado cinco pueblos." According to Lockhart (1972, 192), Hernán Ponce [de León], "though a captain, was less a leader of expeditions than a manager and man of affairs," his business dealings tying him closely to Hernando de Soto, after Pizarro "the most powerful single independent figure" in the conquest of Peru. Alvarado's depiction of Ponce, a ship of whose (co-owned with Soto) the Adelantado (see chapter 7, notes 9 and 10) had commandeered in Realejo, is more in keeping with his own violent tendencies. Ponce had participated in the conquest of Nicaragua before his involvement with Peru, where he remained until 1539 before leaving for Panama and – see Cook and Cook (Cieza de León [1553] 1998, 135n4) – returning to Spain in 1540. The "Puerto Viejo" referred to is the present-day Manta, which lies on the Pacific coast fifty kilometres southwest of Caráquez. San Gregorio de Puerto Viejo was not founded until a year later, on 12 March 1535, by Francisco Pacheco – see Loor (1956, 203) and Newson (1995, 249) – and lies inland fifty kilometres to the south of Caráquez.

8 Alvarado to Francisco de Barrionuevo, governor of Panama, 10 March 1534, in *Libro viejo*, 292, his precise words being: "En este tiempo llegó un barco de Cristoval Rodrigues con veinte españoles, y cinco de caballo, los cuales teniendo de mí noticia se me llegaron y ofrecieron á ir en mi compañia, y por conocer su buena voluntad les socorrí y pagué sus fletes, y otras cosas que debían."

9 San Miguel de Piura, designated by Cieza de León ([1553] 1959, 319) "the first Spanish settlement of Peru," lay inland from the coast, not on it, hence Alvarado's suggestion to found a more functional port town to its north.

Cieza (303) states that San Miguel "was settled and founded by Francisco Pizarro in the name of His Majesty in the year 1533." Citing AGI, Contaduría 1825, Lockhart (1972, 9n14) records it already in existence by 1 August 1532.

10 Alvarado to Francisco de Barrionuevo, governor of Panama, 10 March 1534, in *Libro viejo*, 292, his precise words being: "Los vecinos del San Miguel estan casi desesperados, y como en toda su gobernacion no hay otro pueblo de españoles, y sean tan pocos, y el Sr. Gobernador ande tan absente, parecióme que así para sustentar aquella villa como para el aviamiento y socorro de los que vinieren á estas partes, seria bien hacer un pueblo en esta comarca, no con intento de lo adjudicar, porque esta no me mueve á ello, sino porque S. M. será muy servido, y esta provincia permanecerá en su servicio. En esta Gobernacion quedaban muchos hijos-dalgos, personas de bien detenidas por falta de Naos, y la mucha necesidad que á esta causa pasaban; y puesto que yo tenia ya todas mis Naos á punto para las enviar en el descubrimiento, detuve algunas de ellas, para que fuesen traer esos hidalgos á mi costa sin que paguen fletes de sus personas, caballos y servicio."

11 Newson (1995), Murra (1948), and Jijón y Camaaño (1936, 1941). The place where Alvarado and his men came ashore, and subsequently razed, is the present-day province of Manabí, voiced as Cancebí in Indigenous parlance. It is recorded as such – see Molina Cedeño (2015, 24) – "in the first expeditionary chronicles of Francisco Pizarro upon arrival in Coaque," which lies eighty kilometres north of Caráquez. Loor (1956, 153) maps the territory as explored by the pilot Ruiz in 1526, designating locations with Indigenous place names, Caráquez rendered as Caralobez or Caraslobez.

12 Newson (1995, 61–78 and 247–67) and Jijón y Camaaño (1941, 70–103), the latter an inspiration too for Murra (1948, 791), who considers him "the foremost Ecuadorean student of the nation's Indian past." Saville (1907) remains an indispensable source, the findings of his archaeological survey contextualized by a reading of, and commentary on, historical data. Currie (1995) follows to good effect in Saville's footsteps, as now do a generation or more of Ecuadorian researchers, their work nicely synthesized by Moreno Yañez ([2008] 2015). The assertion made by Saville (1907, 11) – "it is safe to assume that the material in the collection [here] described pertained to a people almost untouched by Inca ideas" – has been borne out. Emblematic "patrimonial artifacts" taken by Saville and in the possession of the Smithsonian Institution in Washington, DC, including massive stone seats

that local lore attributes to giants said to have populated coastal Ecuador in pre-historic times, have been solicited for "repatriation" by the pertinacious Hidrovo Quiñónez (2016).

13 Villamarín and Villamarín (1999, 607–12). "Under the control of the Lord of Salango," the Villamarins state, "the Manteño polity extended from the Esmeraldas to the Ayampe rivers," dominating "culturally and linguistically diverse populations. Salango's domain was a major center of *Spondylus* processing," sea shells from which much-prized "beads of a reddish and white color" were made and traded – see chapter 2, note 8 – far and wide.

14 Newson (1995, 4–8 and 337–52). The contact population for Ecuador as a whole, including the Andean Sierra and the Oriente (eastern lowlands), she reckons to have been around 1.6 million. By the end of the sixteenth century, the population may have dropped to 217,220. Though drastic, an overall decline of 85.5 per cent was not as catastrophic as that experienced by the coast, the most depopulated of the three regional units that make up Ecuador (Newson 1993). Alchon (1991, 18) estimates the population of highland Ecuador to have numbered "approximately 1 million in 1520" and to have fallen to 270,000 by 1559, Indigenous demise brought about primarily because of outbreaks of smallpox, measles, plague, typhus, and influenza. For comparative discussion of epidemic episodes in other parts of Spanish America, see Cook and Lovell ([1992] 2001) and Cook and Lovell (2000).

15 Newson ([1992] 2001, 84–112).

16 Cieza de León ([1553] 1998, 294–5). The designation "prince of chroniclers" is a common but deserving one. Cieza's life and times, and a critical appraisal of his writings, are nowhere better engaged than by Cook and Cook (1998) in their introduction to (and translation of) *The Discovery and Conquest of Peru* (Cieza de León [1553] 1998). Alvarado's delegation of duties is replicated in Herrera ([1615] 1728, 128), as is (see note 6 above) much of Cieza's riveting account, toned down by Herrera so as it make it more palatable for reading by the Crown or officials of its Council of the Indies. Cieza's version of events, much of it based on what members of Alvarado's entourage told him, I draw upon throughout, most appreciatively so. Among those with whom Cieza conversed – see Saville (1907, 103) – the chronicler singles out Alvarado's nephew, "the marshal Alonzo de Alvarado," and the captains Garcilaso de la Vega and Juan de Saavedra.

CHAPTER TEN

1 Hemming ([1970] 1972, 502) and Varón Gabai (1997, 73).

2 Almagro to the Crown, 8 May 1534, in Medina (1889, 219–20). What Almagro had to say is rendered thus: "El gobernador me envió a mí á esta ciudad de San Miguel como á dar órden para que los españoles que por aquí vinieren en los navios sean proveidos de todo lo que hobieren menester para pasar adelante donde anda el gobernador, poblando por manera que estas tierras en breve sean pobladas é pacificas. Llegado á esta ciudad hallé la gente della muy alterada, ansi los españoles como los naturales de la tierra. La cabsa es que ha dos meses que Pedro de Alvarado, gobernador de V. M. de la provincia de Goatimala, con mucha gente de pié é de caballo, desembarcó en la costa de Puerto Viejo, que es en esta gobernacion y en comarca de esta ciudad. Estaban aquellos pueblos de Puerto Viejo de paz é debajo de mamparo real de vuestra católica magestad, porque los pacificó el gobernador don Francisco Pizarro cuando por allí pasó."

3 Almagro to the Crown, 8 May 1534, in Medina (1889, 220), his precise words transcribed thus: "Eran reparo de todos los navios que por allí venian con gente á estas provincias, por ser como la principal escala é puerto que tienen los navios. Cuando allí llegaban siempre traian mucha necesidad, ansi de mantenimientos é otras cosas para el fornecimiento de su viaje. Questos indios han sido tan constantes en las paces que, en viniendo navio por allí, salian á ellos señores é personas principales de los pueblos y llevaban los españoles á sus casas, donde los aposentaban é daban de comer é servian todo el tiempo que allí querian estar."

4 Almagro to the Crown, 8 May 1534, in Medina (1889, 220–2). His allegations are rendered thus: "Al tiempo que llegó allí Pedro de Alvarado quiso entrar la tierra adentro á las espaldas de Puerto Viejo, á una provincia que llaman Quito, porque le dijieron que allí podria haber cierta cantidad de oro. É ataron cuanta gente con cadenas y sogas é los llevaron cargados con su carruaxe. Salieron á robar los indios de un pueblo que está á la Punta de Santa Elena, que estaba de paz, é la gente del pueblo, viendo esto, salieron ellos de guerra y les mataron un español ó dos, y les hirieron otros algunos. Ha sido grande inhumanidad lo que Alvarado ha fecho é hace, que ha de ser cabsa de mucha mal é levantamiento de indios. Dios se lo perdone, que ha metido tanta mal en una tierra tan rica, é ques ya como esta que ya no lo podrá recabar en toda su vida el mal que ha hecho." See also AGI, Patronato 192–1–6 (1534), in which the *cabildo* of San Miguel echoes the concerns of

Almagro about Alvarado's intrusion and devastation. Loor (1956, 208) labels Alvarado "un Atila en miniatura – an Attila [the Hun] in miniature."

5 Almagro to the Crown, 12 October 1534, in Medina (1889, 244–306). The fourteen witnesses, whose testimony was taken by the *teniente de gobernador* (lieutenant governor), Juan de Soto, were in turn: (1) Blas de Atienza, forty-five years of age; (2) Francisco de Villacastin, forty years of age; (3) Bernardo Ramirez, thirty-five or thirty-six years of age; (4) Bartolomé de Segovia, clergyman, thirty-five years of age; (5) Hernando Varela, forty years of age; (6) Alonso Tellez Giron, thirty-three years of age; (7) Juan Avendaño, forty years of age; (8) Francisco Luis de Alcántara, thirty years of age, unable to sign his testimony because "no sabia escribir – he does not know how to write"; (9) Diego de Vega, thirty-four or thirty-five years of age; (10) Andrés Duran, fifty years of age, "alcalde por su Magestad – who serves his Majesty as the mayor of San Miguel"; (11) Pedro Bravo, thirty-five years of age, Franciscan friar and former vicar general of Nicaragua; (12) Vicente de Bejar, forty years of age; (13) Antonio Picado, twenty-six years of age, who at the time of the reported incidents served as Alvarado's secretary; and (14) Álvaro Alonso Prieto, thirty years of age. The "juicio instruido en San Miguel contra Alvarado a petición de Almagro" was also consulted in Seville by Molina ([1986] 2004, 197n3), who located a copy of the deposition in the AGI among the contents of Patronato 185, Ramo 9. He dates the document there to the "últimos meses de 1534."

6 The names of four of the men – Bejar, Picado, Ramirez, and Vega – appear on the *alarde*. Though Bravo's name is not on the list, he is recorded as having been alongside notary Hernando de Sosa when the register was drawn up and boarded ship twelve days later. See Vallejo García-Hevia (2008, vol. 1, 156) for verification, beside Bravo's own disclosure (Medina 1889, 289) that he "vino allí [Peru] con el armada del Adelantado –went there [to Peru] with Alvarado's fleet."

7 Bartolomé García to the Crown, 7 April 1534, from "Información hecha en Panamá al navío llamado *La Concepción*," in Jijón y Camaaño (1936, vol. 1, Documento 6, 41). Testimony is relayed via "el gobernador," Francisco de Barrionuevo, and "el escribano de su Magestad," Hernando del Castillo. The text in the original runs: "Llegaron a Puerto Viejo e pensaron de hallar a los indios de paz [pero] los hallaron los pueblos destruidos e destrozados, e los indios idos por ahí. Había llegado Alvarado e su gente e llevado lo que tenían. [También] habían llevado caciques e indios e indias, e que no

dejó nada. E que aquella lengua les dijo que pués les daban maíz e lo que habían menester. ¿Que por que los mataban? Se quejaban mucho de la gente de Albarado e de lo mal que les había hecho."

8 Molina ([1986] 2004, 196). Cieza de León ([1553] 1998, 295) informs us that the galleon of the fleet, the *San Cristóbal*, was piloted by Fernández himself and sent south "to explore the land beyond Chincha, where the boundaries of Pizarro's governance ended."

9 Almagro to the Crown, 12 October 1534, in Medina (1889, 289–90). Bravo's testimony is transcribed thus: "Visto el mal tratamiento que les hacian, se alzaron el pueblo desde á dos ó tres dias que allí llegaron. Con mucha parte de su gente fue el Adelantado desde su real a los pueblos de Puerto Viejo é Manta, é trajeron mucha gente de indios é indias é muchachos, en cadenas, é atadas." He goes on to say: "Mucha de la gente que se llevaba del dicho Puerto Viejo quedaron muertos é perescieron por el camino: el Adelantado mataban muchos dellos desque se cansaban é no podian llevar las cargas – siempre llevaban la demanda de Quito por donde iban."

10 Almagro to the Crown, 12 October 1534, in Medina (1889, 290). Molina ([1986] 2004, 202) records the *cacique*'s name as Lligua Tohali, who was betrayed "por culpa de un indio traicionero e intricante – by a traitorous and scheming fellow native." Bravo's declaration runs: "Vido este testigo que el Adelantado llevó consigo el dicho cacique y así de allí estaban que se alzasen; é que esto oyó decir este testigo al Adelantado, pero no se sabe si lo hizo el dicho cacique ni si no, no habia lengua con quien bien poderle entender."

11 Almagro to the Crown, 12 October 1534, in Medina (1889, 290). Bravo's testimony is transcribed thus: "Vido este testigo en un pueblo por donde el Adelantado pasó apperear un cacique é quemar á otro indio, é que siempre por donde iban se quemaban é mataban indios sobre que dijesen del camino, así el dicho Adelantado como sus capitanes."

12 Almagro to the Crown, 12 October 1534, in Medina (1889, 299). Picado's testimony is rendered thus: "Vido que cuando el Adelantado partió de Charapotó sacó los dichos indios cargados por la tierra, é por el camino vió quedar gran cantidad de ellos, así indios como indias, muertos unos de estocadas é otros cortadas las cabezas con cuchilladas – é á otros que de cansados se quedaban muertos por el camino. É vido quedarse por ahí perdidas muchas criaturas porque les llevaban sus madres; é que á otras oia que decir por el camino que habia algunas personas de las que

traian indias paridas, que les quitaban los hijos de los brazos é los dejaban para que peresciesen en el camino." He is also recorded as having stated: "Dijo que sabe é vido que el Adelantado é su gente al tiempo que quiso entrar la tierra adentro fué á los pueblos de Puerto Viejo é vido que trajo de allá él y su gente mucha cantidad de indios é indias, é muchachos é niños, que los habian tomado de sus casas estando seguros en ellas. É que despues los vió llevar por el camino cargados é que fué en tanta cantidad que decian que no habia quedado casi casa de indios poblada."

13 Jijón y Camaaño (1936, vol. 1, 59–60). His words in the original run: "Los métodos de Alvarado no diferían de los usados por los demás conquistdores, llámense Pizarro, Almagro, Hernán Cortez o Benalcázar [Belalcázar]: tales inhumanidades contra la masa anónima de la población aborigen son las grandes lacras de la historia de la venida de los castellanos a América."

14 Jijón y Camaaño (1941, 70). His words in the original run: "El primer europeo que se internó por aquellos magníficos bosques y selvas vírgenes del interior de la zona preandina fué Don Pedro de Alvarado, recorriendo así gran parte de la Costa para después andar perdido por las montañas." Of the Adelantado's sinuous foray, it pains the erudite Jijón y Camaaño to note that "there is no account that affords us any ethnographic details – existe ninguna relación que contenga datos etnográficos." The coast of Ecuador, Saucr (1959, 328 and 337) writes, "is neither desert like Perú, nor rain forest like Colombia," though "from south to north shows gradation" from one type of vegetation to the other. "A poorly known hill land stretches along the sea, principally in the Province of Manabí."

15 How long Alvarado's entourage floundered on the Manabí coast before reaching the Andes has yet to be agreed upon (Map 4). According to Saville (1917, 2), Pizarro's secretary, Pedro Sancho ([1534] 1917), states that it was three months, but other sources reckon Alvarado to have been on the coast "five months before beginning the march into the interior." Writing to the Crown from San Miguel on 15 January 1535, Alvarado himself (*Libro viejo*, 1934, 295) says "siete meses – seven months." Jijón y Camaaño (1941, 57n1) believes the trek "could not have lasted more than four months – no pudo durar más que cuatro meses."

16 Cieza de León ([1553] 1998, 295 and 300), who notes also that "Alvarado thanked the Indian who had declared to have seen the treasure and to have been to Quito, and promised him a substantial payment for it." Anticipating

what he later narrates in detail, Cieza continues: "As best as they could, [the Spaniards] set out on the road. Those wretched natives carried most of their loads, so that this expedition cost them dearly, and a prayer to God does not redeem the souls of the Christians who were responsible."

17 Herrera ([1615] 1728, 129) and Loor (1956, 206). The march in a southeasterly direction, Jijón y Camaaño (1936, vol. 1, 60–1) notes, "took Alvarado and his men through the driest part of Manabí," meaning that when they got to Ramadas they were much in need of refreshment – "se dirigieron Alvarado y su tropa al SE y atravestando la parte más seca de Manabí, y en dos jornadas llegaron a un lugar llamado Ramadas, a donde sintieron alguna necesidad de agua."

18 Cieza de León ([1553] 1998, 300–1). He adds: "The natives had no warning of their coming, which was why [the Spaniards] took them by surprise. When they saw the horses among their houses, they lost the strength and spirit to offer resistance. Those who could escape saw themselves as very lucky."

19 Upon entering Paján today, visitors pass through a concrete arch on the edge of town, atop of which four huge, welcoming, sculpted swallows thank one for having come: "Gracias por su visita a San Juan Bautista de las Golondrinas de Paján."

20 Cieza de León ([1553] 1998, 301), commenting further that "the Adelantado was furious, [as the Spaniards] were all thrown into disarray because they did not know the land or which were the right roads." Loor (1956, 206) reckons that the Indian from Manta who led the Spaniards to Paján before abandoning them there did so as a deliberate ploy, one designed to rid his home territory of such a loathsome and destructive presence. Newson (1995, 254), referring to the *Historia del Mondo Nuovo* (1565) of Girolamo Benzoni, notes that the Italian adventurer states that "when the Spanish arrived, Manta had possessed 2,000 inhabitants, but in 1546 contained only 50. He further claimed that this level of destruction was characteristic of all villages in the province."

21 Cieza de León ([1553] 1998, 301) and Herrera ([1615] 1728, 129).

22 Cieza de León ([1553] 1998, 302). "The Indians of all these lands fled," he observes, while "others became prisoners in power of the Spaniards. Some of them took up arms. They did not fare well because most of them were wounded and killed." I have been unable to locate Niza; Loor (1956, 209) had no better luck, Niza not appearing on his map of Alvarado's meanderings.

23 Cieza de León ([1553] 1998, 302), though Daule lies south of Chonana, not to its east. See also Herrera ([1615] 1728, 129); González Suárez (1881, 68–9); Loor (1956, 209–10); and Molina ([1986] 2004, 202–3).

24 Cieza de León ([1553] 1998, 302–3) and Herrera ([1615] 1728, 129).

25 Cieza de León ([1553] 1998, 302–7). Of Gómez de Alvarado's sortie he states: "Those who had been captured said they knew the road to Quito and that they would take them there, that on this highway they would be there shortly. [Gómez] told [Alvarado] that the Indians were saying that where he had explored was the safest way to Quito, that it would be advantageous to take it. In spite of what the captives were declaring, the Adelantado decided that they would take the way Benavides had discovered."

26 González Suárez (1881, 69), the learned archbishop's precise words being: "Perdidos se hallaban en aquel asombroso laberinto que forman las selvas intertropicales." Three and a half decades later, on the other side of the Andes, the excesses of Lope de Aguirre during his descent of the Amazon in search of El Dorado rivalled those of the Adelantado (Vázquez [1562] 1987; Minta 1994; Galster 2011).

CHAPTER ELEVEN

1 Cieza de León ([1553] 1998, 302). What was told to Cieza in this instance was evidently not to his liking, but he felt obliged to record it nonetheless "that the Indians whom [the Spaniards] had brought from Guatemala ate countless native people of these villages, which fall in the district of Puerto Viejo, sins so enormous that they deserved to suffer what they suffered." He adds, for devout measure, "indeed, God permitted it."

2 Cieza de León ([1553] 1998, 65). Of his manner of narration he asserts: "I believe that good writing must be like one person conversing with another – and as one speaks, no more."

3 Cieza de León ([1553] 1979, 1989). According to Cook and Cook (1998, 25), Cantù found the missing manuscript in the Vatican Library "in the 1970s," its whereabouts hitherto "difficult to trace."

4 Cieza de León ([1553] 1998, 304–5). "Indians who had been captured in that land," he states, when asked "to tell where the highway to Quito was, and why they had so few roads, replied [that] they did not know – and other answers that the Indians usually give."

5 Cieza de León ([1553] 1998, 307–8). The volcano in question was probably Cotopaxi, of which Bandelier (1906, 53) confirms "a violent outbreak in

1534." Hemming ([1970] 1972, 161) concurs. Cieza does not mention the volcano by name but says that it was close to Quito, as does Herrera ([1615] 1728, 130). Cotopaxi (elevation 5,897 metres) lies sixty kilometres south of Quito and may be translated from Quechua as "Shining Peak." While not ruling out Cotopaxi, González Suárez (1881, 71) in his *Historia eclesiástica* suggests Pichincha (elevation 4,784 metres) as an option, the twin-peaked volcano located only eight kilometres west of Quito. He records the chronicler Oviedo as having heard Alvarado himself speak of the eruption, one of several "unforeseen circumstances [and] astonishing events that made an already difficult march more painful – circunstancias inesperadas, fenomenos maravillosos [que] contribuían a hacer cada vez más penosa una marcha, ya bajo tantos respectos difícil." In his *Historia general*, González Suárez (1891, 190) proffers Tungurahua (elevation 5,023 metres) as the volcano of choice. It lies 140 kilometres south of Quito, and its name in Quechua means "Throat of Fire." All three volcanoes are still active.

6 Cieza de León ([1553] 1998, 309). Chongos may be the present-day Congo, eighty kilometres upstream from Daule on the Río Congo, a tributary of the Río Daule. I have been unable to locate Noa, though Loor (1956, 209) places it to the north and east of Chongos. Jijón y Camaaño (1936, vol. 1, 65) alludes to a "río Chongo," which he states "today is called Palenque, a wide and powerful river – grande y poderoso." Crossing it, the Adelantado is said to have encountered fierce resistance from local inhabitants, his passage fraught "with great difficulty and danger – con gran dificultad y peligro."

7 Cieza de León ([1553] 1998, 310–11). "Ajo" is the Spanish word for garlic. When Cieza refers to "sheep," he means llamas, alpacas too, there being no sheep in the Americas prior to European intrusion.

8 Jijón y Camaaño (1936, vol. 1, 66) concurs with this designation. "Salinas" is Spanish for salt flats, salt pans, or salt works. Newson (1995, 43) notes salt as being an important item of trade in Tomabela dating back to pre-Inca times. While salt is still produced in Salinas, cheese and dairy products are what the town is famed for today.

9 Cieza de León ([1553] 1998, 311).

10 Cieza de León ([1553] 1998, 311).

11 Cieza de León ([1553] 1998, 312).

CHAPTER TWELVE

1 Molina ([1986] 2004, 207), his words in English meaning "the snowy pass of Tomavela." The mountaineer Edward Whymper (1892, 19–80, 310–19, and 320–34) describes his experiences in ascending both Chimborazo and Carihuairazo – at one point he declared his party "all snow-blind, unable to move" – in gripping prose and captivating sketches. In 1891 and 1892 Whymper confronted the same elements that proved to be Alvarado's undoing, engaging them in scientific experiments related to mountain sickness (*soroche*) and the measurement of atmospheric pressure, especially the altitudes at which the malady occurred and its variable impact on the human body.

2 Hemming ([1970] 1972, 161). Passage betweeen Carihuairazo to the north and Chimborazo to the south Hemming not only ascertains but also (13) diligently maps. Jijón y Camaaño (1936, vol. 1, 67) determined likewise, ruling out passage across the Angamarca region, "which has generally been considered the route taken." His words in the original run: "De Tomabela, siguiendo al NE [noreste], la expedición de Alvarado debió pasar entre el Chimborazo y el Carihuairazo, por una parte elevadísima de la Cordillera, no por la región de Angamarca, como generalmente se ha creído."

3 González Suárez (n.d., 231). The erudite archbishop's exact words – he was forever amending earlier editions of his work – in this instance run: "Pasó la cordillera precisamente a principios del verano, en la época de los mayores vientos y de las más fuertes nevadas." Jijón y Camaaño (1936, vol. 1, 67–8) echoes the words of his teacher and mentor: Alvarado sought to cross the Andes "en una época de fuertes y excepcionales nevadas, por los meses de julio y agosto."

4 Acknowledged by Recinos (1952, 64, 107, 142, and 225) as being the Adelantado's "primo" (cousin), Diego de Alvarado is mistakenly identified as his "hermano" (brother) by (among others) Herrera ([1615] 1728, 141), González Suárez (1881, 77), and Molina ([1986] 2004, 208). Busto Duthurburu (1986, vol. 1, 102) identifies Alvarado as the "sobrino" (nephew) of Diego, which would make Diego the Adelantado's uncle.

5 Cieza de León ([1553] 1998, 331).

6 Cieza de León ([1553] 1998, 331–2). See also Herrera ([1615] 1728, 139).

7 Jijón y Camaaño (1936, vol. 1, 67). Pasa, today San Antonio de Pasa, lies in Ambato province at an elevation of 3,100 metres.

8 Cieza de León ([1553] 1998, 332). See also Herrera ([1615] 1728, 139).
9 Cieza de León ([1553] 1998, 332–3).
10 Cieza de León ([1553] 1998, 335). See also Herrera ([1615] 1728, 140).
11 Cieza de León ([1553] 1998, 335).
12 Cieza de León ([1553] 1998, 335–6).
13 Cieza de León ([1553] 1998, 336). Herrera ([1615] 1728, 139) puts the number of native fatalities at "dos mil Indios – two thousand Indians."
14 Alvarado to the Crown, 15 January 1535, in *Libro viejo* (1934, 294–5). His precise words run: "Hallé pueblos no sabidos y di en muy grandes cienagas y montañas y gentes salvajes que de un pueblo a otro no havia camino y muchas y diferentes lenguas, donde dardé en atravesar esta montaña siete meses y al cabo de esta jornada di en una tierra alta y sin arboleda tan fria que no se podía sufrir. Y a la pasada de un puerto fue tanta la nieve que cayó sobre nosotros questuve en tiempo de perderme y no libré tan bien que no perdí mas de seiscientas anímimas de cristianos y gente de servicio, aunque los españoles no fueron muchos." The "six hundred Christian souls and helpers" is taken to include natives who had been baptized.
15 Alvarado to the Crown, 15 January 1535, in *Libro viejo* (1934, 299–300). His precise words run: "Tope la tierra mas aspera de sierras e ríos y ciénegas e de malezas y espesuras de montañas que ay en estas partes, ni creo que hay en el mundo por donde seguir mi viaxe, abriendo los caminos a espada y a manos, por espacio de más de ciento e sesenta leguas, en que tarde siete meses. En este tiempo, me adolecio mucha xente – la enfermdad era tan grave que a otro día que les dava la primera calentura, murian. Algunos que escapaban perdían el juicio y teniase tal aviso, que cada día se sabía el que caía enfermo, y con esto aunque murieron hasta ochenta hombres. A mi me dio tan rrecia enfermedad que al segundo día estobe desahuciado, y mas de diez días que me duró. Corrí mucho peligro de la vida. Todo mi viaxe fue sin saber parte cierta a donde estava. No havia camino para ir de un pueblo a otro, ni hablaran las lenguas unos de otros, ni ternian ninguno dellos noticia de cristianos que obiesen visto ni oydo. Asi seguí por esta tierra hasta dar en un Puerto adonde hizo tanta ventisca de nieve y granizo e tan grandes yelos e fríos, que se me elaron y murieron mas de nueve hombres e mujeres españoles, e casi todos los negros y otra gente de servicio que llevava – y algunos caballos. Fue tanta la tormenta e trabaxo que desto padecimos, que por salir presto de lugar tan trabaxoso e

peligroso, no obo hombre de nosotros que escapase bastimento ni rropa, ni oro ni plata ninguna. Ansi lo que se havia recoxido en aquellos pueblos, con lo demas que todos traíamos, lo dexé en el Puerto a quien lo quisiese tomar, que arto teníamos que salvarse cada uno. A cabsa de haber perdido los bastimentos, padecimos tan gran hambre que demas de la pasada no comimos sino palmitos cocidos. Si algun caballo se matava, valía la carne dél para comer entre nosotros en dos mil castellanos."

16 Cieza de León ([1553] 1998, 336). See also Herrera ([1615] 1728, 140).

17 Cieza de León ([1553] 1998, 336).

18 Alvarado to the Crown, 12 May 1535, in *Libro viejo* (1934, 300). The words that must have stuck in his throat before being penned are "vio huellas de cavallos rrecien hechas." See also Herrera ([1615] 1728, 140–1).

CHAPTER THIRTEEN

1 It did not take Alvarado long to figure out whose horses must have left the hoofprints. It was months after the fact, however, before he recorded their identity. Writing to the Crown on 12 May 1535 – see *Libro viejo* (1934, 300) – he states: "Supe como eran del Mariscal Almagro, que havia pocos días que era venido con alguna gente a aquella poblacion que se llamava Quito, que estava dos jornadas de alli – I knew they belonged to Mariscal Almagro's people, who had come through here from Quito, a town two days' journey away." Since men affiliated with Belalcázar accompanied Almagro's followers, horses of both contingents would have made their mark on the highway.

2 Loor (1956, 216) is unable to ascribe a precise date for Belalcázar having been sent to San Miguel to serve as lieutenant governor but reckons that it was well before Alvarado's intrusion, "entre julio y noviembre de 1533 – between July and November 1533."

3 Cieza de León ([1553] 1998, 269). According to Cieza, the expedition's conscripts numbered a mere "140 Spaniards, footmen and horsemen," who surely anticipated that fierce opposition awaited them. "Everyone from those regions was distressed when they learned of Atahualpa's death," he states, "and they marveled how, being so few, the Spaniards could defeat so many and capture such a powerful prince. To the last person they all decided to defend the land, not consenting that the Spaniards become masters of it." Loor (1956, 218) puts Belalcázar's Spanish contingent at

"270 hombres, de los cuales setenta eran de a caballo – 270 men, seventy of them horsemen."

4 Hemming ([1970] 1972, 151–68) remains our best account of the Quitan campaign, one engagement of which – at Teocajas on 3 May 1534 – constituted "the greatest pitched battle of the Conquest." Indigenous combatants are estimated by Oviedo to have numbered 50,000, Hemming relates, and the outcome of confrontation was "indecisive – because the Quitans did not stop Benalcázar's [Belalcázar's] invasion and the Spaniards did not destroy the defenders' army." While he laments that the campaign "has received little attention" because of "inadequate records" and "the lack of a chronicler," Hemming's reconstruction of it is most commendable. "The gallant efforts of the native troops, the finest hour of the Inca army," may not be "as well known as they deserve to be," but thanks to Hemming they increasingly are. So, too, the discovery of "a missing work by Pedro Cieza de León," which came to light after Hemming's investigations, has advanced our knowledge considerably. Perusal of it – see especially Cieza de León ([1553] 1998, 268–84, 322–30, and 338–49) – reveals hitherto unknown details of how the Quitan campaign, period by period, place by place, unfolded. See also Loor (1956, 215–44) for further meticulous reconstruction of Belalcázar's campaigns.

5 Cieza de León ([1553] 1998, 329). Cayambe lies sixty kilometres northeast of Quito, forty kilometres southeast of Otavalo. Of Belalcázar's fruitless search for the treasure of Quito, Cieza (323) states: "Belalcázar earnestly asked the Indians whom they met where the treasure of Quito was. They answered, as if astonished, that they knew no more than that Rumiñahui had taken it and that not one of those who carried the loads away was alive because it is rumored that he killed them all to prevent them from revealing where so much wealth had been placed. Although many were asked, none had a different explanation. The Spaniards became dejected and full of melancholy because in order to come on this expedition they had spent and suffered a great deal. They felt enormous hatred for Rumiñahui, about whom news arrived that he was entrenched a little more than three leagues from Quito." Earlier in his chronicle, Cieza (269–70) writes: "It is commonly known that Rumiñahui and other chiefs and priests took more than six hundred *cargas* [loads] of gold that they had collected from the sacred temples of the Sun and that at the time was in the palaces of the Incas. They took it to a lake, according to what some say, and threw it into its deepest part. According to what others say, they buried it in great crags among heaps of snow."

6 Cieza de León ([1553] 1998, 338). He alleges (329) with conspiratorial innuendo: "There were those who were disgruntled with Belalcázar and who, in order to make Almagro even more inflamed against him, declared that he was a rebel and was intending to join Alvarado."

7 Cieza de León ([1553] 1998, 338). See also González Suárez (n.d., 112–13) and Hemming ([1970] 1972, 163).

8 Almagro to the Crown, 12 October 1534, in Medina (1889, 247). His precise words are: "Envié ocho de caballo con una carta mia para que supiesen quien era, é me ofrecía de lo favorecer é ayudar en todo lo que pudiese."

9 González Suárez (n.d., 113).

10 Cieza de León ([1553] 1998, 339). He adds that the Adelantado "gave them some ornaments and jewels from those that had been saved from the snow." See also González Suárez (n.d., 125).

11 Cieza de León ([1553] 1998, 341). "The scouts arrived with these letters," Cieza continues, "and they told the Marshal [Almagro] about the benevolence of the Adelantado and how he had honored them and treated them in a friendly manner. He did not intend to offend or to cause dissension or any scandals, and he would come to Riobamba, where they could discuss honest conditions that would be to the advantage of everyone."

CHAPTER FOURTEEN

1 Sicalpa lies some twenty kilometres west of present-day Riobamba.

2 See the *Libro primero de cabildos de Quito* (hereafter LPCQ). In the LCPQ (1934, 25–9), Gonzalo Farfán and Diego de Tapia are listed as *alcaldes* (a mayor or magistrate) and eight others as *regidores*, aldermen or councillors – Martín Alonso de Angulo, Cristóbal de Ayala, Hernando de Gamarra, Fernando Gallego, Cristóbal Orejón, Lope Ortíz, Hernando de Prado, and Marcos Varela. Almagro's name was signed for him by one Blas de Atiença. Pizarro too – see Lockhart (1972, 277) – was illiterate.

3 LPCQ (1934, 30–5). See also Hemming ([1970] 1972, 164 and 569n164).

4 LPCQ (1934, 36–7). The minutes read: "Es consta de los daños e escándalos que con su benyda e estadía en esta tierra a cavsado el adelantado don Pedro de Alvarado – trae e como a dicho e publicado que a de atravesar e andar por toda esta gouernaçion contra voluntad de la justiçia della. Pide [Almagro] a los dichos señores justiçia e rregidores le den su paresçer de lo que se deve hazer por que mejor se açierte lo que conbyene al seruicio de su magestad e byen desta tierra e que si sera byen estorvalle e rresestille

que no pase ny ande por esta dicha gouernaçion para excusar los daños que a hecho e podia hazer andando por ella. O sy le dexara pasar e se yra delante con alguna gente dexando poblada esta cibdad como agora esta o después del pasado y que gente de pie y de a caballo sera bien que quede en esta dicha cibdad para la guarda e sutentaçion e buen recabdo della."

5 Diego de Tapia to the city council of Santiago de Quito, 19 August 1534, in LPCQ (1934, 37–8). Tapia's words are recorded in the *cabildo* minutes as follows: "El dicho señor mariscal no debe yrse desta probynçia syno estarse en ella con la gente que al presente tiene por que si se fuese o dexaje la dicha gente el dicho Alvarado con el poder que trae de gente podrya venyr a esta çibdad e hallandola desmanparada del dicho señor mariscal podrya estarse en ella y en toda la tierra synque nadie le pudiese yr a la mano. E demas desto es notorio que mucha parte de la gente quel dicho Alvarado al presente tiene esta muy descontenta del e an dicho e publicado que en byendo lugar e tiempo muchos dellos se bendryan a esta dicha cibdad donde el dicho señor mariscal esta. Y con los muchos amygos naturales de la tierra el dicho señor mariscal en nombre se su magestad puede defender el paso al dicho Alvarado e mandalle lo que byere que conbyene al servyçio de su magestad e byen destas partes."

6 Gonzalo Farfán to the city council of Santiago de Quito, 19 August 1534, in LPCQ (1964, 39). Farfán's words are recorded in the *cabildo* minutes thus: "Dixo que le paresçe quel dicho señor mariscal debe yrse delante y rrecojer la gente questa en san myguel para con ella dar la buelta al camyno a donde quyera que topare al dicho Alvarado para le defender e rresystyr que no haga daño en la tierra por que si fuese delante podrya recoger la jente e rehazerce e quytar e hebytar que no bynyese al dicho Alvarado nyngun socoroo de jente ansy por puerto byejo como por otra parte."

7 Cristóbal de Ayala, Martín Alonso de Angulo, Hernando de Gamarra, Lope Ortíz, Hernando de Prado, and Marcos Varela to the city council of Santiago de Quito, 19 August 1534, in LPCQ (1934, 40).

8 Cieza de León ([1553] 1998, 341–2).

9 Cieza de León ([1553] 1998, 343). Felipillo – see Jijón y Camaaño (1936, vol. 1, 92) – was one of the youngsters apprehended by the pilot Ruiz when he seized the native raft off the Manabí coast some eight years before, his Spanish-language skills by now highly developed and equally prized. In his arresting novel about the conquest of Peru, *The Gold Eaters*, Ronald

Wright (2015) leans on the real-life Felipillo to create the fictional Waman, through whose eyes events unfold and the story is told.

10 Molina ([1986] 2004, 212). "Even though he was in Alvarado's service and named as his retainer," Cieza de León ([1553] 1998, 343) reveals, Picado "went to Riobamba [Santiago de Quito] as surreptitiously as he could and appeared before Almagro, offering himself into his service." Upon learning of Picado's defection, "the Adelantado became furious, threatening to kill him if he caught him." Picado went on to become – see Hemming ([1970] 1972, 254), Lockhart (1972, 277), and Varón Gabai (1997, 78) – the influential secretary of Pizarro.

11 Cieza de León ([1553] 1998, 343–4).

12 Alvarado to the Crown, 12 May 1535, as excerpted from the translation by Kelly (1932, 255–6). The Adelantado's more extensive exposition in the original – see *Libro viejo* (1934, 300–1) – runs: "El rrecebió mis cartas y me respondió a ellas [pero] con los mensaxeros que imbió, escribió cartas secretas de creencia y de muchas ofertas e prometimientos a los prencipales e otras gentes que conmigo venían – para que me dexasen y se fuesen a él. Y como veníamos todos tan fatigados e perdidos de los trabaxos pasados, y veían el provecho e las ofertas, hizo tanto fruto en mi gente estas cartas e ofrecimientos, que se alborotaron muchos. Y aún alguno hobo, que sin mas cirtinidad, se salieron escondidamente de mi rreal, para irse con él. En ese medio tiempo, él se dió tal maña, que por su persona y por otros muchos a quien lo él lo encomendó, durante la platica de los conciertos que truxo a su propósito a toda mi gente, con dádivas e ofertas que fablados unos a otros si yo quisiera partir a mi conquista, no hallaria treinta hombres que me siguiera, de mas de ciento e cinquenta de a caballo, e doscientos e cinquenta peones que llo llevaba. Determiné de irme a ver con Almagro, al qual segun me pareció, allé con algun temor e muy recatado de mi, e yo le aseguré que mi venida no hera para perjudicar en cosa nenguna a la Governacion y tierra que pertenecía a Pizarro, sino que iba en seguimiento de la Capitulación que con Vuestra Magestad yo hize."

13 Cieza de León ([1553] 1998, 344–6). He adds: "The Marshal always spoke to those who were with him so that if the Adelantado tried anything, they would be informed. He assured them that if things reached such a pass, he had the word of many of Alvarado's men that they would cross over to him."

14 Cieza de León ([1553] 1998, 346).

15 López de Gómara ([1552] 1991, 188) singles out Caldera, but Wagner (1934, 194–8) presents compelling evidence that favours Fray Marcos. He translates a deposition made by the friar in Santiago de Guatemala on 25 September 1536, culled from a document formerly housed in the AGI as Patronato 2–2–1. In response to being asked if Alvarado, "on reaching the province of Quito, sent to Marshal Diego de Almagro certain messengers," Fray Marcos replied "that he himself was [one of] the messengers." On 26 August he left camp "at daybreak in the morning," a page accompanying him and the Adelantado "to go and discuss with the Marshal as he had sent to tell him." Dated not 25 but 26 September 1536, the testimony of Fray Marcos in this key regard is also featured in Martín Blasco's transcription of Alvarado's *residencia* (Vallejo-García Hevia 2008, vol. 2, 869). For verification, see Clemence, *Harkness Collection* (1936, 219), who notes, however, that only after previous messengers "had returned unsuccessful" was Fray Marcos called upon. In the same vein, Hemming ([1970] 1972, 569–70n167) cautions that "not everything Niza wrote should be believed," echoing the assessment of Sauer (see chapter 8, note 24). Hemming reinforces his point by observing that Velasco ([1789] 1841) "frequently cited a chronicle by Niza," of which Porras Barrenechea (1949/50, 197–202) concluded that "no such work ever existed."

16 Cieza de León ([1553] 1998, 346–7).

17 Cieza de León ([1553] 1998, 347–8). Picado may have been pardoned by Alvarado, but he chose to remain in Almagro's camp: after his defection, he served his new patron faithfully, until his secretarial skills caught the eye of Pizarro. Felipillo was not so lucky. Almagro's pardon – see Hemming ([1970] 1972, 82) – proved not to be long-lasting: "the chief interpreter, an ingratiating youth, [was] garrotted for treachery" in Chile in 1536, by order of the Mariscal.

18 Cieza de León ([1553] 1998, 354). Alvarado's daughter, Leonor, born in Guatemala on 22 March 1524 – see Lovell, Lutz, and Kramer (2020, 19) – would have been ten years of age at the time of her proposed marriage. She and her mother, the Tlaxcalan princess Luisa Xicoténcatl, had survived the ordeal of crossing the Andes along with Alvarado. Almagro's son, Diego, would have been in his mid-teens, Clemence (*Harkness Collection* 1936, viii) recording him "as a twenty-two year old" in 1541, when supporters of Almagro assassinated Pizarro. He may, however, have been older than

that, Clemence (*Harkness Collection* 1936, x) also stating that Diego, "the child of an Indian woman of Panama, was but a youth of twenty-four" when Hernando Pizarro executed his father in Cuzco on 8 July 1538.

19 Cieza de León ([1553] 1998, 354). He adds: "What happened was that before the Adelantado and the Marshal had concluded an agreement, they say that Alvarado tried to form a partnership with Pizarro and Almagro in which he would not receive any money, but would leave with certain stipulations that he asked for. Almagro was not involved in any of this, replying that so many partners could not have peace." The Mariscal's conviction was shared by Juan Morgovejo de Quiñones, a loyal associate of Pizarro's who received a handsome cut of Cajamarca spoils. He is said to have warned Pizarro "that he should be aware and look out for himself because the Adelantado and Almagro had come to an agreement to divest him of the governance and even his life, and that the two of them had made a partnership. Pizarro was disturbed by such talk, although he did not entirely believe it."

20 Jijón y Camaaño (1936, 45), his precise words being "así el verdadero rival de Alvarado era Almagro."

CHAPTER FIFTEEN

1 Clemence, *Harkness Collection* (1932, 17).

2 As rendered from the Spanish original, dated 26 August 1534, by Clemence, *Harkness Collection* (1936, 13).

3 As rendered from the Spanish original, dated 26 August 1534, by Clemence, *Harkness Collection* (1936, 13–17).

4 Clemence, *Harkness Collection* (1936, 15 and 17). A full transcription of the original contract may be consulted in *Revista Peruana* (1880, vol. 4, 196–8), and *Libro viejo* (1934, 293–4). Kelly (1932, 266–7) also renders into English the Spanish original, his translation noting that Domingo de la Presa, "Royal Scribe and Notary Public, empowered to practise in the Court and all portions of the Realm," was also present as both witness and signatory "in testimony of the truth of the matter."

5 Dated 25 September 1536, the testimony of Fray Marcos is from a translation made by Wagner (1934, 197–8) of "an investigation in Guatemala by which Alvarado hoped to escape blame for [his] expedition to Peru."

6 Alvarado to the Crown, 12 May 1535, as rendered by Kelly (1932, 256). The actual words of the Adelantado may be consulted in *Libro viejo* (1934, 301).

In the Spanish original they run: "Quando vio questo estaba desta manera no quiso complir conmigo nenguna cosa de lo Capitulado, yo le moví otros muchos partidos harto en mi perjuicio e provecho suyo. Y a mas que no me salió, hasta que sin poder hacer otra cosa, yo le vendí todos mis navios con todo lo que en ello traía; y mis esclavos y caballos e aderezos de mi persona y casa, en cien mil pesos, que segun el valor de las cosas allí valían, aun por penas me pagó lo demas de los navios que le di. Y esto hize por no quedar del todo perdido – todos los navios con las armas e artilleria e xarcias que llevaban con los socorros que hize a la gente, me costaron harto mas en esta tierra." Varón Gabai (1997, 23–4) sums up thus: "Almagro's negotiating ability proved victorious. First he encouraged desertion among Alvarado's troops and incorporated them into his. Then, with Alvarado weakened, Almagro bought the complete expedition, as well as the privileges received from the emperor for the 'discovery and conquest of the South Seas.' It is quite clear that Alvarado was pressured by the events, and for this reason he would later claim that Almagro had deceived him into accepting the sale."

7 Alvarado to the Crown, 15 January 1535, *Libro viejo* (1934, 295–6). His precise words are: "Me embió a decir que le vendiese mi armada y que me daria por ella cien mill pesos. Yo le respondí que pues havia tomado lo uno, tomase lo otro, que bien conocia la fuerza que se me hacia contra mi voluntad." A fortnight earlier, on 1 January, Alvarado expressed quite contrary sentiments – that Pizarro and Almagro "had delivered and paid the hundred thousand pesos of good gold, each peso minted and marked with a value of four hundred and fifty maravedís, for which I feel most pleased and properly paid, in accordance with my will." Taken from AGI, Patronato 254, Ramo 3, 1, Alvarado's words in the original run: "[L]os anotados Gobernador y Mariscal me han entregado y pagado los anotadoscien mil pesos de buen oro fundido y marcado de un valor de cuatrocientos cincuenta maravedís cada peso en oro y plata, de que me siento muy contento y pagado, de acuerdo a mi voluntad."

8 Almagro to the Crown, 12 October 1534, in Medina (1889, 249). His precise words are: "Sin tener necesidad sino por tener paz le compré seis navios que tenia en la Mar del Sur por cient mill castellanos, que no valian ni pueden valer mas de hasta veinte é cinco ó treinta mill castellanos." Lockhart (1968, 116) reckons that "a large galleon, when new, was worth 6,000 to 8,000 pesos, ordinary ships most often between 1,000 and 2,500

pesos. Boats and frigates brought only about 500 pesos, hardly the price of a good [Black] slave."

9 Cieza de León ([1553] 1998, 348). Molina ([1986] 2004, 220) words the resentment thus: "Alvarado's own men wanted nothing more to do with him, calling him 'Judas' for having abandoned so many ambitious captains and esteemed gentlemen – su propria gente no lo quería y lo llamaba 'Judas' por haber dejado sin cargos a tantos hidalgos y capitanes ambiciosos."

10 Cieza de León ([1553] 1998, 348–51). Almagro entrusted Diego de Agüero as his chief envoy. Representatives of Alvarado accompanied him on the trek south to inform Pizarro of the deal, foremost among them Luis de Moscoso. Given the threats and dangers that lurked while on Inca highways, Agüero and Moscoso presumably counted on being led by well-armed "indios amigos" as well as having in their midst some fellow Spaniards equally well armed.

CHAPTER SIXTEEN

1 Molina ([1986] 2004, 215). His estimate of approximately "trescientas leguas de camino desde Riobamba a Jauja" is made in reference to his citing a document in the AGI, "Probanza sobre la vida de [Pedro de] Alvarado [en el] Perú," written in Santiago de Guatemala in 1536. The Spanish league (*legua*) was a variable unit but officially measured 4.2 kilometres until its abolition by Philip II in 1568. Three hundred leagues would therefore have been roughly 1,260 kilometres. Had Almagro and Alvarado met with Pizarro in Jauja, as originally planned, they likely would have taken the Andean highway of the Incas all the way. Pizarro's decision to beckon them to Pachacamac meant that the second leg of their journey, from San Miguel on, saw the two venture along the coastal road. A map of the "Royal Road of the Incas" may be consulted in Von Hagen's edition of Cieza de León ([1553] 1959, xxxii–xxxiii). In an engaging travelogue, Von Hagen (1955) explores the road network on foot and muleback, and also from the air, threading into his narrative archaeological and historical data that impart a sense of what it must have been like when Almagro and Alvarado were on the road in 1534.

2 Hemming ([1970] 1972, 164) and Molina ([1986] 2004, 217–19), the latter citing a document in AGI, Patronato 185, Ramo 9. For the "Fundaçion de la Villa de Sant Françisco del Quito" on 28 August 1534, including the "Nombramiento de Alcaldes y Regidores," see the minutes of city council in

LPCQ (1964, 45–8). Cieza de León ([1553] 1998, 354–5) writes: "The Marshal believed that because Belalcázar had succeeded in the past, it would be just to leave him in command as lieutenant-captain of that land. Further, because the city of Riobamba was not in a good district, it should be abandoned and established in Quito. Thus, many of those who had come from Guatemala stayed and remained with Belalcázar, and he founded a city in Quito." The *cabildo* minutes make it clear that the decision to found the Villa de San Francisco, named in honour of Governor Pizarro, was taken in the "Çibdad [city] de Santiago," which was never entirely abandoned. Given that "the land has only recently been conquered and pacified," founding elsewhere a seat of authority considered "better to serve the Crown, the conversion of the Indians, and the good of Spanish residents and inhabitants" made practical sense – "quel dicho pueblo se debe mudar a otra parte que al presente a cabsa de ser la tyerra nuevamente conquystada e andar acabandola de paçificar no se a visto ny thiene espiryençia de los sytios donde myjor pueda estar el dicho pueblo en lo que toca al serviçio de su magestad e a la conversyon de los naturales e pro de los vezinos e moradores que en la dicha çibdad se aveçinda." According to Lane (2002, 19), Quito was "renamed in honor of St. Francis," not Pizarro.

3 For a listing of *vecinos* who were among the first residents the Villa de San Francisco, 207 men in all, see LPCQ (1964, 49–57). A "Pedro de Alvarado" appears on the register, but he is not the Adelantado.

4 Hemming ([1970] 1972, 164–8). Quizquiz was killed by dissidents in his own ranks weary of fighting and in favour of seeking a peace accord with the Spaniards. Rumiñahui also "attempted to assemble forces to continue the war, but all were exhausted and wished only to live in peace. In the end someone told Benalcázar [Belalcázar] where he was to be found." The Inca commander was apprehended as he sought to cross "a snow-covered mountain between Panzaleo and Umbicho," doing so in the hope of reaching the hideout of fellow combatant Zope-Zopahua, "fortified in a crag on his hilltop in the Sicchos, probably to the north of Muliambato." After his capture Rumiñahui endured relentless torture but never disclosed the location of the Inca treasure removed from Quito before the arrival of the Spaniards. He was executed in the main square of Quito, burned alive – as was Zope-Zopahua.

5 After escorting Alvarado to San Miguel, Almagro is recorded as having addressed the Crown on two occasions, first on 12 October 1534 (Medina

1889, 244–306) and then on 15 October 1534 (Medina 1889, 306–12). "The city of San Miguel was founded and built," Cieza de León ([1553] 1959, 302) states, "where two or three rivers come together, which is why the valley is so broad. At first it was located on the site known as Tangarara, from which it was moved, because the location was unhealthy to where it is now situated, between two level valleys that are cool and full of shady groves near the city." On the founding of San Miguel, see also Lockhart (1972, 9nn14–15).

6 López de Gómera ([1552] 1991, 190), the chronicler's precise words being that Almagro "hizo grandes dádivas y socorros en dineros, armas y caballos a los suyos y a los de Alvarado" and that "despachó Alvarado a García Holguín a Puerto Viejo a entregar los navíos de su flota a Diego de Mora, capitán de Almagro."

7 López de Gómera ([1552] 1991, 188), the chronicler's precise words being that Alvarado "dejó muchos de su compañía a poblar en Quito con Benalcázar [Belalcázar], y llevó consigo los más y mejores. Benalcázar [Belalcázar] pasó mucho trabajo en su conquista, así por ser la gente muy guerrera."

8 Almagro to the Crown, 12 October 1534, in Medina (1889, 244–306). See chapter 10, note 5 et seq. for incriminating disclosures.

9 Molina ([1986] 2004, 220–3).

10 Cook and Cook, who correct Cieza de León ([1553] 1998, 358 and 359n12) for designating 1534 as the year Lima was founded. Hemming ([1970] 1972, 148–9) writes: "It seemed illogical for the Spanish capital to be so remote from the sea. Pizarro decided to move his capital to the coast, to a climate and altitude more congenial to Spaniards, and to a place where he could never be separated from his maritime lines of communication."

11 Cieza de León ([1553] 1998, 355–6). "When they met," he adds with perhaps too much effusion, "Pizarro and the Adelantado and the Marshal embraced, and the Governor warmly received all the knights who came with them. They went to take up quarters in the lodgings of Pachacamac, where they enjoyed and delighted in being with each other." Cieza ([1553] 1959, 319 and 323–4) puts the distance between San Miguel and the city of Trujillo at "some sixty leagues" and between Trujillo and Lima at "eighty leagues," with "the whole road running through sand and valleys." Named after Pizarro's birthplace in Spain, Trujillo "was founded in the valley of Chimú close to a sizable, beautiful river. It is considered healthy and surrounded on all sides by farms, so it may be said that the Spaniards who live in this city

are supplied with everything, given the abundance of things. And there is no lack of fish, for the sea is only half a league off." Hemming ([1970] 1972, 174) does not align with Cieza regarding how Almagro and Alvarado met up with Pizarro. "In December 1534," he writes, "Almagro sailed down to Pachacamac to ratify his agreement disposing of Alvarado. Pizarro was delighted with the outcome."

12 Cieza de León ([1553] 1998, 356).

13 Alvarado to the Crown, 20 November 1535, in *Libro viejo* (1934, 317), his precise words being: "[Y]o jugué con el Mariscal Almagro e me ganó trece mil e quinientos pesos, en pago de los quales le di ciertos negros e caballos e yeguas e bestidos e aderezos de caza que se tasaron e balian mucha mas cantidad."

14 Alvarado to the Crown, 20 November 1535, in *Libro viejo* (1934, 317), his precise words being: "[Y]ansi mesmo el Adelantado [*sic*] Pizarro me quedó con una rropa de martas, que valia dos mil ducados, sin me pagar cosa neguna por ella."

15 Cieza de León ([1553] 1998, 357).

16 Pizarro to the Crown, 1 January 1535, in Levillier (1921, 5). Penned by a scribe at Pachacamac, the governor's words in the original run: "Bino Alvarado y el Mariscal en mucha conformidad a esta provincia de Pachacamac a verse comigo do rrecibio sus dineros y lo despache con toda brevedad. He ávido mucha alegria en se aver cossa que tanta rrebuelta y alteración – a avia puesto en este rreyno acabado sin muerte ni daño de españoles y con tanta paz. Pareciόle al Mariscal que con cobdigia de dineros podia ganar con el la quietud que el deseava que oviese en la tierra." The "jewels and very valuable stones" that Cieza de León ([1553] 1998, 357) mentions are identified by Clemence (*Harkness Collection*, 1936, 218n5) as "gifts of emeralds, turquoises, and gold and silver vessels."

17 Alvarado to the Crown, 12 May 1535, in *Libro viejo* (1934, 302), the Adelantado's precise words being: "[Y] aun quitandome della de lo que conmigo se contrató, para reacerme y saber de Vuestra Magestad lo que era servido que yo hiziese."

18 Alvarado to the Crown, 12 May 1535, in *Libro viejo* (1934, 313), the Adelantado's precise words being: "Sobre todas las malas obras e agravios que yo recebi del adelantado [*sic*] Pizarro e del Mariscal Almagro [fue] un muy grande engaño: que toda la paga que se me hizo de mis navíos e otras cosas fue en planchas de plata que hizieron de xoyas e baxilla del

Perú. Y al tiempo que las fundían para hacerlas planchas, rrevolvieron con ellas tanto cobre en pedazos, que donde pensé que traya plata, era la mas parte cobre – por manera que yo perdi por este engaño casi la mitad delo que pensé que traía."

CHAPTER SEVENTEEN

1 See Levillier (1921, 5), Pizarro's exact words recorded thus: "Lo despache con toda brevedad y lo enbie a su governacion de Guatemala porque asy me pareció que convenia al serviçio de Vuestra Magestad." The undated "Relación del viaje al Perú de Pedro de Alvarado" (AGI, Patronato 192-1-11) summarizes the entire affair, from word first reaching Pizarro of Alvarado's Peruvian intentions to the governor paying him off and dispatching him back to Guatemala.

2 Velasco ([1789] 1841, 44), his precise words being that Alvarado "partió cuando más tarde al mismo comenzar el 1535." Seldom acclaimed, indeed often reviled, for not citing his sources, the Jesuit father on this occasion attributes his information "to the foremost authority on the matter, [López de] Gómara, who heard it from Alvarado himself – el que mejor escribe este punto es Gómara, quien asegura, por relación verbal del mismo Alvarado."

3 "El gobernador de Guatemala reembarcó hacia América Central el 5 de enero," Lavallé ([2003] 2007, 208) writes, not citing a specific source: "[D]esde un fondeadero en aguas profundas descubierto poco tiempo antes, ligeramente más al norte, y que se bautizó El Callao." A letter that Alvarado wrote from the "Puerto de Lima, çerca de Pachacama" – see chapter 9, note 3 – is dated 4 January 1535.

4 Alvarado to the Crown, 15 January 1535, in *Libro viejo* (1934, 294–6). "Knowing that Alvarado's ships, now under the command of Diego de Moya, were in San Miguel," López de Gómara ([1552] 1991, 190) states, "Pizarro gave the Adelantado all sorts of other things and let him go free – dio otras muchas cosas y lo dejó ir libremente, como supo estar las naos en San Miguel y en poder de Diego de Mora."

5 Alvarado to the Crown, 12 May 1535, in *Libro viejo* (1934, 304). At the start of this missive, the Adelantado states that he was in "the port of Peru" about to board ship for Guatemala "some two months ago." His precise words are: "Estando en el Puerto del Perú para embarcarme para esta Governación, puede haber dos meses."

6 Writing to Alvarado on 9 July 1536 – see *Libro viejo* (1934, 310–12) – Pizarro informs him that "the Inca [Manco Inca Yupanqui] has risen in rebellion and stirred up the land, Spaniards have been killed, Cuzco is under siege, and if no assistance is given, all will be lost. We are few in number, have little weaponry, and the Indians are audacious and daring." Pizarro's plea to Alvarado – come back, your past indiscretions are forgiven – in the original runs: "Se rebeló el Inga e levantó la tierra, e me ha muerto ciertos cristianos y tiene cercada la ciudad del Cuzco. Si no somos socorridos nos perderemos todos, porque somos pocos e tenemos pocas armas e los indios estan atrevidos." Borah (1954, 11–13) notes Pizarro's "desperate appeals" to others besides Alvarado, including Cortés, who "loaded two ships with all the food, men, and arms that he could assemble in haste" and dispatched them from Acapulco to Piura under the command of Hernando de Grijalva. Alvarado chose not to do likewise. Cuzco was eventually relieved by Almagro upon his return to Peru from an expedition to conquer Chile. His entering the city on 18 April 1537 coincided with his deposing two of Pizarro's brothers, Hernando and Gonzalo, from surrogate governance, marking what Hemming ([1970] 1972, 228) identifies as "the moment when the Spaniards were falling into civil war." Fifteen months later, on 8 July 1538, Hernando Pizarro had Almagro garrotted. Three years after that, on 26 July 1541, supporters of Almagro murdered Francisco Pizarro.

7 Alvarado to the Crown, 12 May 1535, in *Libro viejo* (1934, 302). The Adelantado's precise words are: "Di orden en volverme a esta Governación con la paga de mis navios. De concierto se me dió un navío de los que yo le vendí, para que viniese en él, y no permitieron que y viniese a tomar puerto a Panamá, porque sabian que yo iba con intención de ir luego a besar las Reales Manos de Vuestra Magestad, y a pedir se me hiziese xusticia y fuesen castigados los que tantos desservícios hizíeron a Vuestra Magestad y a mi tantos agravios y descomedimientos. Antes dixeron que no me darian pasaxe sino para algun puerto desta Governación, y de secreto mandaron que me dexasen en la Provincia de León de Nicaragua – sin consentir que viniese conmigo nengun español de los que yo llevé y se querían venir conmigo, a fin de que yo no podiese en parte donde hobiese xusticia hacer provanza de lo que conmigo hizieron." Pizarro's rationale for ordering the captain of the ship to sail directly to Nicaragua

was to prevent Alvarado from deboarding in Panama and making his way from there to Spain.

8 Lockhart (1972, 362–5) has a cameo of Trujillo as one of Pizarro's "Men of Cajamarca," placing him in the social group designated "Marginal Hidalgos and Commoners." After escorting "the disgruntled Pedro de Alvarado back to Guatemala," Trujillo headed to Spain with his Cajamarca spoils, as a footman receiving a three-quarter share of gold and a seven-eighth share of silver. He stayed for ten years in his namesake place of birth before deciding that Cuzco, not Trujillo, was the better long-term prospect, returning to Peru around 1546.

9 Cieza de León ([1553] 1998, 357).

10 See the testimony of Gonzalo Ortiz, "Provanza del Adelantado D. Pedro de Alvarado y doña Leonor de Alvarado su hija" ([1563] 1937, 479), his precise words being: "[C]uando el Adelantado volvió del Perú traia consigo a la Doña Luisa y la Doña Leonor." An undated sixteenth-century document transcribed by Medina (1889, 198–202) while working at the Archivo General de Indias simply states that, after going to Pachacamac with Almagro to receive his payment of 100,000 castellanos, Alvarado "boarded ship with his servants and left for Nicaragua – el Adelantado y Almagro se fueron á la provincia de Pachacama, donde hallaran al marques don Francisco Pizarro, é le dieron los dichos cient mill castellanos al Adelantado, y ansy recebidos, se embarcó é se fue con sus criados en su navio a Nicaragua."

11 *Libro Segundo del Cabildo*, folio 79 recto, in Kramer et al. (2018, 139), the minutes reading: "[Q]ue ninguna persona pueda vender cosa ninguna a mas preçios de los que fueron puestos – that no person can sell any item for more than the stipulated price."

12 Alvarado to the Crown, 12 May 1535, in *Libro viejo* (1934, 304–5). The Adelantado's precise words are: "Escrebí a Vuestra Magestad cómo en llegando a esta Gobernacion de Guatymala, daría orden con toda brevedad, de partirme para esos Reynos a besar las Manos de Vuestra Magestad y darle quenta mas entera de lo que me sucedió y a suplicarle se me hiziese xusticia de los agravios que se me hizieron en la tierra del Peru. Yo llegué a esta Cibdad de Santiago a veinte días deste mes de abril, y hallé los indios naturales della algo alterados, que avía pocos días que avían muerto ciertos españoles, de lo qual fueron castigados. Agora con mi

venida estan de mayor voluntad. Al Consexo e Xusticia e Regidóres desta Cibdad, y a los Oficiales de Vuestra Magestad, les ha parecido complir a su Real oficio que por agora no haga absencia desta Governacion; y aun me dan a entender que si de mi voluntad no lo hago, que me lo rrequeriran y lo imbiaran por quexa a Vuestra Magestad. Servicio me ha parescido y aun casi forzado suspender mi partida, hasta que Vuestra Magestad me mande imbiar licencia para que yo vaya a besar sus Reales Manos y a informarle de todo lo que en todo conviene. Y creo de mi ida allá, se seguirá tal fruto, que Vuestra Magestad se tenga por muy servido."

13 A letter written to the Crown by the *cabildo* of Santiago de Guatemala on 14 May 1535 (AGI, Guatemala 41) confirms Alvarado's arrival back. It also notes that the Adelantado's absence coincided five months ago with widespread turmoil, an uprising having occurred on account of Indian towns sensing no heavy hand present to subdue them. Alvarado's timely return would placate resident concerns and put troubled minds at ease, "especially if His Majesty were to hinder any future departure the Adelantado has planned until these disturbances have ceased. His Majesty, furthermore, will better be served by not permitting any more ships to leave this province to explore the Pacific, given the enormous costs and damages such ventures entail." The words of the city council in the original run: "[E]l adelantado volvio aqui por el mes de abril pasado y vino a tiempo a esta ciudad que ansi entre los indios de esta governaçion como entre los vezinos españoles avia algunos desasosiegos que causo su absençia, especialmente abra cinco meses que los mas pueblos desta governacion se alçaron sin mas causa de ver alguna flaqueza en la tierra. Vuestra Magestad sea servido de dilatar su partida hasta tanto que todos estos ynconvenientes çessen y esten mas asentados. [E] si demas de esto cumple al servicio de Vuestra Magestad que el vaya a essos reynos para platicar sobre algun descubrimiento de la mar del sur no permita que de esta provinçia salga mas armada ni navios pues no es tan grande para que muchas vezes se hagan armadas pues no son tan pocos los gastos y trabajos que continuandolo mucho se dexe de reçebir grande perjuicio."

14 Alvarado to the Crown, May 12, 1535, in *Libro viejo* (1934, 301). The Adelantado's precise words are: "Y alli se movieron antél y mi, ciertos partidos por terceras personas, y venimos en conduccion dellos, y los firmamos e otorgamos ante escribano. Quisiera tomar testimonios y de los rrequerimientos que le hize, y no consintió que se me diese, ni

que yo hiziese nengun abto por escrito, para que no podiese mostrar a Vuestra Magestad por escrituras, lo que conmigo hizo, que fue de tan mala disistion. Dexe de hacer lo que complia a mis negocios en el tiempo que podiera hacerlos muy a mi probecho, compliendo tambien con lo que devia al servicio de Vuestra Magestad, aunque no se hiziera sin daño de Almagro y de la gente que con él estava."

15 Alvarado to the Crown, 12 May 1535, in *Libro viejo* (1934, 303–4). The Adelantado's precise words are: "Yo supe que Almagro imbió a suplicar a Vuestra Magestad, le mande proveer de la Governacion de aquellas partes que yo iba a conquistar e poblar. Suplico a Vuestra Magestad, que pues lo que asta agora él a servido, ni la yspiriencia que tiene no es tan bastante. No sé la maña que se dará a ello, ni cómo saldrá con la empresa. Pero yo se dezir a Vuestra Magestad que con mi venida a aquellas partes se aseguró e apaziguó toda la tierra, que segun la poca gente de españoles de píe e de acaballo que tenian todos los que allí havia, estavan puestos en tal necesidad y la tierra tan levantada, que quería que perecieran todos. Con la gente que yo en ella metí, se aseguró todo. Y con la qual se a mudado, la condición a Almagro, de tal manera, que estimo que la llegada de Hernando Pizarro con los despachos que dís que tráe de Vuestra Magestad, no sea parte, para que entre ellos haya alguna gran discordia por donde se pierda todo."

16 Alvarado to the Crown, 12 May 1535, in *Libro viejo* (1934, 302). The Adelantado's precise words are: "En aquella playa donde desembarque, viendo que era imposible seguir mi derrota por la mucha fuerza de las corrientes y vientos contrarios que por allí siempre reinan, yo imbie dos navios de los que llevaba lo mejor abastecidos y bien aderezados que yo pode, para que costeasen toda la costa del Peru, para saber los Puertos délla, y por ver como se corria y adonde llegaba, sin perjudicar cosa nenguna de la Governacion de Pízarro. Y corrieron parte de la Costa; y quando llegavan a algun puerto o playa de la dicha Governación, no les consentian que tomasen puerto, ni les querian provéer por sus dineros de lo necesario. Imbiaban por parte de Pizarro a hablar al Maestre e marinero, e les davan oro y joyas, secretamente, para amontonarlos; y ansi con dádivas, me sacaron los marineros del un navio, y se fueron donde estava Pizarro y por cerca dellos, no pudo pasar adelante, antes se volvió a mucho rriesgo, por la poca gente de marear que traia. Y el otro navio paso adelante y surgió siete leguas adelante de Chincha, que era

la parte donde nengun otro navio hauia llegado; y entraron en él, gente de la Governación de Pizarro; e por su mandado y amenazándoles a los marineros, y a otros dándoles oro, nos sacaron el maestre con dádivas que le dieron, y tomaron la posesión dél, por Pizarro, con todo lo que en él imbiaba; y se alzaron con él; por manera que me fue forzado, yo vendello todo; y a esta cabsa se dexo de navegar e descobrir toda aquella Costa, hasta el Cabo."

17 Alvarado to the Crown, 12 May 1535, in *Libro viejo* (1934, 303). The Adelantado's precise words are: "Yo estoy satisfecho que Vuestra Magestad cree de mi persona, que tengo el deseo que debo a Vuestro Real Servicio y acrezentamiento de su Estado y asi pienso dará credito a lo que aquí digo, pues yo no fui parte ni se me consintio que yo tomase nengun testimonio, ni podiese facer otra provanza, para que mas satisfazirse a Vuestra Magestad; y para enmendar tan gran yerro como contra el Servicio de Vuestra Magestad ellos hizíeron; y para deshazer los agravios que me hizíeron y grandes quexas que yo dellos podría dar."

18 Alvarado to the Crown, May 12, 1535, in *Libro viejo* (1934, 303–4). The Adelantado's precise words are: "Habría hecho informaciones con testigos, de todo lo que habran querido e vieren que les comple, con personas que yo llevava, a quien por pleitos o desmerecimientos de sus personas yo abré castigado; pues nenguno podo ser tan xusto, que governando diversidad de gente no haya quien bien e mal le quiera, especialmente los prencipales, que por los intereses e dádivas me dexaron, culpandome a mi y descargando ansi a aquellos. Suplico a Vuestra Magestad, que considerando esto, no sea culpado sin ser oydo, porque yo espero de dar mis descargos, de tal manera, que con mucha xusticia, Vuestra Magestad los mande castigar por el daño que hizieron; y a mi, restituir lo que por fuerza me tomaron. Lo qual yo espero muy por entero de Vuestra Magestad, pues por solo lo que tocava a su Real Servicio, y por no dar lugar a escandalos que se podieran recrecer si yo quisiera poner en aventura la tierra, e perdido tanto de mi hacienda; y de lo que con servir a Vuestra Magestad yo esperaba ganar."

19 Alvarado to the Crown, 12 May 1535, in *Libro viejo* (1934, 306). The Adelantado's precise words are: "Quedé muy gastado y adebdado; del dinero que truxe quedé deviendo algunos dineros y podránme quedar agora en oro y en plata setenta mil ducados, los quales quería sostener ansi, xuntos, hasta ver lo que Vuestra Magestad es servido se haga."

20 Alvarado to the Crown, May 12, 1535, in *Libro viejo* (1934, 305). The Adelantado's precise words are: "Yo he pensado muchas veces como en esta Mar del Sur debe haber muchas islas y costa de Tierra-firme, de grandísimas riquezas y poblaciones. He mirado la mexor forma que para comenzar lo a hazer se debria tener, y fallo que comenzarlo por la vía que desde la Costa desta Nueva España e provincias délla se comienza, ser a muy gran rriesgo e sin nengun buen fruto por las corrientes contrarias e grandes, y por los vientos contrarios que en esta Mar rreynan. Como se ha visto por yspiriencia, ansi en rebezes, quel Marques de Valle [Cortés] ha imbiado navíos a descobrir, que con las grandes corrientes … no podieron los unos ni los otros correr la Mar adentro, los vientos que se les mandó, y forzados, se volvieron atrás." See Borah (1971) for an extended discussion of the maritime pursuits of Cortés in the Pacific.

21 Alvarado to the Crown, 12 May 1535, in *Libro viejo* (1934, 305–6). The Adelantado's precise words are: "Los flacos navios que en estas partes e costa se pueden hacer … no son tan durables como los de Castilla. Me parece para que este truxese otro muy mayor, haziendose en estos Reynos seis o siete naos gruesas … en que viniesen hasta setecientos hombres en ellas. Y que estas viniesen por el estrecho de Magallanes, hasta pasar en alguna Isla, o Tierra-firme de la otra Costa del Especieria … y que allí quedasen e imbiasen a esta Costa desta Nueva España e provincias, algunas de aquellas naos a hazer saber como estaban allí poblados. Y para en ellas que llevasen cantidad de caballos, pues para aquel tiempo los abrá en corta abundancia; y otros dos mil hombres para buscar todo lo demas que en esta Mar está por descobrir."

22 Alvarado to the Crown, 12 May 1535, in *Libro viejo* (1934, 306). The Adelantado's precise words are: "Y si Vuestra Magestad fuese servido de mandar entender en esto, y lo que digo paresciese allá, que va vien guiado, y viese que mi persona es bastante para ocuparme en la tal xornada, imbiandome a mandar Vuestra Magestad que yo vaya [con] licencia a esos Reynos, que como cosa que yo creo que tanto comple a vuestro Real Servicio, desde agora yo estoy aparexado para en viendo el mandamiento de Vuestra Magestad poner en obra mi partida; y quedará tan bien proveido lo que toca a esta Governacíón, que mi absencia no haga falta."

23 See Vallejo-García Hevia (2008) for full disclosure of Maldonado's findings and Alvarado's defence of his actions. There was little affinity between

the two men, Maldonado doing his best to rein in the worst of Alvarado's excesses, in the end to no avail.

24 Alvarado's positive reception by Emperor Charles V while in Spain, where he was from the latter part of 1536 to early 1539, is noted by Recinos (1952, 170), who also furnishes details about the construction and kitting out of the Adelantado's second armada, estimated by the chronicler Vázquez to have cost some 200,000 gold pesos.

25 According to Kelsey (1986, 77), Alvarado's fleet was made up of "thirteen ships and more than a thousand men, many of whom had come with him from Spain." For the role of Juan Rodríguez Cabrillo in building the vessels and, after the Adelantado's demise, piloting three of them on an exploration of the California coast, see Kramer (2019). Codding (2017, 256–8) grounds what Altman (2010, 147–51) considers Alvarado's "pointless death" in his analysis of the *Mapa de Tequaltiche* (1584), which vividly portrays the armed confrontation between Indigenous and Spanish forces that took the Adelantado's life.

CHAPTER EIGHTEEN

1 Busto Duthurburu (1986, vol. 1, 106–8). Gómez de Alvarado accompanied Almagro when the Mariscal left Cuzco on 3 July 1535 in an attempt to conquer Chile and lay claim to it, his expedition proving as fraught and fruitless as Pedro de Alvarado's invasion of Peru (Vega 2011). Gómez survived what for him was a second crossing of the treacherous, snowy Andes to return with Almagro to Cuzco by way of the Atacama Desert, an equally arduous and debilitating trek. This Gómez de Alvarado is not to be confused with a relative of the Adelantado's (Busto Duthurburu 1986, vol. 1, 108–9) with the same name, and yet another Gómez de Alvarado who may have been related to both. On 18 April 1537, with Gómez among the triumphant victors, Almagro wrested control of Cuzco from Hernando and Gonzalo Pizarro, who had been besieged there by Manco Inca for nine months. Almagro's seizure of the city initiated strife between Spaniards (Almagrists versus Pizarrists) that was to last almost two decades. Cieza de León ([1553] 1998, 381–7, 441–2, and 463–6) documents Almagro's travails in Chile with customary flair, translators Cook and Cook (473) embellishing his narrative with a helpful map. Hemming ([1970] 1972, 174–80 and 223–8) discusses the expedition most diligently, crediting Oviedo y Valdés ([1547/1557] 1959) for much of his data and insight.

2 Busto Duthurburu (1986, vol. 1, 102–3). Diego's poisoning is seen as an act of revenge for testimony he gave that led to the lengthy imprisonment of Hernando Pizarro for the execution of Almagro in Cuzco on 8 July 1538, after the Pizarrist victory at the Battle of Las Salinas two to three months before. This Diego de Alvarado, "El Bueno – the Good One," should not be mistaken for the identically named conquistador (Busto Duthurburu 1986, vol. 1, 103–4) called "El Malo – the Evil One," who served as *maestro de campo* (field commander) for the insurgent Francisco Hernández Girón.

3 Busto Duthurburu (1986, vol. 1, 101 and 113) and Vallejo García-Hevia (2008, vol. 2, 1267). For details of the dissident Francisco Hernández Girón, see Busto Duthurburu (1987, vol. 2, 246–52).

4 Busto Duthurburu (1986, vol. 1, 93–102), Cieza de León ([1553] 1959, 99–100), and Cieza de León ([1553] 1998, 398–405 and 423–6). See also Hemming ([1970] 1972, 236–8 and 247–8), who writes of Chachapoyas: "The area itself is remote, [lying] east of the great canyon of the Marañon and of the road to Quito. It is on the final open stretch of the Andean foothills: a few miles further east the suffocating Amazonian forest takes a firm grip on the land. The Incas added the area to their empire only under Huanya-Capac."

5 Cieza de León ([1553] 1998, 373–4), Hemming ([1970] 1972, 177), Vallejo García-Hevia (2008, vol. 2, 1295), and Weddle (2021). After Soto's death (21 May 1542) during his exploration of southern parts of what was to become the United States, Moscoso assumed command of the expedition and was responsible for it descending the Mississippi on seven crudely built brigantines. From the mouth of the Mississippi, some three hundred survivors of the six hundred or so who had started out in Florida in May 1539 skirted west along the coasts of Louisiana and Texas, reaching the Pánuco River and the northeast frontier of Mexico on 10 September 1543. Soto's is the name customarily associated with this marathon foray, not Moscoso. Like the better known Álvar Núñez Cabeza de Vaca, he was therefore a key player in remarkable feats of exploration (Bishop 1933) not only of North America but of South America as well.

6 In Peru, perhaps the most notable Alvarado of more recent times is General Juan Velasco Alvarado (1910–77), president of the country during a period of military dictatorship between 1968 and 1975. His nationalist agenda divided the country, as did his project of agrarian reform (Seligmann 1995, 56–76). In Ecuador, an Alvarado of renown is one Pío Jaramillo Alvarado (1884–1968). A lawyer, sociologist, politician, and public servant, he

authored several books, among them *La guerra de conquista en América* (1941), about Ecuador's territorial dispute with Peru. This Alvarado is best known, however, for his study of Ecuador's native peoples, *El indio ecuatoriano*, a title that first appeared in 1922 and was republished in a posthumous sixth edition in 1983.

7 López de Gómara ([1552] 1991, 190), his precise words being: "[F]uese Alvarado a Cuauhtemallán [Guatemala] casi solo, y quedaron en el Perú los suyos. Y que como eran nobles y valientes, y aun bravosos, llegaron a ser después muy principales en aquella tierra." Borah (1954, 10) agrees. "Virtually all of the men [Alvarado] took with him," he writes, "remained in Peru." See also Cieza de León ([1553] 1998, 348) and Hemming ([1970] 1972, 164). We should recall, too, the Adelantado's own assertion – see chapter 17, note 7 – that Pizarro did not allow "a single Spaniard of those who came with me" to return to Central America with him. While not entirely the case, the parameters of Alvarado's dismissal are clear.

8 Vega (2011) and Hemming ([1970] 1972, 177–80). "With the arrival of Alvarado's army from Quito," Hemming writes, "the conquerors felt securely in control. The newest arrivals, who had missed the great riches of the first conquistadores, were often the most brutal towards the natives. This was particularly true of Alvarado's men, who had shown such cruelty in the march towards Quito, and who were now on Almagro's Chilean expedition. The priest Cristóbal de Molina was on that expedition and recorded his disgust."

9 Cieza de León ([1553] 1998, 354–5) and Hemming ([1970] 1972, 164–8).

10 Cieza de León ([1553] 1998, 348–9 and 398n12) and Guerra (1951, 289).

11 For a discussion of these "relaciones de méritos y servicios," and the unabashed self-promotion that lay behind them, see MacLeod (1998). "Members of Francisco Pizarro's band present at the seizure of Atahualpa," he observes of the pecking order, "had earlier rights than those who accompanied Diego de Almagro, and they, in turn, had prior claims over the latecomers who arrived with Pedro de Alvarado."

12 Lockhart (1968, 15 and 124). "Though illiterate and known to be of very humble birth," Fernández went on to become "captain as well as master of the Pizarros' galleon *San Cristóbal*, and eventually acquired the signs of complete success: an encomienda, a coat of arms (being a galleon in full sail) and election as alcalde in Lima." Though Lockhart does not specify it, in all likelihood the *San Cristóbal* was the galleon that Fernández had

under his command when serving Alvarado, whose flagship it was and which changed hands – see chapter 15, note 1 – as part of the arrangement struck between the Adelantado and Almagro in Santiago de Quito on 26 August 1534. Fernández is but one example of how loyalties could shift, and old grievances be amended if not completely made right, in the vicissitudes of conquest. It was disgruntlement with Pizarro in the first instance – see chapter 6, note 12, and chapter 9, note 6 – that swayed Fernández to cast his lot with Alvarado, an association whose short-lived duration, three or four years at most, in the end proved not as lucrative and socially enhancing as reconnecting under clearly favourable terms with the governor of Peru.

13 Vallejo García-Hevia (2008). While conducting the *residencia*, Maldonado relieved Alvarado of the governorship of Guatemala for over three years, from 10 May 1536 to 10 September 1539. During that time, the Adelantado was far from the scene, having left Central America to spend time in Spain. There, ingratiating himself once more at court, he convinced Emperor Charles V to trust him with another Pacific seafaring mission. Upon returning to Central America, he appeared before the *cabildo* of Santiago de Guatemala on 26 September 1539, informing its members – see Lovell, Lutz, and Kramer (2020, 88) for elaboration – "of his new (and upgraded) royal credentials, which included being reappointed governor of Guatemala for a further seven years."

14 Vallejo García-Hevia (2008, vol. 2, 758), citing "cargo" (charge) IX from the "Relación de los cargos generales de la pesquisa secreta" made in Santiago de Guatemala on 7 February 1537 by "el Juez de Residencia, Licenciado Alonso Maldonado, contra el Gobernador de la provincia de Guatemala, Pedro de Alvarado." The charge levelled at the Adelantado in the original (AGI, Justicia 295, folio 197 verso) runs: "Al tiempo que salieron con su armada del puerto de la Posesion para el Peru llebo el y los que con el fueron mill y çiento e ochenta a qyatro yndios honbres e mugeres libres y essclavos de los quales se murieron muchos en el Peru e los que no murieron se quedaron alla – that when he left the Puerto de la Posesión [Rialejo] with his armada for Peru, he and those who went with him took 1,184 Indians, men and women, free and enslaved, many of whom died in Peru. Those who did not die remained there, never to return." Herrera ([1615] 1728, 140) puts Indigenous fatalities at two thousand – "dos mil Indios" – while Cieza de León ([1553] 1998, 336) states "more than three thousand." These numbers likely include Ecuadorian as well as Guatemalan and Nicaraguan natives.

15 Guerra (1951, 290). "Durante los años que siguieron," he writes, "se compraron y se vendieron en el Perú muchos esclavos guatemaltecos."

16 Paz Cárcomo (2014, 331). Based on information relayed by Luis Naranjo, a representative of the Guatemalan embassy in Ecuador, twenty-eight individuals are reported to have "Guatemal" as their surname, one "Guatemala."

17 The creation of Spanish sculptor Eduardo Barrón González (1858–1911), the statue of Cortés has been in place since it was unveiled in Medellín, according to Fernández-Daza Álvarez (2013, 12–13), on 2 December 1890. In an act of vandalism on 11 August 2010, the statue was doused in red paint, symbolizing blood, from the chest down. A group calling itself Ciudadanos Anónimos (Anonymous Citizens) declared the sculpture "a cruel and arrogant glorification of genocide, an insult to the people of Mexico – la glorificación cruel y arrogante del genocidio y un insulto al pueblo de México" – and demanded its removal. The statue was cleaned up and remains standing. See www.elmundo.es/elmundo/2010/08/11/espana/1281536193.html (Carvajal 2010) for further details.

18 The creation of American sculptor Charles Cary Rumsey (1879–1922), the equestrian statue of Pizarro has stood in the Plaza Mayor of Trujillo since 1927. It is a copy of the original, which dates from 1920 and stands at the entrance to the Albright-Knox Art Gallery in Buffalo, Rumsey's place of birth. Another copy was donated to the city of Lima by Rumsey's widow, Mary Harriman, and unveiled on 18 January 1935, to mark the four hundredth anniversary of Lima being founded by Pizarro. This replica stood in front of the city cathedral until 1952, when it was moved to an adjacent site in the Plaza de Armas, remaining there until 2003. Since then, the mounted Pizarro no longer atop a pedestal, the statue occupies a remote corner of the Parque de la Muralla, some distance from the Peruvian capital's historic core. See www.sites.utexas.edu/culturescontexts/2013/05/17/pizarro-in-exile/, the *Cultures Contexts* website of Peter Hess.

19 The creation of Spanish painter and sculptor Joaquín García Donaire (1926–2003), the equestrian statue of Almagro (an illegitimate native son) has stood in the Plaza Mayor of Almagro, one of Spain's most elegant civic spaces, since 1980. See www.equestrianstatue.org/almagro-diego-de/, the *Equestrian Statues* website of Kees Van Tilburg, which registers "a badly neglected copy" of the conquistador in Santiago de Chile.

20 Recinos (1952, 205). "El juicio de la posteridad," his words run in the original, "no ha sido favorable a la persona y carácter de Pedro de Alvarado." Neither has posterity been kind to Sebastián de Belalcázar. Statues of him in South America have either been toppled (Popayán, Colombia) or are forever being defaced, as in Quito. I happened to be there on the 485th anniversary of Belalcázar's founding of the city, 6 December 2019, a national holiday. "Quito was not founded," declared a banner draped in front of Belalcázar's paint-smeared figure, reproduced in that day's issue of *La República* online newspaper. "It was invaded and sacked" (www.larepublica.ec/blog/2019/12/06/vandalizan-monumento-sebastian-benalcazar-fundador-quito/).

21 The statue of Alvarado has been a feature of the river walkway in Badajoz since 2003. On the evening of 12 October 2020 the sculpture was vandalized in the same manner as that of Cortés in Medellín some ten years before: red paint was poured on the effigy from the face down. A nearby statue of Pizarro, another cast in bronze by García Olivares (www.estanislaoescultor.com), received the same treatment, which took place on the day that Spain celebrates as the Día de la Hispanidad (www.efe.com/efe/espana/portada/estatuas-de-conquistadores-extremenos-sufren-actos-vandalicos-en-badajoz/10010-4366579).

22 These two stanzas are the first and third of the song "Conquistador," the opening track of the eponymous debut album (Regal Zonophone LRZ 1001, 1967) of the rock group Procol Harum. Lyrics reproduced with kind permission of Keith Reid.

23 In a letter addressed to Cortés on 28 July 1524 – see chapter 1, notes 29 and 30 – Alvarado tells how he sustained the injury, complications from which he later claimed almost proved fatal, confining him to bed and removing him for some time from the field of battle while he recovered. Mackie (1924, 81) translates Alvarado's account of the incident, which occurred at Acajutla on 8 June 1524, as follows: "In this encounter many Spaniards were wounded, myself amongst the rest. They shot an arrow at me that passed through my leg and entered my saddle, from which wound I was made lame, as one leg remained shorter than the other a good four fingers. I was forced to stay for five days in this town to cure our wounds." The Adelantado's aborted campaign in El Salvador – a strategic retreat saw him and his troops back in Guatemala a week before he wrote to Cortés – is discussed in Lovell, Lutz, and Kramer (2020, 25–30).

24 Lured into action during the Mixtón rebellion in Mexico en route to the Spice Islands, the Adelantado failed to heed warnings about adverse weather and battlefield conditions. At Nochistlán, the horse of his secretary, Baltasar de Montoya, lost its footing and fell on him from above. Fatally hurt, he died in Guadalajara on 4 July 1541 from injuries sustained ten days or so before. Simpson (1931, 534–6), Recinos (1952, 193–204), and García Añoveros (1986, 141–9) all draw on the work of Antonio Tello ([c. 1650] 1891) to give an account of Alvarado's final days. On his deathbed, the lieutenant governor of Nueva Galicia, Cristóbal de Oñate, admonished Alvarado for the foolhardy assault on Indigenous rebels he insisted on launching before Spanish reinforcements had arrived from Mexico City. Alvarado is said to have been "so angry and vexed that he would not listen to reason" but saw fit to respond: "The die is cast! I commend myself to God! … It is all over and there is no help for it. It was my fault for not following the advice of those who knew the people and the country. I am tired and dying. Bring me soon to the city so that I may prepare my soul." Simpson (1931, 535–6) considers "the rash Alvarado" himself responsible for the calamity that caused his death, having ignored the counsel of Oñate "not to go on this expedition because the weather was contrary and favorable to the enemy, and this is a very different people from the one you conquered" in Guatemala.

REFERENCES

Before listing and commenting on the array of sources consulted, for the sake of convenience considered primary and secondary in nature, I first address issues of historiography, pointing the reader to contributions that not only pose pertinent questions but also indicate materials upon which answers to them might be based. The distinction between what constitutes a primary source and what constitutes a secondary source can be blurry, if not non-existent. As a rule of thumb, I take the former to mean information that was produced at the time of occurrence, or close to it. The latter I regard as being devised at some stage later – after the fact, possibly with the benefit of hindsight and a period of reflection, perhaps even drawing on pre-existing records, registers, or testimony.

HISTORIOGRAPHY

The historiographical item that most inspired me came my way fortuitously. In October 2018 I attended the annual meeting of the American Society for Ethnohistory, which that year convened in Oaxaca, Mexico. Frank L. Salomon, the John V. Murra Professor Emeritus of Anthropology at the University of Wisconsin-Madison, was in attendance, there to receive the society's Award for Lifetime Achievement. I presented a paper about the topic of this book, then a project in the making. Salomon came along to listen, and we fell into conversation after the session ended. He told me that, as a graduate student of Murra's at Cornell University in the early 1970s, he had undertaken a review of literature pertaining to his research interests, which he believed he still had in his files; I would be welcome to have a copy of it. Two months later, a sixty-four-page scan of "Some Materials for the History of the Native Peoples of Ecuador" arrived in my computer inbox, a paper that Salomon had submitted for his supervisor's scrutiny – most favourable, as comments Murra wrote on it attest – on 16 December 1971. I downloaded what was sent on 11 December 2018. The epiphany of two moments almost a half-century apart is as gratifying as it is giddying, and has stood me in good stead. Advances in the field of Andean studies over the past five decades have been considerable; Salomon's post-graduate work is prominent among them, beginning with *Native Lords of Quito in the Age of the Incas* ([1986] 2007) and ongoing since. His annotated bibliography has weathered well, its longevity a trait my inquiries have profited from.

Seven years before Salomon began his labours, Adam Szászdi (1964) published "The Historiography of the Republic of Ecuador," which also has endured the passage of time extremely well. Opinionated he may be – "Atahualpa, even as the son whom the daughter of the vanquished chieftain of Quito bore to Huayna Capac, represents the imposing will of the conqueror; and as a ruler he is the symbol of the tradition of an alien state" – but well versed in the literature and debates of the day Szászdi most assuredly was. He proves particularly adept at exposing the flaws of the Jesuit priest Juan de Velasco (1727–92), whose *Historia del Reino de Quito* ([1789] 1841) championed "the antiquity and imperial status" of a pre-Inca kingdom encompassing much of what is Ecuador today. Velasco's depictions held sway until being debunked by the man Szászdi (1964, 508) considers "Ecuador's greatest historian," Archbishop Federico González Suárez (1844–1918). His investigations (González Suárez 1881, 1891) and those too of his students, notably Jacinto Jijón y Camaaño (1936, 1941), discern more cultural diversity, spatial nuance, and regional autonomy at play. This has been confirmed by subsequent studies (Ayala Mora [2008] 2015, especially the inset "El reino de Quito y nuestra verdadera historia," 44) that find "ethnic domains in an advanced stage of development, but no unified state – descubren señoríos étnicos de gran desarrollo, pero no un Estado unificado."

Regarding specific focus on the South Sea expeditions of Pedro de Alvarado, above all "the motives behind the Adelantado's penetration of the lands of Quito in 1534," the inventory of Justus Wolfram Schottelius (1938/39) is without equal. His compilation of, and commentary on, 103 primary sources exemplify a dogged penchant for archival foraging. Entries 1 to 36 for the most part deal with Alvarado's Ecuadorian exploits, entries 37 to 103 with the expedition that ended his life in Mexico in 1541. The temporal span of the first batch of documents ranges from 16 May 1531 to 25 September 1536, the second from 10 May 1537 to 18 September 1542. My high-school and first-year university German came in handy when engaging Schottelius, who peppers his text with transcriptions of the original Spanish and accompanies it with two useful maps.

Approaching or entering the third millennium – in Latin America, the benchmark of Christianity is well-nigh indelible – two endeavours stand out to rightful acclaim. The first is the two-volume *Cambridge History of the Native Peoples of the Americas* (1999) devoted to South America. Edited by Salomon and Stuart B. Schwartz, these tomes are far more than mere updates of the still resourceful *Handbook of South American Indians*, vol. 2 of which is dedicated to Andean civilizations (Steward 1946). The modus operandi of *Cambridge Histories* calls for contributors to furnish a bibliographical essay that complements narration, always to positive effect. A second stellar initiative is the three-volume *Guide to Documentary Sources for Andean Studies* (2008) edited by Joanne Pillsbury, in which over 120 scholars exhibit and share their command of the subject.

In terms of historiographical orientation, the eight sources I gained from most are highlighted below. Many others are mentioned throughout the narrative and its attendant endnotes, and listed elsewhere in the references:

Hamerly, Michael T. 2001. *Bibliography of Ecuadorian Bibliographies, 1881–2000*. Austin, TX: Seminar on the Acquisition of Latin American Library Materials.

Hartmann, Roswith, Gertraud Itzstein, Denise Kupferschmidt, and Heiko Prümers. 2005. *Bibliografía básica sobre la arqueología del Ecuador.* Bonn: Bonner Amerikanistische Studien.

Pillsbury, Joanne, ed., 2008. *Guide to Documentary Sources for Andean Studies, 1530–1900*. 3 vols. Norman: University of Oklahoma Press, in collaboration with the Center for Advanced Study in the Visual Arts, United States National Gallery of Art.

Salomon, Frank L. 1971. "Some Materials for the History of the Native Peoples of Ecuador." Unpublished manuscript.

Salomon, Frank, and Stuart B. Schwartz, eds. 1999. *The Cambridge History of the Native Peoples of the Americas.* Vol. 3, *South America,* Part 1 and Part 2. New York: Cambridge University Press.

Schottelius, Justus Wolfram. 1938–39. "Pedro de Alvarado und die Spanische Südseefahrt." *Ibero-Amerikanisches Archiv* 12 (1): 23–67.

Steward, Julian H., ed. 1946. *Handbook of South American Indians.* Vol. 2, *The Andean Civilizations.* Washington, DC: Smithsonian Institution.

Szászdi, Adam. 1964. "The Historiography of the Republic of Ecuador." *Hispanic American Historical Review* 44 (4): 503–50.

PRIMARY SOURCES

For the contact and conquest period, the quarter-century or so between 1519 and 1545, we know more about Mesoamerican peoples than we do about their South American counterparts. The foremost reason for this is that, by the time of the Spanish invasion, the Aztecs, Mayas, and neighbouring societies had developed a strong written tradition that enabled them to record their version of events as they were happening, or soon after subjugation. The Incas and their predecessors kept track by means of *quipus* or *khipus*, knotted-string cords long thought to be devices that registered numerical or statistical data. The narrative and phonetic qualities of these artifacts are being brought to our attention thanks to the insights of Gary Urton (1998, 2017), Salomon (2004) once again, and Sabine Hyland (2017), to name but three scholars who have pursued this line of inquiry. Lack of full-fledged writing systems, however, means that much information about Spanish intrusion from an Indigenous perspective was never recorded, or was put down on paper many years after first contact, with the inevitable drawbacks. There is no native text, for instance, akin to *The Annals of the Cakchiquels* (Recinos and Goetz 1953) that sheds light on Alvarado's comings and goings for Ecuador as it does for Guatemala.

Primary sources were consulted in several repositories, among them the Archivo General de Indias (AGI) in Seville, the Archivo General de Centro América (AGCA) in Guatemala City, and three archives in Ecuador: the Archivo Histórico, the Archivo Histórico Nacional, and the Archivo Metropolitano de Historia (AMHQ), all in Quito, where time spent at the Instituto Geográfico Militar and the Universidad Andina Simón Bolivár also proved beneficial. The same may be said of the Bancroft Library at the University of California in Berkeley and the New York Public Library (NYPL), whose Obadiah Rich Collection (ORC) was well worth persevering with, especially its contents on sometimes difficult-to-read microfilm. Copies of Alvarado's earliest letters about his expedition to Peru are housed in both libraries, transcriptions of some of them more faithful to the originals than versions published in the collections indicated below. Utilitarian and more easily accessible though these transcriptions may be, nothing compares with handling and perusing their first iteration. I was afforded permission to work with original manuscripts from the early sixteenth century, a great privilege, at the AGI, the AGCA, and the AMHQ. The fragility of most of these records, however, and the need to maximize their protection, meant greater dependency on consulting primary sources online or via transcribed editions than ordinarily I would have preferred.

Archivo General de Indias (Seville)

From the teeming contents of the AGI, where I had direct access to pertinent materials, I single out the following:

Guatemala 41: The *cabildo* of Santiago to the Crown, relaying news of Pedro de Alvarado's return from Peru and expressing concern about Indigenous unrest during his absence (14 May 1535)

Guatemala 41, N.1: *Alarde* (roll call) of men who accompanied Pedro de Alvarado on his expedition to Peru (11 January 1534).

Guatemala 45: Francisco de Zurrilla, Francisco de Castellanos, and Gonzalo Ronquillo to the Crown, regarding the armada being built by Pedro de Alvarado and his intent to leave Guatemala for Peru (28 September 1531).

Guatemala 128: Las tasaciones de los pueblos de los términos y jurisdicción de la ciudad de Santiago de Guatemala (1548–51).

Justicia 295 and 296: *Residencia* (judicial inquiry) into the affairs of Pedro de Alvarado, judge Alonso de Maldonado given charge of doing so by royal order on 27 October 1535. The two-volume *Juicio a un conquistador* (Vallejo García-Hevia 2008) has a transcription of the thick and incriminating contents of Justicia 295 and 296, a veritable labour of love undertaken by Julio Martín Blasco.

Patronato 183-1-16: "Descripción de la Bahía de Fonseca y de sus comarcas," a report dated 7 October 1590 in which Juan Bautista Antonelli and Diego López Quintanilla describe the Bay of Fonseca and its environs. Their observations include locational details and site particulars about the port of Iztapa, where ships were built some sixty years before as part of the fleet that Pedro de Alvarado sailed with to Peru.

Patronato 192-1-6: The *cabildo* of San Miguel de Piura alerts the Crown about the arrival of Pedro de Alvarado in Peru and of the destruction this has caused (1534).

Patronato 192-1-11: "Relación del viaje al Perú de Pedro de Alvarado" (n.d.)

Patronato 254-3-1: "Venta de la armada de don Pedro de Alvarado a don Diego de Almagro," concerning the sale of Pedro de Alvarado's armada to Diego de Almagro (1535).

Archivo General de la Nación (Lima)

Obligación N.1, Pac.1 0, 717–488: Pedro de Alvarado agrees to pay the heirs of Juan de la Parra, deceased, 4,500 pesos for the horse with which Parra boarded ship on his way to Peru (4 January 1535).

Archivo Metropolitano de Historia (Quito)

From the AMHQ, where I also had direct access to materials, I single out the following:

"Acta de fundación de la ciudad de Santiago de Quito" (15 August 1534).

"Título del Libro de Cabildo de la ciudad de Santiago de Quito" (17 August 1534).

"Padrón de los primeros vecinos de Santiago de Quito" (17 August 1534).

"Acerca de lo que se debía hacer con don Pedro de Alvarado" (19 August 1534).

COLLECTIONS OF PRIMARY SOURCES IN PUBLISHED FORM

From documentary compilations, not all of which (alas) indicate archival provenance, or do so only vaguely, I draw the attention of readers to the following:

Colección de documentos inéditos para la historia de Chile, vol. 4 (1889)

"Carta de Pedro de Alvarado al Rey" (25 April 1533).

"Relación de los encuentros que tuvieron en el Perú el Adelantado Benalcázar [Belalcázar], don Pedro de Alvarado, Almagro, Pizarro y otros capitanes" (AGI, Patronato 1–1–1/28, n.d. 1534).

"Relación de varios sucesos en la conquista del Perú" (AGI, n.d. 1534?).

"Carta de Diego de Almagro al Rey" (8 May 1534).

"Información hecha a pedimento del Mariscal Don Diego de Almagro contra el Adelantado Pedro de Alvarado sobre haberse introducido en la gobernación de Don Francisco Pizarro" (12 October 1534).

"Carta de Diego de Almagro al Rey" (15 October 1534).

Colección Somoza, vol. 3 (1954)

"Información legalizada en la Ciudad de Panamá contra el Adelantado Pedro de Alvarado por haber tomado, en el Puerto de la Posesión, los navíos que debieren conducirse los auxilios que enviaría a Pizarro el Gobernador de Nicaragua" (AGI, Justicia 1051, 23 October 1533).

"Carta de Sebastián de Benalcázar [Belalcázar] a Su Magestad dando cuenta de como Pedro de Alvarado se apoderó de los navíos que habían de conducir, al mando del Capitán Gabriel de Rojas, para defensa del Gobernador del Perú, Francisco Pizarro" (AGI, Patronato 27, Ramo 11, 11 November 1533).

"Carta del Adelantado Pedro de Alvarado, informando el Gobernador de Castilla del Oro de varios sucesos, entre otros de la venta de sus navíos en pública almoneda, en donde él los adquirió" (AGI, Guatemala 39, 10 March 1534).

"Testimonio de [Pedro de Alvarado] cómo no tomó por fuerza ni contra la voluntad de su dueño, un navío, surto en el Puerto de la Posesión" (AGI, Guatemala 965, 13 May 1535).

Colección Somoza, vol. 4 (1955)

Declaration of Francisco de Castañeda, "Governador e Alcalde Mayor por su Magestad en estas probinçias de Nicaragua – that no assistance be afforded Pedro de Alvarado in his preparations to mount an expedition to Peru" (AGI, Justicia 293, 30 September 1533).

Gobernantes del Perú (1921)

"Carta de Don Francisco Pizarro a Su Magestad, refiriendo [a] la llegada de Pedro de Alvarado a su Gobernación de Quito e todo lo acaccido" (1 January 1535).

Harkness Collection (1932)

"Carta de cesión y traspaso" from the Adelantado Don Pedro de Alvarado to Francisco Pizarro and Diego de Almagro, ceding the rights granted him by Emperor Charles V for discovery and conquest in the South Sea (26 August 1534).

"Carta de venta" from the Adelantado Pedro de Alvarado to the Mariscal Don Diego de Almagro. Sale of fleet built by Alvarado for discovery in the South Sea (26 August 1534).

"Carta de poder" from the Adelantado Don Pedro de Alvarado to Francisco Pizarro and Diego de Almagro. To take possession of the ships of the aforementioned fleet with everything pertaining to them (27 August 1534).

Harkness Collection (1936)

Pedro de Alvarado. Sale of armada to Almagro and Pizarro, with cession of privileges for exploration and settlement in the South Sea. Three instruments (26 August 1534).

Libro viejo (1934)

"Carta de D. Pedro de Alvarado al Emperador Carlos V" (1 September 1532). A fuller text of this letter is housed in the NYPL/ORC (Rich 1–4).

"Carta a Su Magestad del Adelantado don Pedro de Alvarado" (18 January 1534, erroneously dated in the transcription 7 or 8 January).

"Carta del Adelantado don Pedro de Alvarado al Ayuntamiento de Guatemala, anunciándole su embarco en la Posesión para el Sur" (20 January 1534).

"Carta del Adelantado don Pedro de Alvarado al Gobernador de Panamá, don Francisco de Barrionuevo" (10 March 1534). See also entry 3 in the *Colección Somoza*, vol. 3 above.

"Contrato de compra-venta de la armada del Adelantado Don Pedro de Alvarado" (26 August 1534). See also entry 2 in the *Harkness Collection* (1932) and the entry from the *Harkness Collection* (1936) above.

"Carta de D. Pedro de Alvarado al Emperador Carlos V" (15 January 1535).

"Carta a Su Magestad del Adelantado don Pedro Dalvarado (*sic*), sobre las contrariedades que el mismo sufría de Pizarro" (12 May 1535, the year erroneously indicated twice in the transcription as 1536).

"Carta del Adelantado Don Pedro de Alvarado al Real Consejo de Yndias" (20 November 1535, the year erroneously indicated twice in the transcription as 1536).

"Carta de D. Francisco Pizarro a D. Pedro de Alvarado pidiéndole vaya al Perú en su auxilio" (9 July 1536).

Sebastián de Benalcázar (1936)

"Treslado bien y fielmente sacado de una capitulación que su Magestad hizo con el Adelantado Don Pedro de Alvarado" (AGI, 1532).

"Información hecha en Panamá al navío llamado *La Concepción*, que es del Adelantado Francisco Pizarro, y sobre lo que pasaba en el Perú" (AGI, 7 April 1534).

DOCUMENTARY COMPILATIONS AND OTHER PRIMARY SOURCES

Full citations to documentary compilations for early colonial times follow, including some not among those referred to above. Also listed are other primary sources available for consultation in published form.

Alvarado, Pedro de. [1524] 1944. "Dos cartas de Pedro de Alvarado a Hernán Cortés." *Anales de la Sociedad de Geografía e Historia de Guatemala* 19 (5): 386–96.

– [1534–35] 1880. "Cartas del Conquistador Pedro de Alvarado." Transcribed by J.E. [Ephraim George] Squier from the Archivo [General] de Indias. *Revista Peruana* 4: 191–8 and 327–37.

Clemence, Stella Risley, ed. and trans. 1932. *The Harkness Collection in the Library of Congress: Calendar of Spanish Manuscripts Concerning Peru, 1531–1651*. Washington, DC: United States Government Printing Office.

– 1936. *The Harkness Collection in the Library of Congress: Documents from Early Peru, the Pizarros and the Almagros, 1531–1578*. Washington, DC: United States Government Printing Office.

Garcés, Jorge A.G., ed. 1936. *Colección de documentos inéditos relativos al adelantado capitán don Sebastián de Benalcázar, 1535–1565*. Quito: Archivo Municipal.

Jijón y Caamaño, Jacinto. 1936. *Sebastián de Benalcázar*. Vol. 1. Quito: Imprenta del Clero.

Kramer, Wendy, coordinator. 2018. *Libro Segundo del Cabildo*. Paleographic transcription by Wendy Kramer with Edgar F. Chután Alvarado. Edited by Jorge Luján Muñoz and Wendy Kramer. Introduction by Christopher H. Lutz with Wendy Kramer. La Antigua, Guatemala: Centro de Investigaciones Regionales de Mesoamérica; Guatemala City: Universidad del Valle de Guatemala and the Academia de Geografía e Historia de Guatemala; New York: Hispanic Society of America; and Wellfleet, MA: Plumsock Mesoamerican Studies.

Levillier, Roberto, ed., 1921. *Gobernantes del Perú: Cartas y papeles, siglo XVI. Documentos del Archivo de Indias*. Tomo 1. Madrid: Sucesores de Rivadeneyra (S.A.).

Libro primero de cabildos de Quito. 1934. Transcribed by José Rumazo González. Quito: Archivo Municipal.

Libro viejo de la fundación de Guatemala y papeles relativos a D. Pedro de Alvarado. 1934. Prologue by Jorge García Granados. Guatemala: Tipografía Nacional.

Medina, José Toribio. 1889. *Colección de documentos inéditos para la historia de Chile.* Vol. 4. *Almagro y sus compañeros.* Santiago de Chile: Imprenta Ercilla.

Porras Barrenechea, Raúl, ed., 1959. *Cartas del Perú* (1524–34). Lima: Edición de la Sociedad de Bibliófilos Peruanos.

"Provanza del Adelantado D. Pedro de Alvarado y doña Leonor de Alvarado su hija." [1563] 1937. *Anales de la Sociedad de Geografía e Historia de Guatemala* 13 (4): 475–87.

Ramírez, José Fernando, ed. [1847] 1930–33. "Proceso de residencia contra Pedro de Alvarado." *Anales de la Sociedad de Geografía e Historia de Guatemala* 7 (1– 4): 95–122, 210–39, 360–87, 513–28; 8 (2–4): 254–67; 9 (1–2): 121–9, 256–64.

Recinos, Adrián and Delia Goetz, eds. and trans. 1953. *The Annals of the Cakchiquels.* Norman: University of Oklahoma Press.

Vallejo García-Hevia, José María. 2008. *Juicio a un conquistador: Pedro de Alvarado, su proceso de residencia en Guatemala, 1536–1538.* Transcription of AGI, Justicia 295 and 296, by Julio Martín Blasco. 2 vols. Madrid: Marcial Pons.

Vega Bolaños, Andrés, ed. 1954–57. *Colección Somoza: Documentos para la historia de Nicaragua.* 17 vols. Madrid.

SECONDARY SOURCES

Of several biographies of Pedro de Alvarado in Spanish, that of Adrián Recinos (1952) remains the most insightful and informative, the monograph of John E. Kelly (1932) still the only one in English. Each devotes a chapter, or the better part thereof, to Alvarado's expedition to Peru. Rarely cited today, Kelly's work has much to commend it, including translations of two of the Adelantado's letters to Emperor Charles V, the first drafted before he set sail in 1534, the second after the debacle in 1535. Kelly renders with a flourish the contract struck between Alvarado and Almagro on 26 August 1534; its arrangements saw the fleet of the former change hands, the allegiance of his followers likewise. Recinos (1952, 238) is the more inclined of the two biographers to pass judgment, believing that the Adelantado's faults and flaws, "sus faltas" as he discreetly puts it, "history has not forgiven" – nor is likely to.

Jijón y Caamaño (1936, 6) does not shy from passing judgment either, his biography of Sebastián de Belalcázar (see above) also devoting a chapter to Alvarado's designs on Peru, the Kingdom of Quito foremost of all. He considers the conquest an "immense evil – mal inmenso" for the peoples it dominated and oppressed. Ecuadorian historians of previous and subsequent generations would not disagree, the most candid among them González Suárez (1881, 1891), Wilfrido Loor (1956), Gonzalo Molina García ([1986] 2004), and Ramiro Molina Cedeño (2015). In English, John Hemming ([1970] 1972) has long since replaced William H. Prescott (1847) as the gold standard in grappling with conquest writ large, deservedly and enduringly so. A half-century later, R. Alan Covey (2020) echoes Hemming in emphasizing sustained native resistance to Spanish intrusion; Pizarro may have won the day at Cajamarca on 16 November 1532, but he and those who followed him faced fierce opposition elsewhere for years, indeed for decades. The work of Linda A. Newson (1995) on Ecuador specifically may be said to complement and enhance that of Murra (1946) rather than supersede it, her analyses of the impact of disease outbreaks on Indigenous peoples likewise echoing and elaborating the contribution of Suzanne Austin Alchon (1991). Of the Spanish chroniclers, Pedro de Cieza de León ([1553] 1998) is unrivalled, in a class of his own.

Alchon, Suzanne Austin. 1991. *Native Society and Disease in Colonial Ecuador*. New York: Cambridge University Press.

Altman, Ida. 2010. *The War for Mexico's West: Indians and Spaniards in New Galicia, 1524–1550*. Albuquerque: University of New Mexico Press.

Altolaguirre y Duvale, Ángel de. 1927. *Don Pedro de Alvarado, Conquistador del Reino de Guatemala*. Madrid: Editorial Voluntad.

Anderson, Arthur J.O., and Charles E. Dibble., ed. and trans. [1555] 1978. *The War of Conquest: How It Was Waged Here in Mexico*. Salt Lake City: University of Utah Press.

Asselbergs, Florine. 2004. *Conquered Conquistadors: The Lienzo de Quauhquechollan – A Nahua Vision of the Conquest of Guatemala*. Leiden: CNWS.

– 2008. *Conquered Conquistadors: The Lienzo de Quauhquechollan – A Nahua Vision of the Conquest of Guatemala*. Boulder: University Press of Colorado.

– [2010] 2018. *Los conquistadores conquistados: El Lienzo de Quauhquechollan – Una visión nahua de la conquista de Guatemala*. Translated by Eddy H. Gaytán. La Antigua, Guatemala: Centro de Investigaciones Regionales de Mesoamérica; South Woodstock, VT: Plumsock Mesoamerican Studies.

Ayala Mora, Enrique, ed. [2008] 2015. *Historia del Ecuador*. Vol. 1, Época Aborigen y Colonial, Independencia. Quito: Universidad Andina Simón Bolivar.

Ayón, Tomás. [1882] 1977. *Historia de Nicaragua*. Vol. 1. Managua: Colección Cultural, Banco de América, Serie Histórica 10.

Ballesteros Gaibrois, Manuel. 1987. *Diego de Almagro*. Historia 16. Madrid: Ediciones Quorum.

Bancroft, Hubert Howe. 1883. *The Works of Hubert Howe Bancroft*. Vol. 7, *History of Central America*, vol. 2. San Francisco: A.L. Bancroft and Company.

Bandelier, Adolph F. 1906. "Traditions of Precolumbian Earthquakes and Volcanic Eruptions in Western South America." *American Anthropologist* 8 (1): 47–81.

Barón Castro, Rodolfo. 1943. *Pedro de Alvarado*. Madrid: Ediciones Atlas, Colección Vidas.

Benzoni, Girolamo. [1565] 1572. *La Historia del Mondo Nuovo*. 2nd ed. Venice: Tini Fratelli.

Bishop, Morris. 1933. *The Odyssey of Cabeza de Vaca*. New York and London: Century Company.

Borah, Woodrow. 1954. *Early Colonial Trade and Navigation between Mexico and Peru*. Ibero-Americana 38. Berkeley and Los Angeles: University of California Press.

– 1971. "Hernán Cortés y sus intereses marítimos en el Pacífico: El Perú y la Baja California." *Estudios de Historia Novohispana* 4: 7–25.

Bravo Guerreira, María Concepción. 1976. "¿Fue Francisco de Xerez el autor de la Relación Sámano? Anotaciones al viaje de descubrimiento del Perú." *Anuario de Estudios Americanos* 33: 33–55.

Briggs, Kate. [2017] 2020. *This Little Art*. London: Fitzcarraldo Editions.

Busto Duthurburu, José Antonio del. 1986. *Diccionario histórico biográfico de los conquistadores del Perú*. 2 vols. Lima: Librería Studium.

Cabezas Carcache, Horacio. 2019. *Pedro de Alvarado, Gobernador y Adelantado de Guatemala: Galán de corazón temerario, rapaz y cruel*. Guatemala: Edición Privada.

Carvajal, Álvaro. 2010. "Manchan con pintura roja una estatua de Hernán Cortés." *El Mundo* 12 (August).

Castro, Felipe. 2008. "In Search of Unique Iberian Ship Design Concepts." *Historical Archaeology* 42 (2): 63–87.

Cieza de León, Pedro de. [1553] 1959. *The Incas*. Edited and introduced by Victor Wolfgang von Hagen. Translated by Harriet de Onis. Norman: University of Oklahoma Press.

– [1553] 1979. *Pedro de Cieza de León e il "Descubrimiento y conquista del Perú."* Edited by Francesca Cantù. Rome: Instituto Storico Italiano.

– [1553] 1984–85. 3 vols. *Obras Completas*. Edited and introduced by Carmelo Sáenz de Santa María. Monumenta Hispano-Indiana. 3 vols. Madrid: CSIC.

– [1553] 1989. *Crónica del Perú: Tercera Parte*. Edited by Francesca Cantù. Lima: Universidad Católica del Perú.

– [1553] 1998. *The Discovery and Conquest of Peru: Chronicles of the New World Encounter*. Edited and translated by Alexandra Parma Cook and Noble David Cook. Durham, NC: Duke University Press.

Codding, Mitchell A., ed. 2017. *Tesoros de la Hispanic Society of America: Visiones del Mundo Hispánico*. Madrid and New York: Museo Nacional del Prado and Hispanic Society of America.

Cook, Alexandra Parma, and Noble David Cook. 1991. *Good Faith and Truthful Ignorance: A Case of Transatlantic Bigamy*. Durham, NC: Duke University Press.

– 1998. Introduction to Cieza de León [1553] 1998. In *The Discovery and Conquest of Peru: Chronicles of the New World Encounter*, 5–35. Edited and translated by Alexandra Parma Cook and Noble David Cook. Durham, NC: Duke University Press.

Cook, Noble David, and W. George Lovell, eds. 2000. *Juicios secretos de Dios: Epidemias y despoblación indígena en Hispanoamérica colonial*. Translated by Jorge Gómez. Quito: Ediciones Abya-Yala.

– 2001. *"Secret Judgments of God": Old World Disease in Colonial Spanish America*. 2nd ed. Norman: University of Oklahoma Press.

Covey, R. Alan. 2020. *Inca Apocalypse: The Spanish Conquest and Transformation of the Andean World*. New York: Oxford University Press.

Currie, Elizabeth J. 1995. "Archaeology, Ethnohistory, and Exchange along the Coast of Ecuador." *Antiquity* 69 (264): 511–26.

DeBoer, Warren R. 1996. *Traces behind the Esmeraldas Shore: Prehistory of the Santiago-Cayapas Region, Ecuador*. Tuscaloosa: University of Alabama Press.

Díaz del Castillo, Bernal. [1632] 1963. *The Conquest of New Spain*. Translated and introduced by J.M. Cohen. London: Penguin Books.

– [1632] 1970. *Historia verdadera de la conquista de la Nueva España*. Introduction and notes by Joaquín Ramírez Cabañas. 8th ed. Mexico: Editorial Porrúa.

Diccionario de Autoridades. [1726] 1984. *Edición facsimíl*. 3 vols. Madrid: Editorial Gredos.

Dunlop, Robert Glasgow. 1847. *Travels in Central America*. London: Longman, Brown, Green, and Longmans.

Edwards, Clinton R. 1965. *Aboriginal Watercraft on the Pacific Coast of South America*. Ibero-Americana 47. Berkeley and Los Angeles: University of California Press.

Fernández-Daza Álvarez, Carmen. 2013. *Medellín y Hernán Cortés en la obra de dos escritoras extremeñas del siglo XIX: Carolina Coronado y Vicenta García Miranda*. Almendralejo: Imprenta Félix Rodríguez.

Fuentes y Guzmán, Francisco Antonio de. [1690–99] 1969–72. *Recordación florida*. In *Obras históricas de Don Francisco Antonio de Fuentes y Guzmán*, edited and introduced by Carmelo Sáenz de Santa María. 3 vols. Madrid: Biblioteca de Autores Españoles.

Galeano, Eduardo. 1983. *Memoria del fuego*, vol. 1, *Los nacimientos*. Madrid: Siglo Veintiuno.

– 1985. *Memory of Fire*, vol. 1, *Genesis*. Translated by Cedric Belfrage. New York: Pantheon.

– [1989] 1991. *The Book of Embraces*. Translated by Cedric Belfrage. New York: W.W. Norton and Company.

Galster, Ingrid. 2011. *Aguirre o La posteridad arbitraria*. Bogotá: Editorial Universidad del Rosario y Editorial Universidad Javeriana.

García Añoveros, Jesús María. 1987a. "Don Pedro de Alvarado: Las fuentes históricas, documentación, crónicas y bibliografía existente." *Mesoamérica* 13: 243–82.

– 1987b. *Pedro de Alvarado*. Historia 16. Madrid: Ediciones Quorum.

García Olivares, Estanislao. n.d. *Acerca de Estanislao García Olivares*. estanislaoescultor.com.

García de Palacio, Diego. [1587] 1944. *Instrucción náutica para navegar*. Madrid: Ediciones Cultura Hispánica.

Garcilaso de la Vega, El Inca. [1609/1616] 1966. *Royal Commentaries of the Incas and General History of Peru*. Translated and introduced by Harold V. Livermore. 2 vols. Austin and London: University of Texas Press.

González Suárez, Federico. 1881. *Historia eclesiástica del Ecuador*. Vol. 1. Quito: Imprenta del Clero.

– 1891. *Historia general de la república del Ecuador*. Vol. 2. Quito: Imprenta del Clero.

– n.d. *Historia general de la república del Ecuador*. Vol. 2. Segunda Edición. Guayaquil: Publicaciones Educativas Ariel.

Guerra, Eduardo. 1951. "Quito y Pedro de Alvarado." *Anales de la Sociedad de Geografía e Historia de Guatemala* 25 (3): 288–90.

Hemming, John. [1970] 1972. *The Conquest of the Incas*. London: Abacus Sphere Books.

Herrera, Antonio de. [1615] 1728. *Historia general de los hechos de los castellanos en las Islas y Tierra Firme del Mar Océano: Década Quinta*. Madrid: Francisco Martínez Abad.

Hess, Peter. 2013. *Cultures Contexts*. www.sites.utexas.edu/culturescontexts/2013/05/17/pizarro-in-exile/.

Hidrovo Quiñónez, Tatiana M. 2016. *Tras las huellas de la Ciudad de los Cerros*. Montecristi, Ecuador: Centro Cívico Ciudad Alfaro.

Hirth, Kenneth G., and Joanne Pillsbury, eds. 2013 *Merchants, Markets, and Exchange in the Pre-Columbian World*. Washington, DC: Dumbarton Oaks Research Library and Collection.

Hyland, Sabine. 2017. "Writing with Twisted Cords: The Inscriptive Capacity of Andean Khipus." *Current Anthropology* 58: 412–19.

Jaramillo Alvarado, Pío. [1922] 1983. *El indio ecuatoriano: Contribución al estudio de la sociología indoamericana*. 6th ed. 2 vols. Quito: Corporación Editora Nacional.

– 1941. *La guerra de conquista en América*. Guayaquil, Equador: Editorial Jouvin.

Jijón y Caamaño, Jacinto. 1941. *El Ecuador interandino y occidental antes de la conquista castellana*. Vol. 2. Quito: Editorial Ecuatoriana.

Kelly, John E. 1932. *Pedro de Alvarado, Conquistador*. Princeton, NJ: Princeton University Press.

Kelsey, Harry. 1986. *Juan Rodríguez Cabrillo*. San Marino, CA: Huntington Library.

Kirkpatrick, Frederick A. [1934] 1970. *Los conquistadores españoles*. Madrid: Espasa-Calpe.

Kistler, S. Ashley, ed. 2018. *Faces of Resistance: Maya Heroes, Power, and Identity*. Tuscaloosa: University of Alabama Press.

Kramer, Wendy. 1994. *Encomienda Politics in Early Colonial Guatemala, 1524–1544: Dividing the Spoils*. Dellplain Latin American Studies, no. 31. Boulder, CO: Westview Press.

– 2019. *Juan Rodríguez Cabrillo: A Voyage of Rediscovery*. San Diego, CA: Maritime Museum of San Diego.

Laanella, Erika Elizabeth. 2008. "Instrucción náutica (1587) by Diego García de Palacio: An Early Nautical Handbook from Mexico." MA thesis, Texas A&M.

Lane, Kris E. 2002. *Quito 1599: City and Colony in Transition*. Alburquerque: University of New Mexico Press.

Larraín Valdés, Gerardo. 1996. *Diego de Almagro*. Santiago de Chile : Editorial Luxemburgo.

Las Casas, Bartolome de. [1552] 1977. *Brevíssima relación de la destrucción de la Indias*. Edited and introduced by Manuel Ballesteros y Gaibrois. Madrid: Fundación Universitaria Español.

Lavallé, Bernard. [2003] 2007. *Francisco Pizarro y la conquista del imperio inca*. Barcelona: Editorial Planeta DeAgostini.

León Borja de Szászdi, Dora. 1964. "Prehistoria de la costa ecuatoriana." *Anuario de Estudios Americanos* 21: 381–436.

León Sáenz, Jorge. 2009. "Los astilleros y la industria marítima en el Pacífico americano: Siglos XVI a XIX." *Diálogos, Revista Electrónica de Historia* 10 (1): 44–90.

Livermore, Harold V. 1966. Introduction to Garcilaso de la Vega, El Inca. 1609/1616. *Royal Commentaries of the Incas and General History of Peru*. Translated and introduced by Harold V. Livermore. Part 1, xv–xxxi, and Part 2, vii–xxvi. Austin and London: University of Texas Press.

Lockhart, James. 1968. *Spanish Peru, 1532–1560: A Colonial Society*. Madison: University of Wisconsin Press.

– 1972. *The Men of Cajamarca: A Social and Biographical Study of the First Conquerors of Peru*. Austin: University of Texas Press.

Loor, Wilfrido. 1956. *Manabí: Prehistoria y conquista*. Quito: Editorial La Salle.

López de Gómara, Francisco. [1552] 1863. *Historia general de las Indias*. Madrid: M. Rivadenyra.

– [1552] 1966. *Cortés: The Life of the Conqueror by His Secretary*. Translated and edited by Lesley Byrd Simpson. Berkeley: University of California Press.

– [1552] 1991. *Historia general de las Indias y vida de Hernán Cortés*. Prologue by Jorge Gurría Lacroix. Caracas: Biblioteca Ayacucho.

Loredo, Rafael. 1958. *Los repartos: Bocetos para la nueva historia del Perú*. Lima: D. Miranda.

Lovell, W. George, and Christopher H. Lutz. 2018. "Unsung Heroes: Cahí Ymox, Belehé Qat, and Kaqchikel Resistance to the Spanish Invasion of Guatemala." In S. Ashley Kistler, ed., *Faces of Resistance*, 37–60. Tuscaloosa: University of Alabama Press.

Lovell, W. George, Christopher H. Lutz, and Wendy Kramer. 2020. *Strike Fear in the Land: Pedro de Alvarado and the Conquest of Guatemala, 1524–1541*. Norman: University of Oklahoma Press.

MacCormack, Sabine. 1999. "Ethnography in South America." In Frank Salomon and Stuart B. Schwartz, eds., *The Cambridge History of the Native Peoples of the America*. Vol. 3, *South America*, Part 1: 96–187. New York: Cambridge University Press.

Mackie, Sedley J., ed. and trans. 1924. *An Account of the Conquest of Guatemala in 1524 by Pedro de Alvarado*. New York: Cortés Society.

MacLeod, Murdo J. 1970. "Las Casas, Guatemala, and the Sad but Inevitable Case of Antonio de Remesal." *Topic: A Journal of the Liberal Arts* 20: 53–64.

– 1998. "Self-Promotion: The *Relaciones de Méritos y Servicios* and Their Historical and Political Interpretation." *Colonial Latin American Historical Review* 7 (1): 25 42.

Marroquín, Francisco. [1545] 1949. "An Unpublished Letter of Don Francisco Marroquín, First Bishop of Guatemala, to the Emperor Charles V." *The Americas* 5 (3): 344–5.

Meade de Ángulo, Mercedes. 1992. *Doña Luisa Teohquilhuastzin, Mujer del Capitán Pedro de Alvarado*. Mexico: Gobierno del Estado de Puebla.

Medina, José Toribio. 1919. *Bartolomé Ruiz de Andrade: Primer piloto del Mar del Sur*. Santiago de Chile: Imprenta Elzeviriana.

Meide, Chuck. 2002. *A Plague of Ships: Spanish Ships and Shipbuilding in the Atlantic Colonies, Sixteenth and Seventeenth Centuries*. Williamsburg, VA: College of William and Mary.

Minta, Stephen. *Aguirre: The Re-creation of a Sixteenth-Century Journey across South America*. New York: Henry Holt and Company.

Molina Cedeño, Ramiro. 2015. *De historias documentadas a crónicas noveladas*. Quito: Casa de Cultura Ecuatoriana Benjamín Carrión.

Molina García, Gonzalo. [1986] 2004. *El capitán Francisco Pacheco en la conquista de América: Fundador de Portoviejo*. Portoviejo: Casa de la Cultura de Manabí.

Moreno Yánez, Segundo E. [2008] 2015. "Sociedades agrícolas supracomunales." In Enrique Ayala Mora, ed., *Historia del Ecuador*, vol. 1, Época Aborigen y Colonial, Independencia, 33–44. Quito: Universidad Andina Simón Bolivar.

Murphy, Robert C. 1941. "The Earliest Spanish Advances Southward from Panama along the West Coast of South America." *Hispanic American Historical Review* 21 (1): 3–28.

Murra, John. 1948. "The Historic Tribes of Ecuador." In Julian H. Steward, ed. *Handbook of South American Indians*, vol. 2, *The Andean Civilizations*, 785–851. Washington, DC: Smithsonian Institution.

Newson, Linda A. 1987. *Indian Survival in Colonial Nicaragua*. Norman: University of Oklahoma Press.

– [1992] 2001. "Old World Epidemics in Early Colonial Ecuador." In Noble David Cook and W. George Lovell, eds. *"Secret Judgments of God": Old World Disease in Colonial Spanish America*, 84–112. Norman: University of Oklahoma Press.

– 1993. "Highland-Lowland Contrasts in the Impact of Old World Diseases in Early Colonial Ecuador." *Social Science Medicine* 36 (9): 1187–95.

– 1995. *Life and Death in Early Colonial Ecuador*. Norman: University of Oklahoma Press.

Padden, R.C. 1967. *The Hummingbird and the Hawk: Conquest and Sovereignty in the Valley of Mexico, 1503–1541*. Columbus: Ohio State University Press.

Paz Cárcamo, Guillermo. 2014. *Kaji' Imox: El camino del pueblo kaqchikel*. Guatemala: Editorial Cholsamaj.

Ortuño Sánchez Pedreño, José María. 2005. "Los afanes del Adelantado de Guatemala, Pedro de Alvarado, por descubrir y poblar en el Mar del Sur." *Revista de Estudios Histórico-Jurídicos* (Valparaíso) 27: 251–79.

Oviedo y Valdés, Gonzalo Fernández de. [1547/1557] 1959. *La historia general y natural de las Indias*. Biblioteca de Autores Españoles, vols. 117–21. Madrid: Ediciones Atlas.

Porras Barrenechea, Raúl. 1962. *Los cronistas del Perú, 1528–1650*. Lima: Sanmartí Impresores.

Prescott, William H. 1847. *History of the Conquest of Peru*. 3 vols. London: George Routledge and Sons.

Radell, David R. [1976] 1992. "The Indian Slave Trade and the Population of Nicaragua during the Sixteenth Century." In William M. Denevan, ed. *The Native Population of the Americas in 1492*, 67–76. Madison: University of Wisconsin Press.

Radell, David R., and James J. Parsons. 1971. "Realejo: A Forgotten Colonial Port and Shipbuilding Center in Nicaragua." *Hispanic American Historical Review* 51 (2): 295–312.

Rahn Phillips, Carla. 2019. "A Translation of Pedro de Alvarado's 1526 Contract with the Spanish Crown: Pacific Exploration and Territoriality." *Terrae Incognitae* 51 (3): 235–53.

Recinos, Adrián. 1943. "Dos expediciones del Gobernador don Pedro de Alvarado." *Anales de la Sociedad de Geografía e Historia* 19 (1): 62–8.

– 1952. *Pedro de Alvarado, conquistador de México y Guatemala*. Mexico: Fondo de Cultura Económica.

Remesal, Antonio de. [1619] 1932. *Historia general de las Indias Occidentales y particular de la gobernación de Chiapa y Guatemala*. 2 vols. Biblioteca "Goathemala," vol. 4. Guatemala: Sociedad de Geografía e Historia.

– [1619] 1964–66. *Historia general de las Indias Occidentales y particular de la gobernación de Chiapa y Guatemala*. 2 vols. Biblioteca de Autores Españoles, vols. 175 and 183. Madrid: Ediciones Atlas.

Restall, Matthew. 2018. *When Montezuma Met Cortés: The True Story of the Meeting That Changed History*. New York: Ecco Press.

Rowe, John H. 1946. "Inca Culture at the Time of Spanish Conquest." In Julian H. Steward, ed. *Handbook of South American Indians*, vol. 2, *The Andean Civilizations*, 183–330. Washington, DC: Smithsonian Institution.

Rubio Sánchez, Manuel. 1956. "Puerto de Iztapa o de la Independencia." *Antropología e Historia de Guatemala* 8 (2): 24–50.

– 1977. *Historial de el Realejo*. Notas del Dr. Eduardo Pérez-Valle. Managua, Nicaragua: Colección Cultural, Banco de América, Serie Fuentes Históricas 4.

Sáenz de Santa María, Carmelo. 1964. *El Licenciado Don Francisco Marroquín, Primer Obispo de Guatemala (1499–1563)*. Madrid: Ediciones Cultura Hispanica.

– 1983. "La hueste de don Pedro de Alvarado en la historia del Perú." *Revista de Indias* 43 (171): 315–25.

Salomon, Frank. [1986] 2007. *Native Lords of Quito in the Age of the Incas: The Political Economy of North Andean Chiefdoms*. New York: Cambridge University Press.

– 2004. *The Cord Keepers: Khipus and Cultural Life in a Peruvian Village.* Durham, NC: Duke University Press.

Sancho, Pedro. [1534] 1917. *The Conquest of Peru.* Translated by Philip A. Means. New York: Cortés Society.

Sauer, Carl O. 1932. *The Road to Cíbola.* Ibero-Americana 3. Berkeley: University of California Press.

– 1950. "Geography of South America." In Julian H. Steward, ed., *Handbook of South American Indians*, vol. 6, *Physical Anthropology, Linguistics, and Cultural Geography of South American Indians*, 319–44. Washington, DC: Smithsonian Institution.

– 1966. *The Early Spanish Main.* Berkeley: University of California Press.

Saville, Marshall H. 1907. *The Antiquities of Manabí, Ecuador: A Preliminary Report.* New York: Irving Press.

– 1917. "A Letter of Pedro de Alvarado relating to his Expedition to Ecuador." *Contributions from the Museum of the American Indian* 5 (1): 1–6.

Seligmann, Linda J. 1995. *Between Reform and Revolution: Political Struggles in the Peruvian Andes, 1969–1991.* Stanford, CA: Stanford University Press.

Sherman, William L. 1979. *Forced Native Labor in Sixteenth-Century Central America.* Lincoln: University of Nebraska Press.

Simpson, Lesley B. 1931. "The Death of Pedro de Alvarado: A Study in Legend-Making." *Hispanic American Historical Review* 11 (4): 529–38.

Smith, Cameron M., Greg Baker, John F. Haslett, and Iliana López. 2008. "On the Vessel Sailed by Bartholome Ruiz in 1526: Characterization and Significance for the Pre-Columbian Archaeology of Northwestern South America." *Terrae Incognitae* 40 (1): 47–59.

Spilbergen, Joris Van. [1619] 1943. *De Reis om de Wereld van Joris van Spilbergen, 1614–1617.* s'Gravenhague: J.C.M. Warnsinck.

Squier, Ephraim George. 1852. *Nicaragua: Its People, Scenery, Monuments, and the Proposed Interoceanic Canal.* 2 vols. New York: D. Appleton and Company.

Szászdi, Adám. 1978. "En Torno a la Balsa de Salango, Ecuador, Que Capturó Bartolomé Ruiz." *Anuario de Estudios Americanos* 35: 453–554

Taylor, William B. 1980. Review of Sherman, *Forced Native Labor in Sixteenth-Century Central America*, in *Hispanic American Historical Review* 60 (2): 324–5.

Tello, Antonio. [c.1650] 1891. *Historia de la Nueva Galicia.* In *Crónica miscelánea, en que se trata de la conquista de la Santa Provincia de Xalisco.* Guadalajara: Imprenta de la República Literaria.

Thomas, Hugh. 1993. *Conquest: Montezuma, Cortés, and the Fall of Old Mexico*. New York: Simon and Schuster.

Topic, John R. 2013. "Exchange on the Equatorial Frontier: A Comparison of Ecuador and Northern Peru." In Kenneth G. Hirth and Joanne Pillsbury, eds. *Merchants, Markets, and Exchange in the Pre-Columbian World*, 335–60. Washington, DC: Dumbarton Oaks Research Library and Collection.

Torres Lanzas, Pedro. [1903] 1985. *Catálogo de mapas y planos de Guatemala en el Archivo General de Indias*. Madrid: Ministerio de Cultura, Dirección de Bellas Artes y Archivos.

Urton, Gary. 1998. "From Knots to Narratives: Reconstructing the Art of Historical Record Keeping in the Andes from Spanish Transcriptions of Inka *Khipus*." *Ethnohistory* 45 (5): 409–38.

– 2017. *Inka History in Knots*. Austin: University of Texas Press.

Valcárcel Martínez, Simón. 1995. "Fray Antonio de Remesal, 1575–1627." *Caravelle* 64: 9–29.

Van Tillburg, Kees. n.d. *Equestrian Statues*. www.equestrianstatue.org/almagro-diego-de/.

Varón Gabai, Rafael. 1997. *Francisco Pizarro and His Brothers: The Illusion of Power in Sixteenth-Century Peru*. Translated by Javier Flores Espinoza. Norman and London: University of Oklahoma Press.

Vaz Mingo, Milagros del. 1986. *Las capitulaciones de Indias en el siglo XVI*. Madrid: Instituto de Cooperación Iberoamericana.

Vázquez, Francisco. [1562] 1987. *El Dorado: Crónica de la expedición de Pedro de Ursua y Lope de Aguirre*. Introduction and notes by Javier Ortiz de la Tabla. Madrid: Alianza Editorial.

Vega, Alejandra. 2011. "Experiencias de cordillera, ecos de frío: Relatos cruzados entre Chile y Quito en el siglo XVI." *Revista Chilena de Literatura* 80: 223–42.

Velasco, Juan de. [1789] 1841. *Historia del reino de Quito*. Clásicos Ariel: Biblioteca de Autores Ecuatorianos 5. Quito: Imprenta de Gobierno, por Juan Campuzano.

Villamarín, Juan, and Judith Villamarín. 1999. "Chiefdoms." In Frank Salomon and Stuart B. Schwartz, eds., *The Cambridge History of the Native Peoples of the Americas*. Vol. 3, *South America*, Part 1: 577–667. New York: Cambridge University Press.

Von Hagen, Victor. 1955. *Highway of the Sun*. New York: Duell, Sloan, and Pearce.

Wagner, Henry R. 1934. "Fray Marcos de Niza." *New Mexico Historical Review* 9 (2): 184–227.

– 1946. "The Last Will of Pedro de Alvarado." *California Historical Society Quarterly* 25 (4): 309–10.

Weddle, Robert S. 2021. "Luis de Moscoso Alvarado." *Handbook of Texas Online*. Accessed 26 May. www.tshaonline.org/handbook/entries/moscoso-alvarado-luis-de.

Werner, Patrick S. 2004. *Derecho indiano en la Nicaragua temprana: Una guía para la Colección Somoza*. Managua, Nicaragua: Instituto Nicaragüense de Cultura.

West, Robert C. 1961. "Aboriginal Sea Navigation between Middle and South America." *American Anthropologist* 63 (1):133–5.

Whymper, Edward. 1892. *Travels amongst the Great Andes of the Equator*. London: John Murray.

Wright, Ronald. [1992] 2003. *Stolen Continents: Conquest and Resistance in the Americas*. Toronto: Penguin Canada.

– 2015. *The Gold Eaters*. New York: Riverhead Books.

Ximénez, Francisco. [1715–20] 1929–31. *Historia de la provincia de San Vicente de Chiapa y Guatemala de la Orden de Predicadores*. 3 vols. Guatemala: Sociedad de Geografía e Historia.

Zárate, Agustín de. [1555] 1968. *The Discovery and Conquest of Peru*. Translated with an introduction by J.M. Cohen. Harmondsworth, UK: Penguin Books.

INDEX